SINGER®

simple sewing

Creative Publishing international

First published in the United States of America by Creative Publishing international, Inc., a member of Quayside Publishing Group
400 First Avenue North
Suite 300
Minneapolis, MN 55401
1-800-328-3895
www.creativepub.com

ISBN-13: 978-1-58923-474-1
ISBN-10: 1-58923-474-X

10 9 8 7 6 5 4 3 2 1

Printed in China

Library of Congress Cataloging-in-Publication data available

Book Design: Mary Rohl, Tina R. Johnson, and Susan Gilday
Illustrator: Heather Lambert
Tech Editor: Carol Fresia

SINGER®

simple
sewing

Beth
Baumgartel

THE **COMPLETE**
ILLUSTRATED
MACHINE-SIDE
REFERENCE
OF **TIPS AND**
TECHNIQUES

contents

the basics 7

all about sewing machines

the sewing machine 8
machine features 9
machine needles 10
bobbins 11
presser feet 12
specialty accessories 13
stitch patterns 14
the serger 15
serger stitches 16

tools of the trade

hand-sewing tools 17
measuring tools 18
cutting tools 19
marking tools 20
all about thread 21
pressing tools 22
pressing pointers 23
interfacing, stabilizers & fusibles 24
how to apply interfacing 25
lining in garments 26
lining & interlining in home décor 27
functional trim 28
decorative trim 29
elastics 30

working with patterns 31

commercial patterns 32
pattern sizing 33

finding the right size 34
design & wearing ease 35
the pattern envelope 36
the instruction sheet 37
the pattern pieces 38
simple length adjustments 40

getting set to sew 41

choosing the right fabric 42
preparing your work space 43
winding & loading the bobbin 44
threading the sewing machine 46
checking stitch tension 47
preparing your fabric 48
straightening fabric grain 49
preparing & laying out the pattern 50
pinning the pattern 51
cutting the fabric 52
marking the fabric 53
check before you sew 55

essential techniques 56

construction stitches 57
the perfect seam 59
trimming a seam 60
types of seams 61
seam finishes 64
hand-sewing 66
hand stitches 67
securing hand stitches 69

basting methods 70
machine-sewing 71
machine stitches 72
sewing darts 74
stitching & mitering corners 75
making bias binding 76
mitering bias trim 77
attaching trims 78
sewing elastic to fabric 81
inserting elastic in a casing 82
making welting 84
attaching welting 85
making piping 86
making fabric bows 87
making tassels 88
forming gathers 89
sewing ruffles 90
sewing pleats 91
easing 92
marking & preparing hems 93
hemming methods 94

zippers

zippers 96
inserting a zipper 98
inserting a lapped zipper 100
inserting a centered zipper 102

closures

buttons & fasteners 103
attaching fasteners 105
buttonhole tips 106
making buttonholes 107

sewing on buttons.........................108
reinforcing buttons 110

working with fabrics...............111

fabric glossary
woven fabrics.............................112
knit fabrics 113
cotton....................................114
linen.....................................115
silk......................................116
wool.....................................117
rayon, acetate & triacetate..............118
synthetic fibers..........................119

sewing special fabrics
sewing stretch fabrics....................120
sewing slippery fabrics...................122
sewing sheer & lace fabrics 124
sewing textured fabrics 126
sewing striped, plaid & print fabrics....128

home décor 132

before you begin
choosing the right fabric..................133
trims 135
cutting the fabric........................136
piecing fabric widths 137

pillows & cushions
selecting a pillow style...................138
fabric choices 139
pillow forms & fillings 140

closures 141
fabric requirements.......................142
sewing a knife-edge pillow 143
sewing a boxed pillow 145

bedroom & bath accents
bedroom fashions and fabrics.............147
measuring the bed.......................148
fabric requirements for bed covers 149
sewing a duvet cover.....................150
sewing a dust ruffle......................151
bathroom fashions & fabrics 153
sewing a shower curtain 154
sewing bath towels 155

kitchen & dining room accents
table fashions & fabrics 156
fabric requirements for tablecloths......157
shaping tablecloths 159
hemming tablecloths 160
sewing a ruffled tablecloth................161
sewing placemats & table runners 162
sewing napkins 164

window treatments
basic window treatments 165
formal window fashions 166
casual window fashions...................168
fabrics for window treatments............170
hardware for window treatments.........171
decorative hardware 173
mounting boards.........................174
measuring windows 176
fabric requirements.......................178

sewing edge-to-edge lining................180
sewing interior lining 181
sewing unlined rod-pocket curtains 183
making tabs 185
sewing tab curtains.......................186
heading tapes 187
attaching heading tapes 188

mending & repair...................190

mending basics
assessing the damage 191
checklist of considerations 192
common repairs..........................193
notions 194
tools 195
general guidelines 197
fixing with fusibles........................198
fusing tips 199

darning
about darning 200
darning by hand 202
darning knit fabrics 203
darning by machine......................204

patching
about patches............................206
fusing an iron-on patch 207
patching on the right side.................208
finishing the edges 209
patching on the wrong side 210

surface & seam fixes

thread snags & pulls 212

repairing straight seams 213

reinforcing stressed seams 214

mending patch pockets 215

repairing in-seam pockets 216

reattaching decorative trim 217

repairing edge finishes 218

closures

about closures 219

choosing replacement buttons 220

multiple buttons & fabric mends 221

fixing frayed buttonholes 222

making a new buttonhole 223

quick fixes for buttonholes 224

creative buttonhole repairs 225

replacing elastic 226

replacing snaps 228

replacing hook fasteners 229

fixing drawstrings 230

zippers

zipper care 231

repairing a zipper 232

fixing a zipper slider 233

about replacing zippers 234

replacing a centered zipper 235

replacing a lapped zipper 237

replacing a fly-front zipper 239

replacing a separating zipper 241

construction & fit fixes

repairing lining 243

guidelines for adjusting fit 244

when it's too tight 245

when it's too loose 246

when it's too wide 247

stretched & frayed necklines 248

hemming

fixing a torn hem 249

repairing hems by hand 250

repairing hems by machine 251

making a simple hem 252

shortening with fabric tucks 254

hemming decorative edges 255

shortening tapered or flared garments .. 256

lengthening at the hem 257

lengthening with a facing or ruffle 258

lengthening with a cuff 259

specialty repairs

camouflaging flaws 260

adding an appliqué 261

adding beads, sequins & stones 262

decorative stitching 264

decorative trim 265

adding a patch pocket 266

adding a pocket flap 267

refolding pleats 268

mini makeovers 269

mending lace 270

mending leather & suede 271

mending pile fabrics 272

mending stretch knits 273

care & prevention

washing & drying 274

fixing ironing accidents 276

storing garments 277

fabric-cleaning products 278

how to treat a stain 279

caring for carpets & upholstery 280

stain removal chart 281

index 283

the
basics

the sewing machine

The function of every sewing machine is the same: to interlock top and bottom threads quickly and precisely to form a series of stitches. In addition to the basic straight stitch, all modern machines sew a zigzag stitch, and most of them sew several decorative stitches, too.

There are fabulous sewing machines for every budget, with user-friendly features that make sewing practically goof-proof. Computerized machines have an amazing variety of stitches and many automatic features. Some are sold with an embroidery module that lets you create professional-quality embroidery at the push of a button.

Every machine is different, so study your owner's manual and learn all the features of your machine to maximize its efficiency and your creativity.

machine features

Every machine operates differently, but they all have similar features, thread guides, and controls. Refer to your owner's manual for specific operating instructions.

automatic needle threader	a button or lever that inserts the thread through the eye of the needle
automatic presser foot pressure	automatically adjusts for different fabric thicknesses
automatic thread cutter	cuts top and bottom threads when a button or knob is pushed or turned
feed dogs	metal teeth below the presser foot that grip the fabric and move it along the bed of the machine
LED or LCD information screen	provides information and guidance but does not adjust or control the machine
low bobbin indicator	beeps or flashes when the bobbin is low
needle stop up/down	presets the needle to stop in the up or down position as needed
presser foot	keeps the fabric flat and guides it over the feed dogs
presser foot knee-lift lever	allows you to lift the presser foot with your knee so you can keep your hands on your work
stitch length and width	adjusts stitch size from 0 to 7 mm wide and from 0 to 6 mm long (range varies by machine)
thread guides	series of guides that control the upper thread to help form stitches and balance tension
throat plate	fits over the feed dogs with an opening for the needle, usually marked with seam allowance lines
variable stitch speed	allows you to speed up the machine for long, repetitive sewing or slow it down for precise, intricate work

machine needles

Always use the sewing machine needles recommended by the manufacturer of your machine. This information is in your manual. Keep an assortment of needle sizes in your supply box. Start every sewing project with a new needle, or change the needle after eight hours of sewing. Dull needles cause skipped stitches and snagged fabric.

The upper portion of the sewing machine needle is called the shank, and the lower portion is called the shaft. The flat area on the back of the shank almost always faces the back of the machine (check your manual). If you insert the needle incorrectly, your stitches will be inconsistent and you could damage the machine.

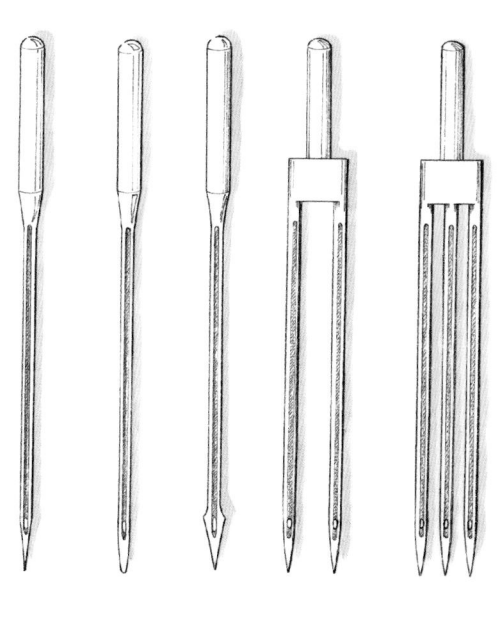

Needle Style

There are four basic needle styles. Fabric type and the purpose of the stitches determine which style you should use.

sharp point needles: for woven fabrics—the sharp point pierces the fabric cleanly

ballpoint needles: for knit fabrics—the rounded tip slips through the knit fabric loops

wedge point needles: for leather—the wedge cuts a tiny slit for each stitch

twin or triple needles: for two or three parallel rows of decorative stitches

Needle Size

Needle size is indicated by two numbers—the American sizes (9, 11, 12, 14, 16, 18) and the European (60, 70, 80, 90,100, 110)—with the smaller numbers representing thinner needles. As a general rule, the heavier the fabric, the larger the needle you'll need. The most widely used needle sizes are 12/80 and 14/90.

If you aren't sure which size to use, start with 12/80. If the thread shreds, try a larger size. If the seam puckers or the machine skips stitches, you may need a smaller needle.

bobbins

Bobbins are small metal or plastic spools that hold the lower thread in a cavity under the needle plate. There are two styles of bobbin: side or front loading, and top loading.

A side- or front-loading bobbin sits inside a bobbin case, which has thread guides to control the lower thread tension. Then the bobbin case fits into the side or front of the machine. Top-loading bobbins simply drop into the cavity below the throat plate (which is sometimes clear plastic, so you can see when the bobbin needs to be rethreaded). The thread is then drawn through built-in tension guides.

Keep a supply of bobbins on hand, wound with the colors you use most often so you won't have to wind a new bobbin mid-seam. Thread the top of the machine and the bobbin with the same type of thread to ensure a balanced stitch.

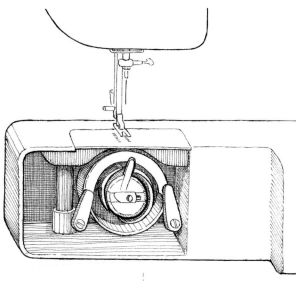

front-loading bobbin

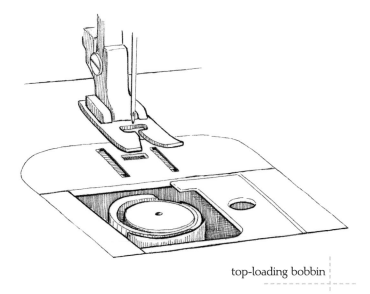

top-loading bobbin

presser feet

A presser foot holds the fabric in place as the feed dogs move it along the bed of the machine. Different feet are suited to different sewing tasks. You'll definitely need an all-purpose foot and a zipper foot, which are included with every machine.

If you buy a special presser foot, make sure the foot shank matches the feet that came with your machine—high shank, low shank, or slanted shank (as shown at left)—or buy a shank adaptor kit to make it fit correctly.

blind hem foot
forms stitches that are not visible from the right side of the fabric

general purpose foot
works well for most sewing purposes, with straight or zigzag stitch

piping foot
makes and applies corded piping

straight stitch foot
sews straight stitches only—good for sheer, lightweight fabrics

buttonhole foot
sews buttonholes automatically in various sizes and shapes

narrow hem foot
double-folds light-weight fabric as the needle stitches a very narrow hem

quarter-inch seam foot
sews ¼" (6 mm) seams quickly and accurately—ideal for quilting

zipper foot
accommodates zippers, piping, and cording

walking foot (even feed)
helps feed the top layer of fabric at the same rate as the bottom layer when stitching several thicknesses or when matching patterns or plaids

overedge/overcast foot
forms stitches over the raw edge to prevent fraying and curling

satin stitch or decorative stitch foot
features a wide, underside groove that glides over decorative stitching

darning foot
holds the fabric surface taut for machine darning and free-motion embroidery

specialty accessories

There are several specialty attachments that make sewing easier and are especially useful for home décor sewing.

bias binder:

- folds and attaches bias binding to unfinished edge in one step
- works with premade bias or self-fabric bias-cut strips

ruffler:

- folds fabric to form evenly spaced gathers or pleats
- some styles gather/pleat and attach to fabric in one step
- best for light- to medium-weight fabrics

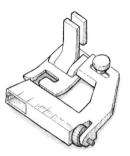

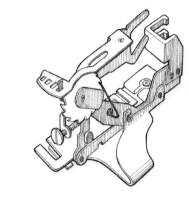

seam guide:

- attaches to machine bed with screw or magnet
- guides edge of fabric so seam allowance is consistent
- provides wider seam guide than the standard marks on the throat plate

quilting guide bar:

- attaches directly to a quilting foot (and usually sold together)
- guides parallel rows of stitching, for channel quilting and topstitching

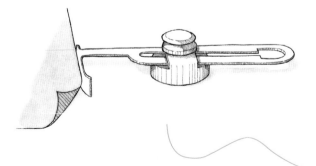

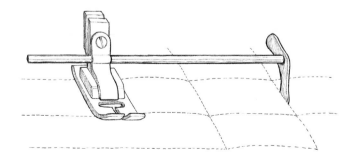

stitch patterns

Even the most basic sewing machine has several stitch patterns. Some computerized machines have more than 500 stitches! Utility stitches are suitable for construction and seam finishing. Decorative stitches are meant to be seen. Many machines also stitch alphabets, numbers, and small motifs.

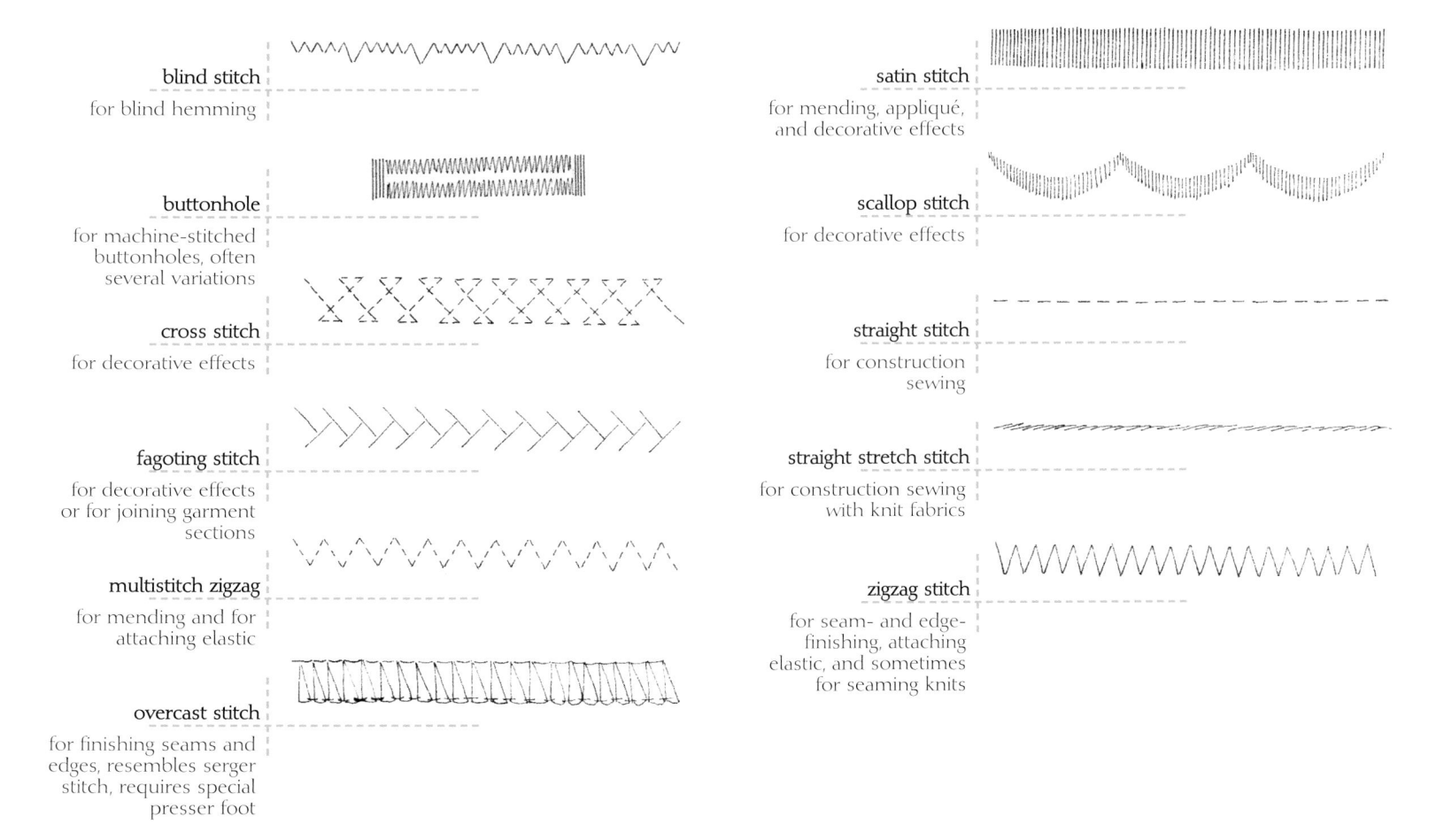

blind stitch
for blind hemming

buttonhole
for machine-stitched buttonholes, often several variations

cross stitch
for decorative effects

fagoting stitch
for decorative effects or for joining garment sections

multistitch zigzag
for mending and for attaching elastic

overcast stitch
for finishing seams and edges, resembles serger stitch, requires special presser foot

satin stitch
for mending, appliqué, and decorative effects

scallop stitch
for decorative effects

straight stitch
for construction sewing

straight stretch stitch
for construction sewing with knit fabrics

zigzag stitch
for seam- and edge-finishing, attaching elastic, and sometimes for seaming knits

the serger

The serger—also called an overlock machine—creates a professional-looking edge finish. It sews, trims, and overcasts the fabric edge in one step at a very high speed (about 1,600 stitches per minute).

Of course, you still need your sewing machine, but the serger is helpful for some types of construction and embellishment and for finishing seam allowances. Most have a differential feed feature that prevents puckers and stretched seams.

The major difference among sergers is the number of threads they can handle. They have either one or two needles and two or three loopers. Loopers work together with the needles to form the stitches in much the same way the bobbin works with the needle on the sewing machine. You can thread the loopers with decorative threads for special effects. Always thread the serger needles with utility thread.

All sergers sew a basic, three-thread overlock stitch, which is ideal for edge-finishing and for seaming knit fabrics.

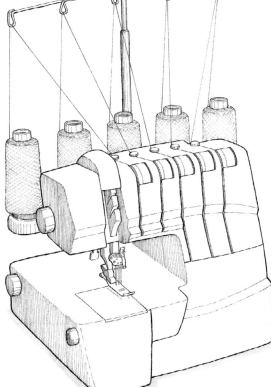

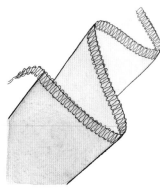

To secure the thread ends of a serged seam:
- dab on liquid fray preventer or fabric glue
- lift the presser foot, flip the fabric, and stitch over the last few stitches
- weave a long thread tail through the stitches with a tapestry needle

serger stitches

To form stitches, sergers use two, three, four, or five threads, which run through one or two needles and two or three loopers. The loopers deliver the thread to interlock with the needle threads—but they do not pierce the fabric. Instead, the looper threads sit on the top or underside of the fabric and wrap around the fabric's cut edge.

With your serger, you can sew and clean-finish window treatments, bed and bath linens, tablecloths, and pillows. Overlock and overedge stitches add strength, stability, and a more professional-looking finish. Other stitches, such as the flatlock and cover stitch, are more suitable for garment construction and embellishment.

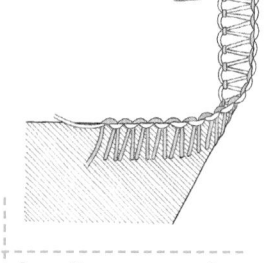

two-thread overedge — for lightweight seam finishing only, woven fabrics | **threading:** one needle, one looper

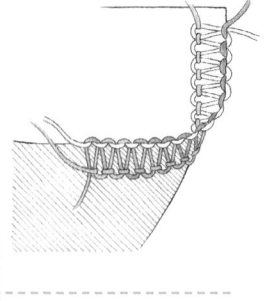

three-thread overlock — most common stitch, for seaming knit fabrics only, edge-finishing woven fabrics | **threading:** one needle, two loopers

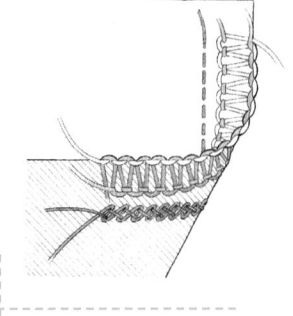

four-thread safety — for seaming and overedge-stitching; ideal for lightweight woven fabrics | **threading:** two needles, two loopers

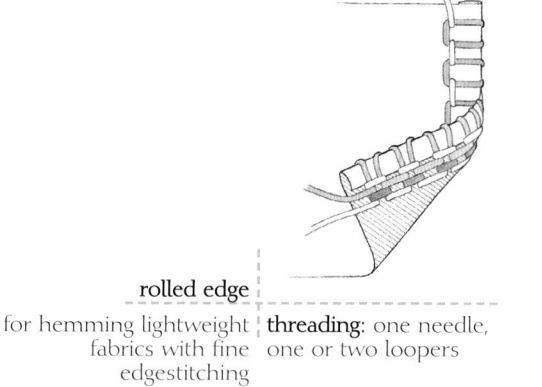

rolled edge — for hemming lightweight fabrics with fine edgestitching | **threading:** one needle, one or two loopers

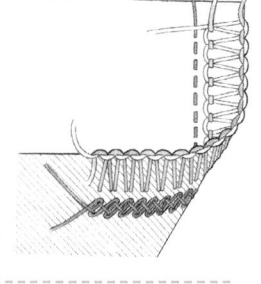

five-thread safety — for seaming and overcast-stitching woven fabrics | **threading:** two needles, three loopers

hand-sewing tools

You can sew almost anything by machine, but you still need a supply of hand needles and pins. You'll also need a pincushion or magnetic pin dish or two—one near the machine and one near the ironing board.

Pins

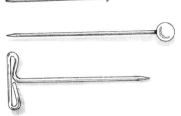

dressmaker straight pins: 1¹/₁₆" (2.7 cm) long, sometimes with large, colored glass heads that are easy to see and grasp

pleating pins: about 1" (2.5 cm) long, used on delicate fabrics

quilting pins: 1¼" (3.2 cm) long, ideal for pinning bulky fabrics or multiple layers

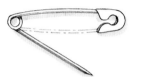

t-pins: large with a wide, crossbar head that won't get lost in heavy drapery fabrics and bulky knits or fall out of open-weave fabrics

safety pins: with sharp points that lock into covered ends; helpful when inserting elastic into a casing

Hand-sewing Needles

Hand-sewing needles, sized from 1 to 26, are often sold with several sizes in one package. The larger the needle size, the shorter and finer the needle.

betweens: short with round eyes and commonly used in quilting

embroidery or crewel needles: medium length with larger eyes to accommodate decorative thread or yarn

sharps: all-purpose, medium-length needles with sharp points

milliner's needles: long with round eyes and handy for basting

Rough, bent, or rusty pins and needles ruin fabric, so toss them out.

measuring tools

Careful, accurate measuring is key to sewing success. Once you have cut the fabric, there's no turning back. Be sure you have a seam gauge, a flexible tape measure, and a rigid straightedge ruler. For quilting, you'll want a see-through, acrylic ruler marked with ¼" (6 mm) parallel lines for quick, accurate measuring.

seam gauge: great for small measurements, especially seam allowances and hems

flexible tape measure: 60" (152.4 cm) soft (but not stretchy) tape measure for body measurements or curved seams

transparent ruler: 2" (5.1 cm) wide transparent ruler with horizontal and vertical measurement markings for easy measuring and marking

yardstick: helpful when you are laying out pattern and fabric, locating grainline, and marking hems

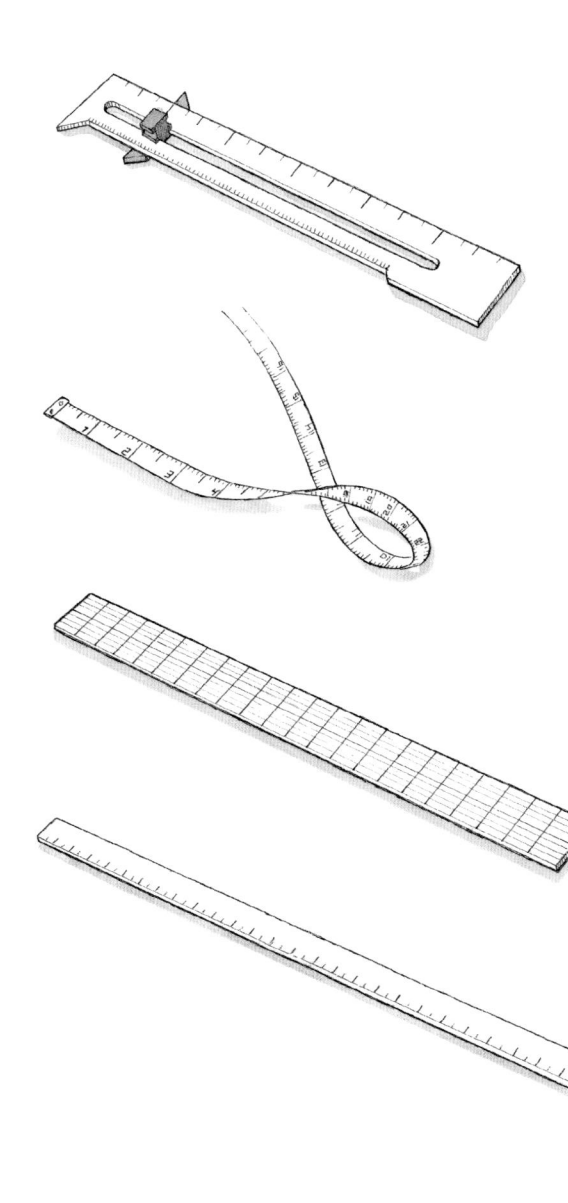

For tailoring and pattern making, there are curved rulers that help you draw shaped seam lines.

cutting tools

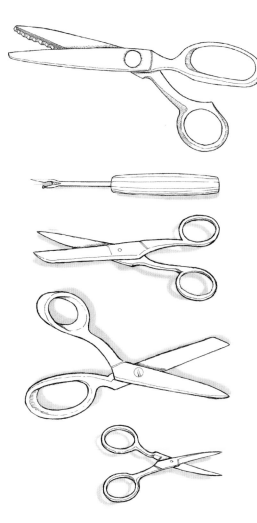

There are many types of cutting tools, but here are some you'll use often. Invest in high-quality tools—it's worth it!—and keep them sharp. Working with dull tools just makes the work harder, and they are more likely to snag or damage fabric. Keep your sewing scissors separate from your household scissors, and never let anyone use them to cut paper!

pinking shears: Pinking shears have zigzag blades that cut a "pinked" edge. Pinking is one way to finish seam allowances to keep them from raveling.

seam ripper: With this precise tool, you can remove unwanted stitches without ripping the fabric. You can also cut open stitched buttonholes.

sewing scissors: You need scissors to trim, grade, and clip seams. Most sewing scissors are 6" (15.2 cm) long with one sharp point and one blunt, rounded point.

sewing shears: Shears are usually 7" to 8" (17.8 to 20.3 cm) long. They have bent handles and a small hole for the thumb. The bottom blade rests on the work surface so the fabric lies flat, which makes it easier to cut long lengths of fabric accurately.

embroidery scissors or thread snips: These small scissors are for precision cutting (trimming seams, cutting corners, and snipping thread ends, for example). They are about 3" to 4" (7.6 to 10.2 cm) long with two sharp points. Some sewers wear them around their necks on a ribbon or string to keep them handy.

Work a seam ripper on the outside of the seam, not between the layers of fabrics. Slide the sharp point under the stitch to cut. Repeat every 1" (2.5 cm) along the seam.

marking tools

Marking tools allow you to transfer symbols and other information from the sewing pattern onto the fabric. These temporary marks help you accurately assemble the fabric pieces after you remove the pattern. Test any marking tool on a scrap of your fabric first to make sure the marks will come off later and won't harm the fabric.

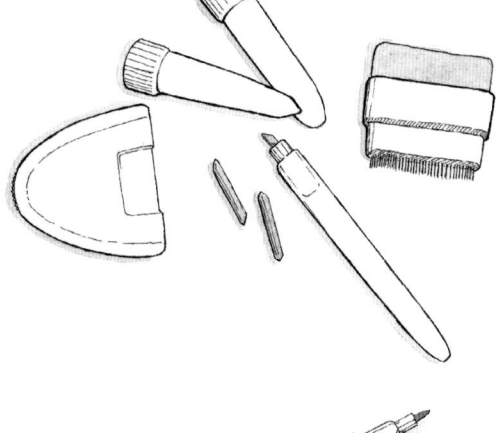

chalk wedge or pencil: With these tools, it's simple to accurately copy design lines and construction markings. Chalk rubs off easily, so mark the fabric just before you're ready to sew.

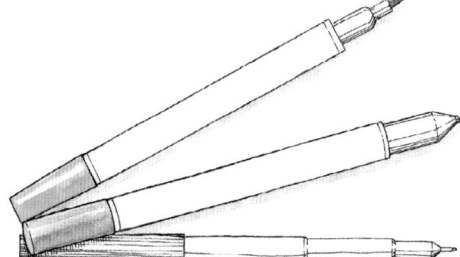

fabric-marking pens: Water-soluble ink pens usually have blue ink that you can remove from the fabric with a damp sponge when you no longer need the markings. (Do not use water-soluble pens on very lightweight fabrics or on fabrics that need to be dry-cleaned.) Air-soluble ink simply disappears on its own within 48 hours.

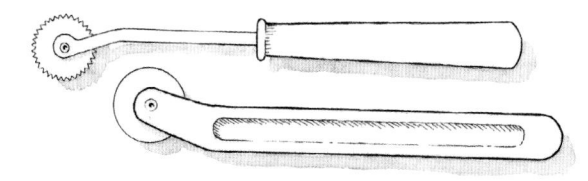

tracing wheel and tracing paper: A tracing wheel has either a smooth edge, which is best for delicate fabrics, or a notched edge, which works well for most other fabrics. The wheel is used with dressmaker's tracing paper to mark large areas and long seam lines. The paper has colored wax on one side and is positioned on the fabric with the wax side down. Roll the tracing wheel over the paper, to transfer the marks. Choose a wax color that is a shade or two different from your fabric so it is clearly visible.

The sharp edge of a sliver of dry bath soap makes an excellent marking tool! Carefully shave it with a knife if you need a finer line.

all about thread

High-quality thread might be your most important sewing tool! It should be smooth and strong with uniform thickness. Color is the most obvious difference between threads, but fiber content is equally important. As a general rule, match the fiber content of the thread with that of the fabric. Use the same type of thread in the needle and in the bobbin (unless sewing with decorative thread).

Common Threads

Cotton-wrapped polyester thread	Cotton thread	Polyester thread	Silk thread
• general-purpose thread • used for most sewing and dressmaking • suitable for natural or man-made fibers, knit or woven fabrics	• best with cotton, linen, or wool fibers • good with woven fabrics	• suitable for fabrics made of man-made fibers, especially knits	• expensive • suitable for garment sewing on silk and wool fabric

Specialty Threads

Basting thread	Hand-quilting thread	Invisible thread	Machine embroidery thread	Metallic thread	Serger thread	Topstitching thread	Upholstery thread
• lightweight thread, usually 100 percent cotton • used for temporary stitches • breaks easily so you can pull out the stitches	• has a waxy coating to prevent tangles • strong enough to pass through multiple layers of fabric	• usually nylon • used for mending, machine-quilting, and attaching trim	• high-gloss thread • available in a crayon-box assortment of colors, textures, and sizes • designed to fill a specific area smoothly	• has a lovely shimmer • ideal for decorative stitching	• sold on large cones • designed for high-speed sewing • decorative threads, such as wooly nylon, nylon, metallic, cotton, and rayon, can be threaded in loopers	• strong and heavy • produces a well-defined stitch • works well for sewing on buttons	• 100 percent nylon or polyester • strong and resistant to chemicals and mildew • suitable for upholstery fabrics

pressing tools

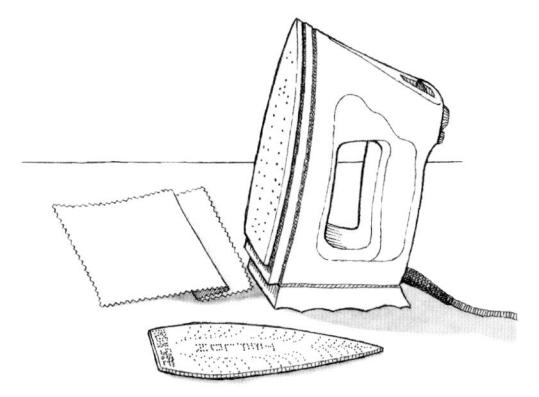

Pressing is the key to professional-looking projects—every step of the way. Pressing and ironing are different processes. To press, lift the iron and firmly place it on the fabric (instead of gliding it over the fabric as you do when you iron). Take the time to press each seam after you stitch it.

You need an iron that steams, mists, sprays, and surges at any temperature setting. The ironing board should be sturdy. Press cloths, such as muslin or cheesecloth, protect the fabric and the iron's sole plate, especially when working with fusibles. Or you can substitute a Teflon-coated cover that fits over the sole plate.

There are several optional pressing tools to help you press shaped seams, corners, and tight areas.

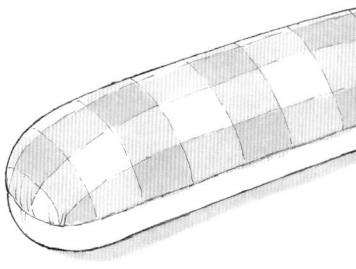

needle board: flexible bed of steel needles for pressing pile fabrics, especially velvet, without crushing the pile (or you can use a fluffy towel)

seam roll: firmly packed, long cushion (half wool, half cotton) for pressing seams open without leaving an imprint on the right side of the fabric

tailor's ham: firmly packed, rounded cushion (half wool, half cotton) for pressing shaped and curved seams and sections

point presser: multipurpose, wooden tool for pounding creases in heavy fabric and pressing different-shaped seams and small areas, such as collar points

sleeve board: narrow, mini ironing board for pressing narrow, tubular garment sections, such as sleeves

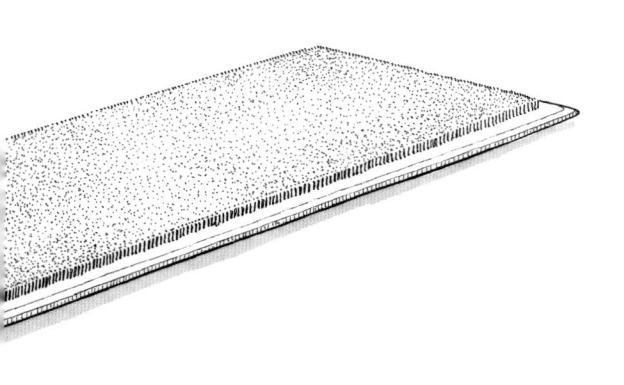

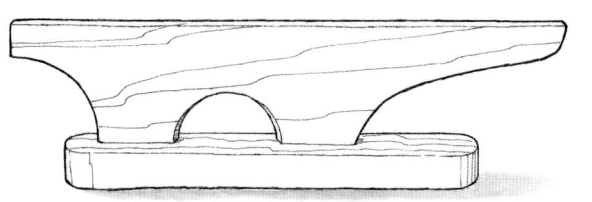

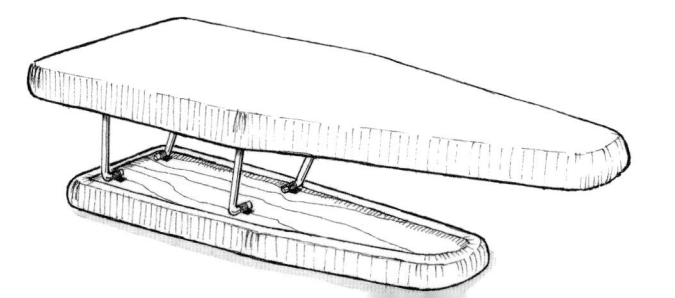

pressing pointers

Careful and frequent pressing is the key to great-looking garments. Pressing is not the same process as ironing. When pressing, lift and firmly place the iron—do not glide over the fabric, as when ironing.

- [ ] Always test the heat setting on scrap fabric first to make sure the iron is the correct temperature for your fabric.

- [ ] Press after completing each step of the construction process.

- [ ] Always use a press cloth to prevent heat shine and water spotting. A scrap of muslin makes a good press cloth.

- [ ] Seam allowances might leave an impression on the right side of delicate fabrics, so insert strips of brown paper between the seam allowances and the garment.

- [ ] Whenever possible, press on the wrong side of the fabric.

- [ ] When pressing curves, take care not to pull or stretch the fabric.

- [ ] Press seams and darts before stitching another seam across them.

- [ ] Do not press over basting threads or pins—they might leave marks in the fabric.

Pressing Straight Seams

1. Press along the stitching line to embed the stitches into the fabric.

2. Press the seam open, creasing the folds with the tip of the iron.

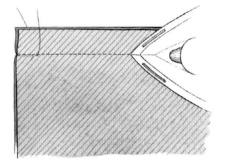

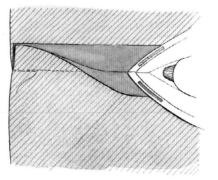

Pressing curved seams

1. Press the seam flat along the stitching line, to embed the stitches. Clip or notch the curve, as needed (see page 60).

2. Press the seam open on a tailor's ham or seam roll (see page 22), pressing with only the tip of the iron.

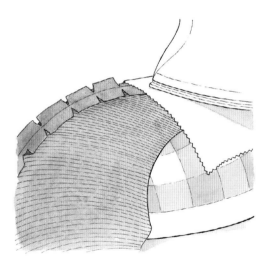

interfacing, stabilizers & fusibles

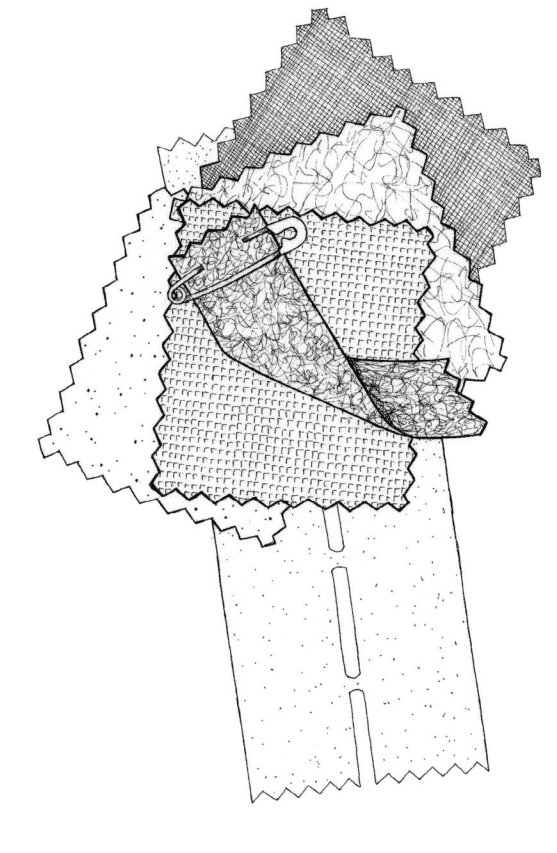

Interfacing is sewn or fused (see page 25) to the wrong side of fabric to add body, stability, and shape to garment pieces. It is used within collars, cuffs, lapels, waistbands, and pockets, behind buttons and buttonholes, and around necklines to prevent stretching. Choose interfacing that is lighter weight than the fashion fabric. To make sure they are compatible, hold them together and make sure the interfacing supports the fabric but doesn't change the way it hangs.

Interfacing is either woven, nonwoven, or knit. Woven interfacing should be cut on the same grain as the fabric. Nonwovens can be cut in any direction. Knit interfacing stretches on the crosswise grain and is suitable for lightweight knits and woven fabrics.

Interfacing Type	Uses
sheer or featherweight	lightweight woven and knitted fabrics
lightweight	dress-weight fabrics
medium-weight	suitings and medium-weight to heavy fabrics
heavyweight	accessories, toys, and craft
waistbanding (precut)	waistbands, cuffs, plackets, and straight facings
hair canvas	tailoring

Stabilizers & Other Fusibles

Fusible web bonds together two layers of fabric. It is used instead of stitching for hemming and for securing trim and appliqués before sewing them in place. Fusible web is available with or without paper backing. Hemming tape, which is similar to fusible web, is used specifically to fuse hems. Stabilizers provide extra stability behind decorative stitching. Fabric adhesives, such as fabric glue or glue sticks, temporarily hold fabric layers or permanently secure trim on items that won't be washed or handled excessively.

how to apply interfacing

Sew-in interfacing looks more natural than fusible (iron-on) interfacing, and it's the only choice if your fabric can't withstand high heat. Fusible interfacing has a resin on one side, which bonds to the wrong side of the fabric with the application of heat, moisture, and pressure. Always follow the manufacturer's directions. Fusibles do change the hand of the fabric, so test any fusible on a scrap of the fabric you're using for your project.

sew-in, lightweight interfacing: Hand- or machine-baste the interfacing to the wrong side of the fabric, next to the seam line and inside the seam allowance. Trim away the interfacing close to the stitching.

sew-in, medium- to heavy-weight interfacing: Trim the interfacing to fit inside the seam line and hand-baste it to the wrong side, to minimize bulk in the seam.

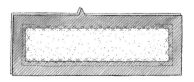

fusible interfacing: Place the interfacing adhesive side down on the wrong side of the fabric. Cover it with a damp press cloth. With a dry iron on a warm setting, press (do not iron) one area for about 15 seconds. Lift the iron, reposition it, and repeat the pressing until the whole piece is fused in place.

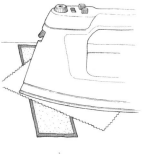

fusible web: Fusible web is placed between two fabrics to bond them together. Methods and heat settings differ from brand to brand, so follow the manufacturer's directions for application.

lining in garments

Lining is most commonly used in tailored garments, such as jackets, coats, trousers, and skirts. A lining prolongs the life of the garment by enclosing and protecting the inner construction details and the interfacing. A commercial pattern will provide pattern pieces and sewing instructions if the garment should be lined.

Lining fabric is tightly woven and lightweight. It has a silky, slippery hand, which makes it easy and comfortable to put on and take off the garment. Lining is sold in different weights and colors and is color-fast, perspiration proof, and wrinkle resistant. It often has a cling-free finish. Choose lining fabric that is softer and lighter weight than your fabric, but has the same care requirements.

What Does a Lining Do?
- makes the garment more comfortable
- makes the garment warmer
- protects the interior surface of the fabric
- hides interior construction details and interfacing
- helps keep the garment from wrinkling
- helps garment hang better and gives fabric more body
- minimizes stretching and wear
- provides structural stability and helps maintain shape
- reduces clinging and makes it easier to slip garment on and off

lining & interlining in home décor

Lining creates a professional, custom-made finish for your home décor. Drapery lining fabrics are available in the same widths as decorator fabrics. They are treated to resist stains and repel water, and some also block light.

For items like table runners or placemats, which have visible linings, choose lighter weight decorator fabric that has the same care requirements as the main fabric. (For instructions on how to line curtains, see pages 181-182; for placements, see page 163.)

What Does a Lining Do?

- protects the decorator fabric from soil and abrasion
- improves the way the item hangs or drapes
- neatens the wrong side and hides construction details
- adds to the longevity of the item
- protects decorator fabric from fading with sunlight
- helps maintain shape and provides stability
- gives windows a neat appearance from the outside
- blackout linings block light and increase opacity
- thermal lining adds insulation

Interlining is a fabric that is inserted and stitched between the main fabric and the lining. It adds extra body and insulation. It also makes fabrics with a printed design more opaque when light shines through. Plain drapery lining fabric can serve as interlining.

functional trim

Some trims help with the construction of a garment. They are sold in packages in convenient lengths. When applying trims, mark their placement with a water- or air-soluble pen. Pin or glue the trim in place and sew slowly, easing around the corners. Do not pull the trim taut as you stitch. For more about attaching trims, see pages 78 to 80.

seam binding

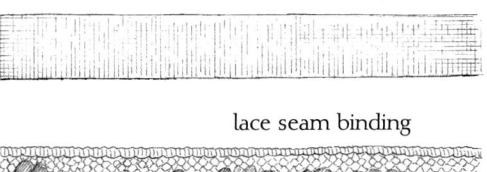

Seam binding is a woven tape, usually 1/2" (1.3 cm) wide. It helps to finish hem edges, reinforce seams, or extend seam allowances.

lace seam binding

single-fold bias tape

double-fold bias tape

fold-over braid

twill tape

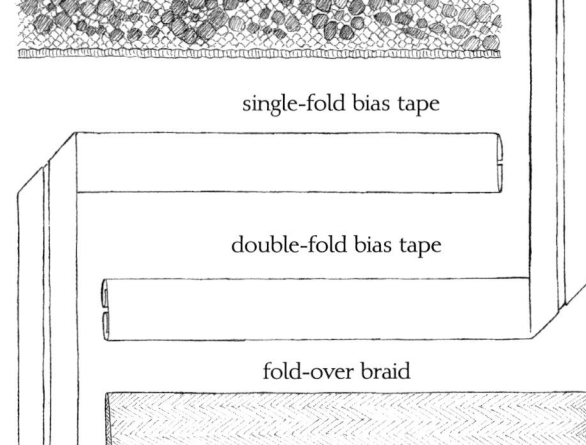

Lace seam binding is also a decorative trim. It's suitable on hem edges of knit or stretch woven fabrics.

Single-fold bias tape is a flexible, pre-folded tape that is used to encase raw edges. It is simply a bias strip with edges pressed to the wrong side so that they meet in the center. Single-fold bias tape is available ready-made or you can make it from bias-cut strips of fabric (see page 76).

Double-fold bias tape is similar to single-fold bias tape, but is folded a second time slightly off center, so the top is marginally narrower for easier application.

Fold-over braid is a pre-folded, decorative braid trim that is used to encase raw edges.

Twill tape is a strong cotton or polyester tape with a diagonal weave. It's best for making casings and for stabilizing and reinforcing seams.

decorative trim

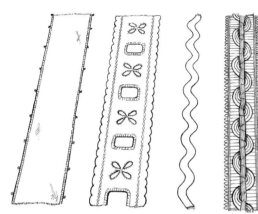

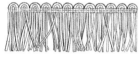

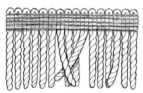

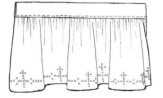

Choosing trim is a matter of personal taste, however, it's important to match the care requirements and weight of the trim with your fabric.

Band trims have two finished edges and should be topstitched in place.

braid: three or more strands plaited together; available in many widths and variations

gimp: narrow braid made of thin cording

middy braid: narrow, flat braid; sold off a bolt or in packages of precut lengths

ribbon: narrow, woven fabric with two finished edges; wide range of widths, weaves, and fibers

rickrack: flat zigzag; many widths and colors

soutache: very narrow braid woven with a center indentation for stitching

Edgings are flat or gathered with one finished edge. The other edge is meant to be caught in a seam or stitched to an edge.

beading: flat trim with openings through which a ribbon can be inserted; can be edging or band trim

eyelet: traditionally white, lightweight, with embroidered holes

fringe: variations include ball, bullion, brush, and chainette; all have a flat heading for application and loose, hanging threads

lace: openwork trim, can be flat or gathered; edging or band trim

piping: fabric-covered cord with a fabric extension for insertion into a seam

ruffling: lace or other fabric gathered onto a heading (extra fabric for insertion into a seam)

Insertion trims are used as narrow, decorative connecting strips between two fabrics.

lace: flat openwork trim; used for lingerie

fagoting: flat strip with continuous crosswise bars of thread, meant to mimic hand-stitched, heirloom fagoting

elastics

Elastic is a narrow, flexible, stretchable strip that is enclosed in a casing or stitched directly onto a garment. Elastic helps create shape at the waist, wrist, ankle, or neckline (see page 81). Standard widths range from 1/4" to 2 1/2" (6 mm to 6.4 cm). You can also buy elastic thread and wide, decorative, waistband elastic. Look for non-roll elastic, which is extra-heavy to prevent it from rolling in a waistband.

High-quality elastic stretches to more than twice its length. Most elastic is a rubber/polyester blend, which can be machine-washed and dry-cleaned.

braided elastic: Braided elastic becomes narrower when it's stretched. This style is used inside casings on sleeve and leg hems and also on swimwear.

knitted elastic: Knitted elastic is soft and strong. It retains its width when stretched and is good for casings and direct-fabric application on light- to medium-weight fabrics.

woven elastic: Woven elastic is the strongest elastic. It retains its width when stretched and is good for casings and direct-fabric application on light-, medium-, or heavyweight fabrics.

working
with
patterns

commercial patterns

The beauty of working with commercial patterns is that the hard work is done for you! You are free to focus on the creative decisions—the type and color of the fabric; the style of the buttons and embellishments.

Brand-new pattern catalogs hit the stores either monthly or seasonally. Each catalog contains more than 500 patterns, including a large selection of classic styles and off-season styles, too. So, if you need a heavy jacket in July or a bathing suit in November, you can always find one! The newest styles are in the first few pages of each tabbed section of the catalog and are usually featured in several spreads of fashion photography.

The pattern catalog is divided into sections, each for a specific category: dresses, eveningwear and bridal, sportswear, active sportswear, separates, outerwear, lingerie and sleepwear, women and half-sizes, maternity, men and boys, juniors or preteens, childrenswear, crafts, home decorating, and costumes.

Each pattern has its own style number and is featured on its own page or half-page with a photograph or illustration that shows what the finished garment will look like. There are often alternative views, which show different constructions and minor style variations in length, fullness, decorative stitching, collars, and pockets.

The back of the catalog has an index of pattern style numbers, a fitting measurement chart, and an explanation of figure types and sizing.

pattern sizing

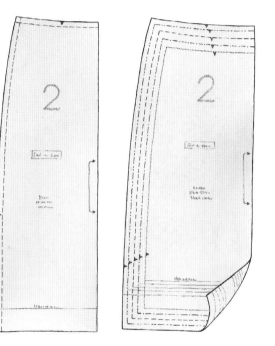

Pattern sizing is different from ready-to-wear sizing. Compare your actual body measurements to the fitting/measurement chart at the back of the catalog. Choose the pattern size that most closely matches your body measurements (see page 34). If all your measurements don't match up with one size, choose a pattern that matches your bust size when making dresses, blouses, and jackets. Choose a pattern that matches your hip size when making skirts and pants.

Many patterns are multisize, with several sizes printed on the same tissue paper. If you have a size 10 waist and size 12 hips, for example, you can easily draw alteration lines from one seam line to the other, tapering gently to maintain the garment's shape. Or, if the pattern includes several garments, you can make a size 10 jacket and size 12 skirt. Loose-fitting items are sometimes sized extra-small, small, medium, and large, and those four sizes are often printed on one tissue.

To avoid confusion, seam lines are usually not printed on multisize patterns. Sometimes the different sizes have different types of cutting lines—one solid, one dashed, and one with a dot/dash pattern—to make each size easier to cut accurately.

Multisize patterns are great for children. Don't cut away the larger size cutting lines. Fold them under or trace the size you're making. This way, you can use the same pattern through several growth spurts!

finding the right size

The key to determining the correct size pattern is accurate body measurements. Have someone take your measurements for you, if possible. To do it yourself, stand in front of a full-length mirror and make sure the tape measure is always flat and straight.

Wear a leotard or underwear and tie a string or ribbon around your waist. The string will roll to your natural waist, making an easy reference point. Stand up straight with your shoulders back. Hold the tape measure snug, but not tight, and parallel to the floor for circumference measurements. Measure twice to double-check. Record your measurements on an index card and bring it with you when you go shopping for your pattern.

1 Bust:
   a. Full bust: Measure around the torso over the fullest part of the bust and straight across the back.
   b. High bust: Measure across the top of the bust, above the full bust line, just under the arm and across the widest part of the back.
      If your high-bust measurement is at least 2" (5.1 cm) more than your full-bust measurement, use the high-bust measurement to determine your pattern size for blouses, dresses, and jackets. If the high-bust measurement is not 2" (5.1 cm) more than the full-bust measurement, use the full-bust measurement.

2 Waist: Measure around your natural waist, directly over the string, around the thinnest part of your body.

3 Hips:
   a. Measure around the fullest part of your hips, usually 7" to 9" (17.8 to 22.9 cm) below the string that marks your waist.
   b. If your waist and hip measurements are not both included in one pattern size, choose the pattern for your hip measurement. It is easier to adjust the pattern at the waist than it is at the hips, particularly if it is a multisize pattern.

4 Back waist length: Measure from the most prominent bone at the base of your neck to the string at your waist.

5 Height: Remove your shoes, stand up tall with your eyes straight ahead, and measure your height against a wall.

design & wearing ease

Design ease and wearing ease affect how close or loose fitting the finished garment will be. Design ease is the extra fullness the designer adds to the pattern to create a garment's silhouette and style. Wearing ease refers to the extra room or space in the garment beyond your body measurements.

Every garment made of woven fabrics needs wearing ease to allow for movement and comfort. A close-fitting top doesn't need much wearing ease, for example, but a coat or jacket does. Knit fabrics stretch, so they don't require wearing ease.

Use your body measurements to determine the correct size pattern. Then consider how the designer intended the garment to fit to help you decide if you will like the finished results. The following terms indicate how much ease is in the pattern. You'll find them in the pattern description on the back of the envelope. The photo or illustration on the front of the envelope will help you visualize the fit, too.

close fitting: little or no wearing ease and no design ease

fitted: minimal wearing ease and little or no design ease

semi-fitted: up to 4" (10.2 cm) of design and wearing ease in the bust area

loose fitting: up to 8" (20.3 cm) of design and wearing ease in the bust area

very loose fitting: more than 8" (20.3 cm) of design and wearing ease in the bust area

the pattern envelope

The pattern envelope is designed to give you all the information you need to decide whether the pattern is right for you.

The envelope front is all about fashion—what the finished garment or project will look like. The back of the envelope provides all the important information you need to sew all the items included in the pattern.

Elements on the Front

☐ Fashion photograph(s) or illustration(s)

☐ Name of the pattern company and pattern style number

☐ Figure type (misses, women's, half-sizes, etc.) and size

☐ Identifying logos (such as for petite, multisize, easy to sew, and knits only)

Elements on the Back

☐ Line drawings—of the back views and sometimes front views—show the shape and outline of the design, seams, details, pocket placement, zipper location, etc.

☐ Garment caption is a written description of the garment.

☐ Number of pattern pieces required for the garment.

☐ Finished garment measurements, indicating how long and how full the finished garment will be.

☐ Recommended fabrics and information about fabric suitability. Fabrics with a nap or a one-way design require extra fabric, so follow the "with nap" yardage suggestion (see page 50.)

☐ Notions are the necessary items you need to complete the design, including thread, zipper, buttons, and seam binding.

☐ A body measurement chart may be printed on the envelope flap or on the instruction sheet. It is always printed in the back of the catalog.

☐ The yardage block indicates how much fabric, interfacing, and lining you need to make the items in the pattern. Highlight the information for your size and the variation you plan to make.

☐ Style number, size, and price.

the instruction sheet

Inside the envelope, folded with the pattern pieces, you'll find the instruction sheet, which explains how to lay out the pattern, cut the fabric, and sew the pieces together.

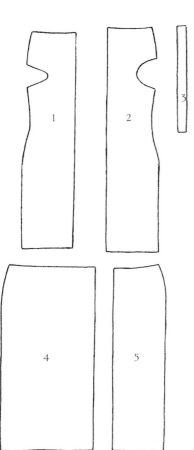

pattern pieces key: This key includes a list and line drawings of all the pieces. The drawings help you visualize the pieces you will be using. Usually there is a list of which pieces are needed for each particular item. Circle the pieces you'll use.

general sewing information: Here you'll find important tips and basic cutting and sewing techniques. This section explains the symbols on the pattern pieces and also includes a brief glossary of terms. Sometimes there is a body measurement chart.

cutting layouts: There is a cutting "map" for every size, every fabric width, and every item shown on the front of the envelope. The layouts show you how to fold the fabric and position the pieces for the most economical use of the fabric (see pages 50 and 51). Layout guides for lining, interfacing, or contrast fabric are provided, too, if needed.

step-by-step sewing guide: This section provides step-by-step, clearly written instructions with construction sketches. If a step is complex, there is often a secondary, enlarged sketch.

Read through all the construction steps before starting. It's easier to get where you're going when you know the path!

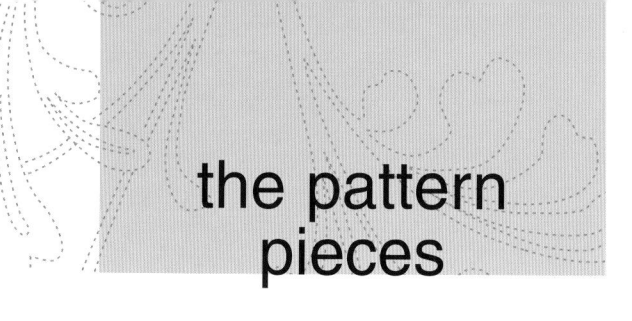

the pattern pieces

Pattern pieces are printed on lightweight tissue paper. In the center of each printed piece is a section with general information, including the pattern style number, size, the name of the piece (skirt front, waistband, etc.), and its assigned number. Cutting information ("cut one on fold," "cut two," etc.) is also printed on the pattern piece. All pattern companies use a universal system of marking symbols.

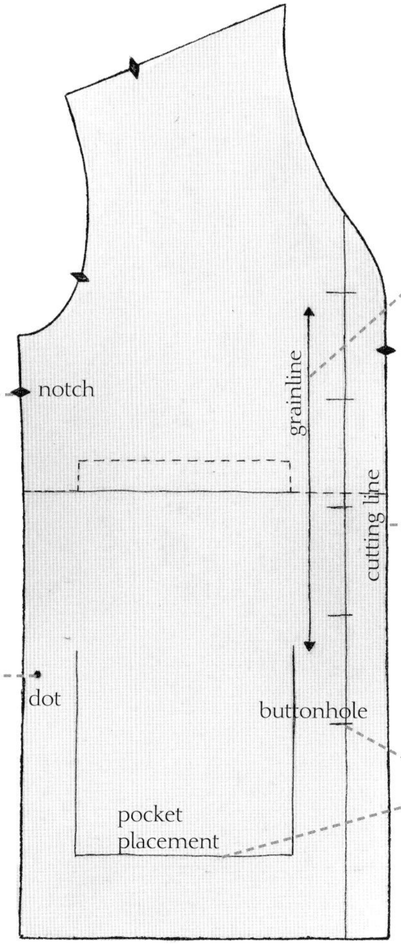

notches

Diamond shapes—single, double, or triple—help you match pattern pieces along the seam lines.

notch

dots

These marks—large or small (sometimes squares or triangles)—indicate special construction areas that require matching, clipping, gathering, and stay-stitching.

dot

grainline

cutting line

pocket placement

buttonhole

grainline

The suggested direction of the fabric grain is indicated with a heavy solid line with arrows at each end. Align this grainline with the lengthwise grain (parallel to selvage) of the fabric, unless otherwise noted. Measure from the selvage with a ruler to make sure the grainline is straight.

cutting line

The cutting line is a heavy solid line around the outer edge (sometimes with a drawing of a tiny scissors). Multisize patterns have a different line for every size. Highlight the line you want to follow.

construction and detail placement lines

Lines indicate dart, zipper, pocket, button, and buttohole placement.

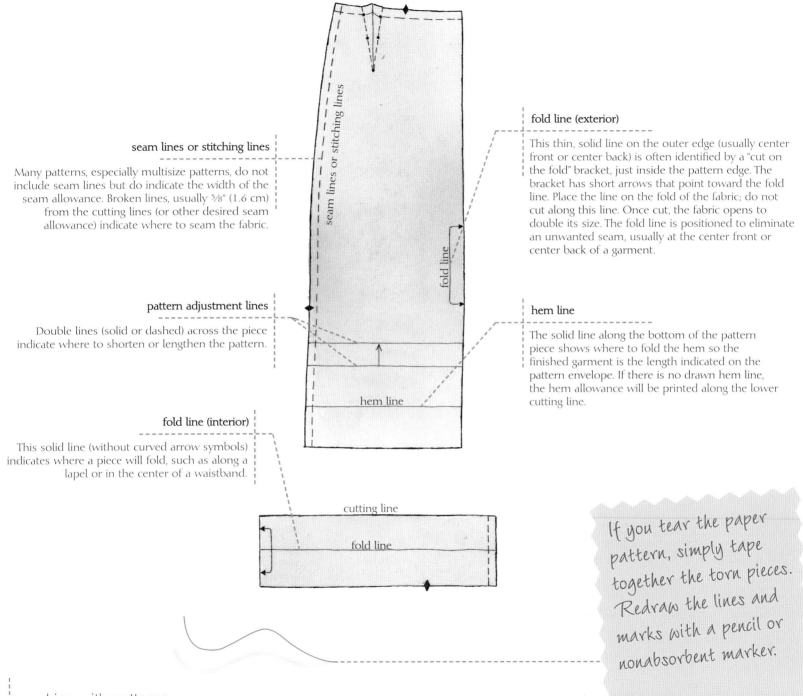

seam lines or stitching lines

Many patterns, especially multisize patterns, do not include seam lines but do indicate the width of the seam allowance. Broken lines, usually 5⁄8" (1.6 cm) from the cutting lines (or other desired seam allowance) indicate where to seam the fabric.

pattern adjustment lines

Double lines (solid or dashed) across the piece indicate where to shorten or lengthen the pattern.

fold line (interior)

This solid line (without curved arrow symbols) indicates where a piece will fold, such as along a lapel or in the center of a waistband.

fold line (exterior)

This thin, solid line on the outer edge (usually center front or center back) is often identified by a "cut on the fold" bracket, just inside the pattern edge. The bracket has short arrows that point toward the fold line. Place the line on the fold of the fabric; do not cut along this line. Once cut, the fabric opens to double its size. The fold line is positioned to eliminate an unwanted seam, usually at the center front or center back of a garment.

hem line

The solid line along the bottom of the pattern piece shows where to fold the hem so the finished garment is the length indicated on the pattern envelope. If there is no drawn hem line, the hem allowance will be printed along the lower cutting line.

seam lines or stitching lines

fold line

hem line

cutting line

fold line

If you tear the paper pattern, simply tape together the torn pieces. Redraw the lines and marks with a pencil or nonabsorbent marker.

simple length adjustments

You can save time and fabric—and get a better fit—by making pattern length adjustments before you cut your fabric. Before you begin, press the pattern piece with a dry, warm iron to remove wrinkles and folds.

Compare your body measurements (see page 34) with the measurement of the pattern from seam line to hem line to decide how much to shorten or lengthen. If the pattern doesn't have specific pattern adjustment lines, you can lengthen or shorten it at the hem without drastically changing the shape of the finished garment. Simply cut away or draw in the desired amount of length.

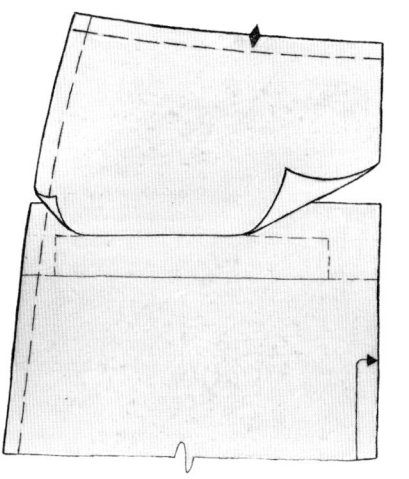

To Shorten a Pattern

Cut along the pattern adjustment line and overlap the cut edges the desired amount. Measure with a ruler or tape measure to be sure that the pattern is overlapped uniformly along the cut. Tape the edges together. With a shaped ruler and pencil or marker, redraw and blend the cutting lines. Repeat for corresponding pieces (for example, skirt front and back, both sleeve pieces for a two-piece sleeve, bodice front and back).

To Lengthen a Pattern

Cut along the pattern adjustment line and place a wide strip of paper under the cut edges (be sure the paper is wide enough to accommodate the extra length). Spread the cut pattern apart the desired amount of adjustment and tape each edge to the paper. Measure the gap with a ruler or tape measure to ensure that the pattern is spread uniformly along the cut. With a pencil or marker, redraw and blend the cutting lines and any other markings. Repeat for corresponding pieces.

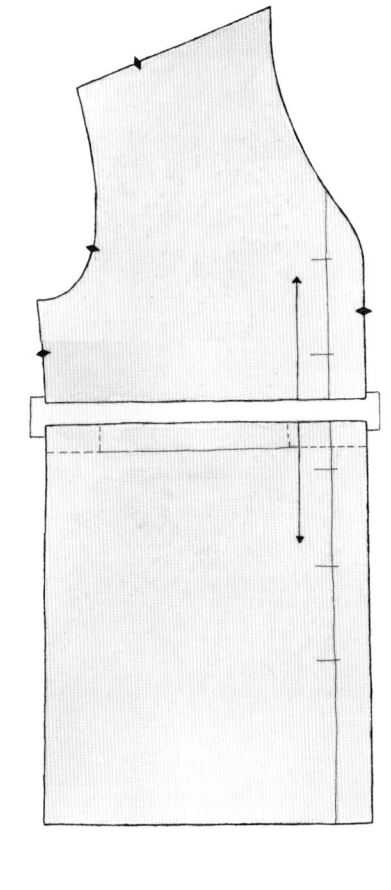

getting
set to sew

choosing the right fabric

A trip to the fabric store is inspirational! From cotton broadcloth to fuzzy fleece, every fabric has its own personality. The way it looks, feels, drapes, launders, and wears is determined by several characteristics: fiber content, construction (woven or knitted), and finishes. This information is often listed on the end of the fabric bolt. (See pages 112 to 119 for more information about fabric characteristics and care.)

Fibers are either natural or man-made, and a fabric can be made entirely from one fiber or from a combination of fibers. Natural fibers come from plants (cotton and linen) or animals (wool and silk). They tend to shrink and lose shape, but are comfortable and absorbent.

Man-made fibers, produced through chemical processes, are designed to mimic natural fibers. They retain their shape and are shrink and stain resistant, but they aren't as comfortable as natural fibers. By blending fibers, manufacturers maximize the positive characteristics of each to create more comfortable, durable, and pleasing fabrics.

How to Choose Fabric

☐ Check the back of the pattern envelope for suggestions.

☐ Certain fabrics have nap (see page 126) so be sure to buy the extra yardage that nap fabrics require.

☐ Consider your wardrobe—which fabrics are most comfortable and flattering?

☐ Understand the properties of the fibers to know how the fabric will perform.

☐ Handle the fabric and see how it falls over your hand. Does it drape or is it crisp and stiff?

☐ Crush a corner with your hand. Does it bounce back or does it wrinkle?

☐ Do the edges ravel excessively? How tight is the weave? A tightly woven fabric is easier to sew and maintain.

☐ Is the color or pattern consistent across the whole length of fabric?

☐ How much does the fabric stretch (and do you want it to stretch)?

☐ Do you notice any pilling or loose threads? Fabrics with this tendency may not wear well.

preparing your work space

Organize your sewing space and equipment so you are ready to sew whenever the urge strikes. If you are lucky, you can leave your sewing machines and supplies set up in a space of their own. Most sewers, though, sew on their kitchen or dining room tables.

If this is the case, at least commandeer a shelf in a closet and keep all your supplies and machines together. Visibility is key—keep thread, notions, and tools in clear, plastic, labeled boxes. Store your prewashed (and labeled) fabric with matching thread, buttons, interfacing, and other related notions in clear, self-sealing plastic bags.

Your sewing table should be large enough to fit your sewing machine and your fabric and supplies. You'll also need a comfortable chair—preferably swivel—and adequate lighting. An extra gooseneck lamp directs task lighting where you need it. Set up an ironing board nearby your sewing table so you can use it frequently.

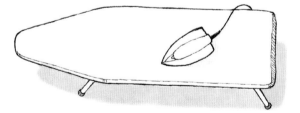

When you're not using your sewing machine, cover it to keep dust out. Most machines have a soft or hard cover. Or you can simply drape the machine with a cloth — or sew your own quick cover!

winding & loading the bobbin

The methods for winding thread onto a bobbin and for loading the bobbin into the machine are different for every machine—so check your owner's manual. Begin with an empty bobbin and wind at a constant, medium speed so the thread winds evenly. Do not overwind the bobbin.

wind on top: Most machines have a mechanism on top for bobbin winding. The machine is threaded specifically to wind the bobbin.

wind in place: Top-loading bobbins often wind in place with the machine threaded as if to sew. This system is convenient because you don't have to unthread the machine each time you need to refill the bobbin.

wind with separate motor: Some new machines feature a second motor for winding bobbins.

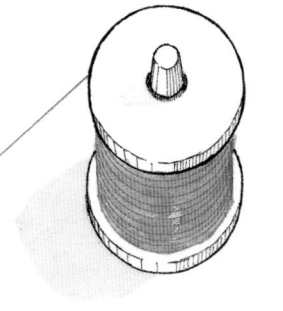

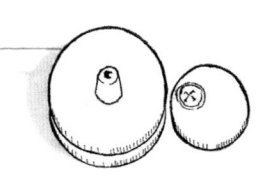

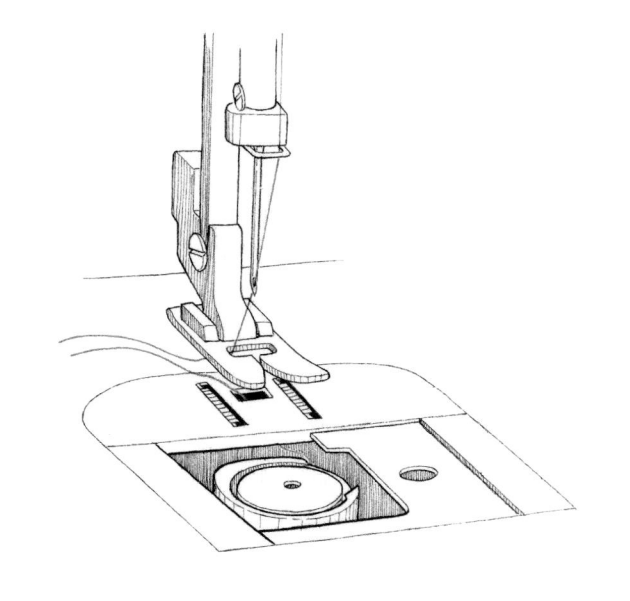

load at top: Drop the bobbin in the top of the machine bed and draw the thread through the tension guide.

load at front or side: Place the bobbin in the case and slide the thread under the bobbin-case tension spring. Place the bobbin case in the machine cavity.

drawing bobbin thread to top: Hold the needle thread while turning the balance wheel toward you one full rotation. As the needle goes down, the top thread interlocks with the bobbin thread and brings it up through the needle hole. Pull both threads together under the presser foot and off to the side or back.

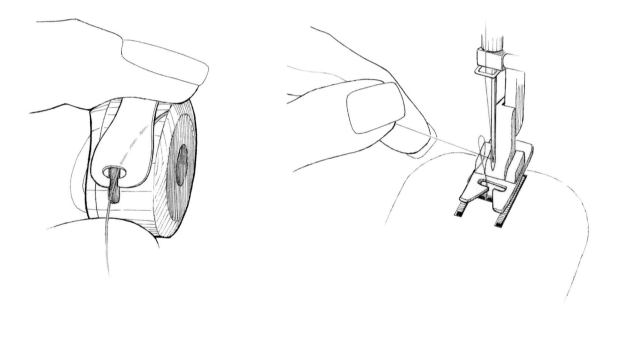

threading the sewing machine

To ensure a good stitch, you must thread the machine correctly. The thread path is usually marked somewhere on the machine. If the path is unclear, refer to the manual.

1 Insert a new needle. Loosen the needle clamp, slide the old needle out and the new one in, and tighten the clamp. Usually the flat side of the shank goes toward the back of the machine, and the groove in the needle shaft faces the front.

2 Wind the bobbin and install it (see pages 44 and 45).

3 Raise the presser foot to open the tension discs, and raise the needle to its highest position.

4 Place the spool on the spool pin, and pull the thread to the left through the first thread guide.

5 Continue to draw the thread through the guides and the tension discs, following the marked thread path or the instructions in your manual. Make sure you don't skip a thread guide or you will distort the tension.

6 Pass the thread through the eye of the needle.

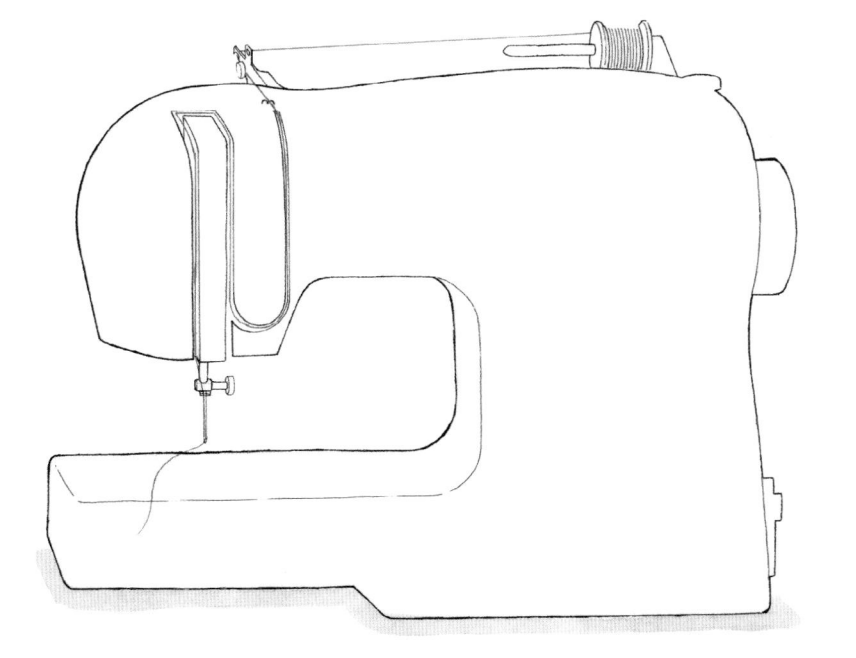

checking stitch tension

For a perfect, balanced stitch, the top and bobbin threads must interlock midway between the fabric layers. Only the needle thread should show on top of the fabric, and only the bobbin thread should show underneath. If the upper thread tension is too tight, the fabric may pucker. If it's too loose, unsightly loops may form on the underside.

To check your stitch tension, sew a seam with different colors of thread in the needle and bobbin. If both thread colors are visible on top, loosen the upper thread tension slightly. If you see both threads on the underside, tighten the tension slightly.

When manually adjusting the upper thread tension, make only a slight adjustment and then test it by sewing a seam on a scrap piece of your fabric. (The bobbin tension is factory-set and shouldn't be adjusted.)

As a general rule, loosen the tension for heavy fabrics and increase it for lightweight fabrics. Some machines have automatic tension control—the machine senses the fabric thickness and self-adjusts.

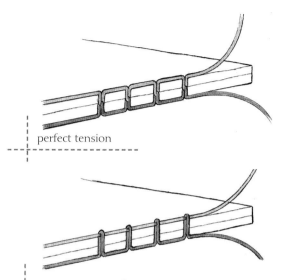

perfect tension

top tension too tight

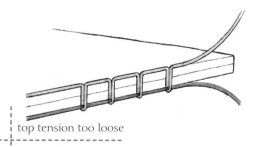

top tension too loose

If stitch tension is off:
- rethread the machine
- take out the bobbin and put it in again
- check that the needle isn't damaged
- adjust the upper thread tension slightly

preparing your fabric

Preshrink your fabric—and lining, zipper, and trims—so the finished project won't shrink later. Launder everything as you intend to launder the finished item. Thoroughly steam-press any fabric that will be dry-cleaned. Machine-wash washable fabric in cold water with mild detergent and machine-dry.

Check the care instructions printed on the end of the fabric bolt. Machine-washing is convenient, but it may remove sizing and other finishes that enhance the fabric's beauty and performance.

If you aren't sure whether your fabric is washable, launder a 6" (15.2 cm) square. Remove it from the dryer, press, and measure. Is it still 6" (15.2 cm) square? Did it fade? Did it ravel? If the results are good, preshrink the entire length of fabric the same way.

If the fabric ravels, zigzag-stitch the cut edges before laundering. Press the dried fabric to eliminate wrinkles. Carefully press out the crease that formed on the bolt.

If the fabric can't be laundered, steam to preshrink it or have it dry-cleaned. To preshrink with steam, first steam-press a small scrap of the fabric to test for damage. Dampen the fabric (or a press cloth) and press on the wrong side until the water evaporates. Shoot steam into the fibers as you press.

If your fabric is identical on both sides, choose one side as the right side and then mark the wrong side with tailor's chalk or a fabric-marking pen so you won't confuse the sides when sewing.

Don't use the selvage as an edge. For projects that require full fabric widths, trim away the selvages before or after seaming or before hemming sides.

Determine whether the surface fibers have a definite up and down direction. Cut fabrics that have nap, pile, shine, shading, and one-way printed or woven designs so the fibers in all the pieces run the same direction (page 136).

Find the straight grain of the fabric and straighten the cut ends (page 49).

Dry-clean window treatments and machine-wash bed, bath, and table linens and pillow covers.

straightening fabric grain

Grain refers to the direction of the fabric threads. Lengthwise grain is parallel to the selvages. Crosswise grain is perpendicular to the selvage. Bias grain is diagonal, and the grain of the fabric with "true bias" runs 45 degrees to the lengthwise and crosswise grains.

Most garments are cut so the lengthwise grain runs from the top of the garment to the hem (see page 50). This layout produces the most stable fabric pieces and the most economical use of the fabric. Garments made from border print fabrics are usually cut on the crosswise grain.

Bias-cut garments stretch in both directions, so they require special techniques for seaming and hemming (see pages 61, 95, and 120). They hang beautifully and tend to skim the body with a fluid elegance, so skirts and eveningwear are often cut on the bias.

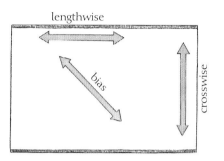

lengthwise

bias

crosswise

Checking the Grain

Woven fabric must be "on-grain"—with lengthwise and crosswise yarns at right angles to each other—so garments hang smoothly and seams are straight. Here's how to check your fabric:

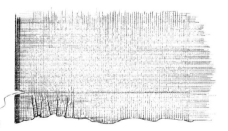

1   Snip into the selvage and pull a crosswise yarn so the fabric puckers. Cut along the puckered yarn to the opposite selvage. The cut creates a perfectly straight grainline in the crosswise direction.

2   Fold the fabric in half lengthwise, aligning the selvages, and smooth it flat. The cut ends should be even. If the ends don't align, shift the layers until they do. Pin the layers together along the selvages and ends at frequent intervals. Steam-press the fabric to align the fibers along the grainlines.

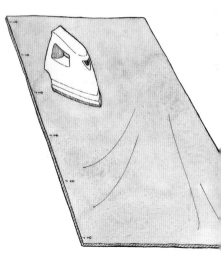

preparing & laying out the pattern

Check the pattern instruction sheet to determine which pattern pieces you need. Cut them apart, leaving extra pattern tissue beyond the cutting lines in case you need to lengthen or widen a piece. The extra tissue also makes it easier to cut the fabric. Press the pattern pieces with a warm, dry iron so they are flat. Make any necessary fitting adjustments (see page 40).

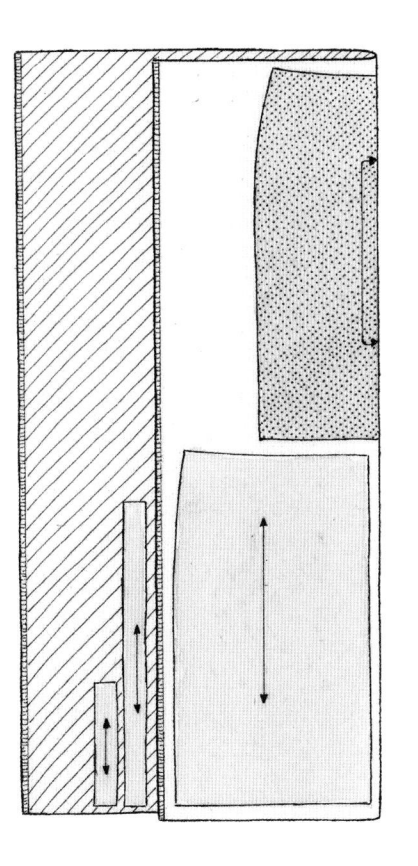

On your instruction sheet, circle or highlight the cutting layout for the fabric width, size, and view of the items you are making. Follow the "with nap" layout if the fabric is a directional print—has a definite up and down—or has a surface pile (see pages 126 and 127). Position all the pieces in the same direction, so the top of each piece is near the same end of the fabric.

Clear a large, flat surface so you can lay out the fabric so it is straight and smooth. If the fabric looks the same on both sides, choose and mark the wrong side with tailor's chalk or a fabric-marking pen. After you cut the pieces, make sure there's a mark on each piece.

Fold the fabric as the layout indicates (most often with selvages and right sides of the fabric together). Do not use the fabric selvage as a straight edge. Position the pieces away from the selvages to avoid puckered seams.

Arrange the pattern pieces on the folded fabric, following the layout guide and beginning with the largest pieces. If the pattern piece is shaded in the guide, place the piece with the printed side down. Place unshaded pieces face up. Leave room to cut any pieces that need more than two fabric pieces. Refer to the section on matching prints, plaids, stripes, and napped fabrics, if it applies (see pages 126 to 128 and page 131).

pinning the pattern

If you adjusted the pattern tissue and the pieces don't fit on the fabric, overlap the tissue pieces—but only outside the cutting lines. If the pieces still don't fit on the fabric, consider shortening the garment slightly at the hem.

Pin all pieces before cutting. To make sure all the pieces are straight, pin the pieces along the fold first. Then pin the largest of the remaining pattern pieces. Put a pin at the center of the grainline. Measure from the edge of the fabric to each end of the grainline to make sure the piece is straight, as shown in the drawing below.

Pin the corners and then the edges, smoothing the pattern as you work. Place the pins within the seam allowance, diagonal to the corners and perpendicular to the edges, with points toward the cutting lines. Space pins about 3" (7.6 cm) apart (but slightly closer together on slippery fabrics and curved cutting lines). Fill in the unused areas of fabric with the smaller pattern pieces. Pin them as you did the larger pieces.

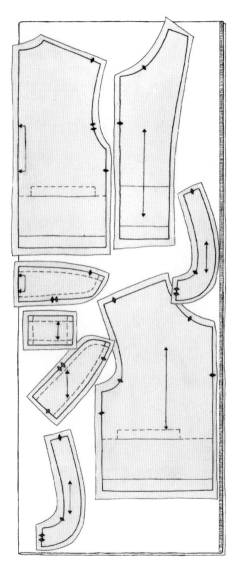

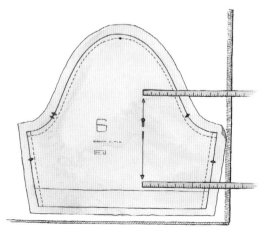

If the entire length of fabric doesn't fit on your cutting surface, pin the pattern pieces at just one end. Fold the fabric, with the pieces inside, and pin the remaining pattern pieces onto the next section of fabric.

cutting the fabric

Double-check that the pattern pieces are positioned correctly and pinned securely before you begin to cut. Place one hand on the table, close to the cutting line to hold the fabric flat. Work with a sharp, dressmaker's shears (page 19)—the bent handle helps keep the fabric flat. Hold your shears to the right of the cutting line for greatest accuracy. Cut with long, firm strokes on straight edges and with shorter ones around curves.

Cut notches outward, if that is how they are drawn. Or you can make short snips into the seam allowance at the notch location. To snip, cut 1/8" (3 mm) into the seam allowance with only the tips of the scissors, taking care not to cut through the seam line. Snips are a perfect way to mark notches, the ends of darts, fold lines, and the center front and back.

Save your fabric scraps so you can later test interfacing weight, stitch quality, pressing, and buttonholes.

marking the fabric

Transfer key markings from the pattern to the fabric after cutting and before removing the tissue.

You should always test any type of marking tool (except thread basting) on a scrap piece of your fabric. For a description of the various types of marking tools, see page 20. The markings are temporary so you should be able to remove them easily, but make sure they stay on for as long as you need to refer to them. Chalk rubs off easily, and air-soluble marking pens disappear in 24 to 48 hours, so mark close to sewing time.

Transfer darts, tucks, gathering and pleat lines, buttonholes, and pocket or other placement lines. If the marks are more helpful on the right side of the fabric (for example, the placement of patch pockets), transfer them with a marking pen or tracing wheel to the wrong side. Then hand-baste over the marks to mark the right side with thread.

chalk and fabric-marking pens: To mark with chalk and fabric marking pens, first place pins at the symbols through the pattern and fabric layers. Carefully pull the pattern away from the fabric and over the pins. Mark the pin location on the top layer of the fabric with the chalk or marking pen. Turn the fabric over and mark the same pin locations on that side. Remove the pins, separate the layers, and connect the markings (if necessary—for example, for darts).

tracing wheel and tracing paper: To mark with a tracing wheel and tracing paper, insert two pieces of dressmaker's tracing paper so the carbon or wax side of the paper faces the wrong side of each fabric layer. Roll the tracing wheel over the mark. Use a ruler as a guide when marking long straight lines. Mark dots, notches, or other small symbols with short lines or Xs. Remove the pattern tissue and tracing paper.

snips, basting, and tacks: You can mark notches, dots, center back and center front markings with snips into the seam allowance.

You can also mark construction elements by hand-basting with thread. Thread a needle with a single, unknotted strand. Take long running stitches to mark straight lines. Leave long thread tails.

You can mark pattern symbols with thread tacks. With double, unknotted thread, insert the needle in and out of the symbol, through pattern and both layers of fabric. Cut the thread, leaving 1" (2.5 cm) tails. Carefully remove the pattern, slightly separate the fabric layers, and clip the thread, leaving thread tufts on each layer.

check before you sew

- [ ] Organize your sewing area. Position the sewing machine on the right side of your worktable so the bulk of the fabric can rest on the left side. Keep a wastebasket nearby or tape a small trash bag to the edge of the worktable to catch thread snips and fabric scraps.

- [ ] Throughout your work area, provide adequate overhead lighting and task lighting for close-up work.

- [ ] Set up an iron and ironing board. Keep a press cloth handy, too (a scrap of muslin works well).

- [ ] Gather all the necessary sewing tools and notions before you start your project. Keep sewing scissors, pins, a pincushion, and a seam ripper within reach.

- [ ] Prepare and preshrink your fabric. Press out the center crease and make sure the fabric grain line is straight (see page 49).

- [ ] Read the pattern instruction sheet from beginning to end.

- [ ] Cut out the necessary pattern pieces and press out any wrinkles with a warm, dry iron.

- [ ] Put a new needle in the machine (the rule of thumb is: a new needle after every eight hours of use).

- [ ] Fill a bobbin with the same thread that is on the thread spool.

- [ ] Brush the bobbin area and feed dogs to remove lint (most machines come with a small lint brush).

- [ ] Raise the presser foot and thread the machine, referring to your machine manual for accuracy.

- [ ] Practice stitching on a scrap of your fabric. Notice the length and tension of the machine stitches. Make any necessary adjustments.

- [ ] Take a deep breath, relax, and begin—but, most important, have fun!

essential techniques

construction stitches

Most sewing machines have a variety of built-in stitches, but you can accomplish anything with just a simple straight stitch. Straight stitches form the basis for several construction techniques, each with its own purpose and finished effect.

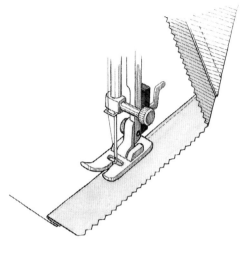

edgestitching: Stitch close to the seam line or edge to make a seam lie flat, as shown above. To create a sharp crease, stitch along a fold very close to the edge. Stitch from the bottom toward the top of a garment.

understitching: To prevent a facing from rolling to the right side of the garment, sew the seam, trim and grade the seam allowances, and press them toward the facing. Working from the right side, stitch through the facing and seam allowances close to the seam line.

staystitching: Stitch just inside the seam line of a single layer to prevent fabric from stretching out of shape. Curved seam lines—such as necklines, facings, armholes, waistlines, and side seams over the hip area—require staystitching.

To turn a corner, leave the needle in the fabric, lift the presser foot, and turn the fabric. Lower the presser foot and continue stitching.

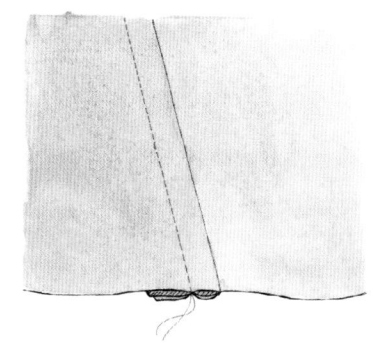

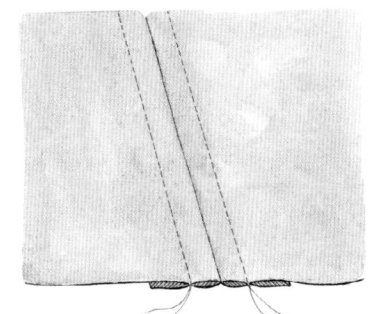

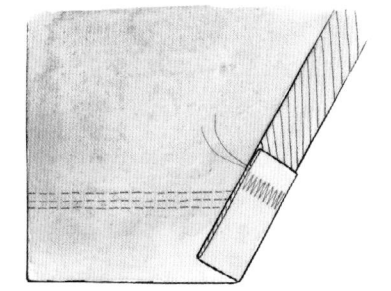

topstitching: Straight stitches are stitched on the right side of the fabric to emphasize a detail, to hold seam allowances in place, and/or to create design interest. Work with topstitching thread and a stitch length of 6 to 8 stitches per inch (2.5 cm).

single topstitched seam: Press both seam allowances toward one side of the seam. Stitch through all the layers ¼" to ³⁄₈" (6 mm to 1 cm) from the seam, catching the seam allowances underneath.

double topstitched seam: Press open the seam allowances. Topstitch ¼" to ³⁄₈" (6 mm to 1 cm) from the seam line on each side, catching the seam allowances underneath. Stitch both sides in the same direction—from the bottom toward the top.

multiple rows of topstitching: Work with a twin or triple needle for perfectly parallel topstitching rows (see page 10). The stitches will have some give, so this method is useful for knits and stretch woven fabrics.

the perfect seam

Seams are the basic construction elements that hold fabric pieces together. Most often, you will sew a straight-stitch seam with a stitch length of 8 to 12 stitches per inch (2.5 cm). If the fabric is heavy, set the machine for a longer stitch length—6 to 10 stitches per inch (2.5 cm). If the fabric is lightweight, set the stitch length to a shorter length—about 12 to 14 stitches per inch (2.5 cm). The seam allowance is ⅝" (1.6 cm) unless otherwise noted on the pattern tissue and instruction sheet.

Test the stitch on a scrap piece of your fabric before you begin sewing. You may need to adjust the presser-foot pressure and the stitch tension if you are sewing different fabric thicknesses. If the stitches look too tight, loose, or uneven, rethread the machine—nine times out of ten rethreading will fix the problem.

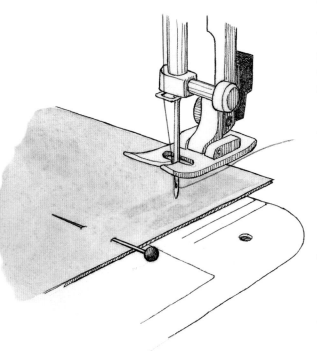

1 Pin the fabric layers with right sides together (unless otherwise noted) and raw edges even. Insert pins perpendicular to the edge about every 2" (5.1 cm), with all the heads facing in the same direction so you can remove them easily as you come to them.

2 Lift the presser foot and raise the needle to its highest position by turning the handwheel toward you.

3 Position the fabric under the presser foot so the cut edges align with the ⅝" (1.6 cm) seam allowance marking on the throat plate and the top edges are slightly behind the presser foot.

4 Lower the presser foot. Adjust the machine setting to stitch in reverse. Backstitch to the top edges of the fabric, holding the thread tails for the first few stitches.

5 Change the machine setting to stitch forward. Stitch over the backstitches and continue stitching to the end of the seam.

6 Backstitch again for about ½" (1.3 cm). Raise the presser foot and pull the fabric out from under it. If the bobbin thread does not release easily, turn the handwheel toward you slightly. Clip the threads close to the stitching.

To avoid tangles, hold the bobbin and top threads to the back or side until you take the first few stitches.

trimming a seam

Pressing is often enough to make seams lie flat—but sometimes you need to trim the seam allowances to reduce bulk. Trimming also helps smooth curves and sharpen corners.

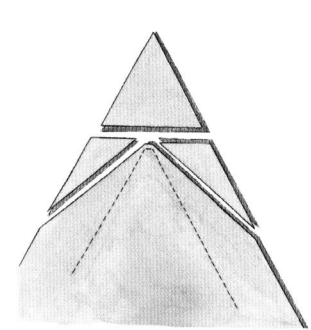

trimming a point or corner: Trim the seam allowances straight across the point or corner first. Then taper the allowances along each side.

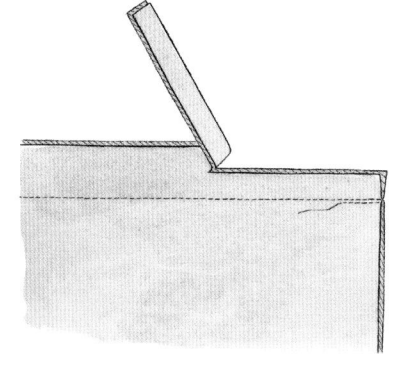

trimming: Cut away half of the seam allowance width.

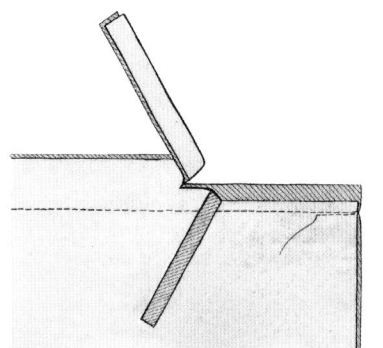

grading: Grade enclosed seams (waistbands) and garment edges (lapel, front opening) to eliminate a thick ridge. After trimming both seam allowances, trim the seam allowance that will lie nearest the inside of the garment again, by about half its width.

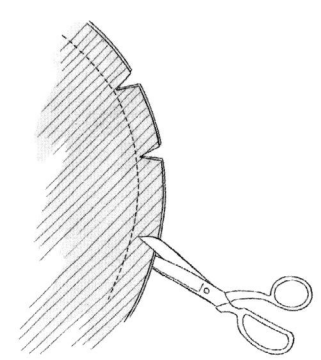

notching: Cut wedges out of the seam allowances of outward curves to remove extra fullness.

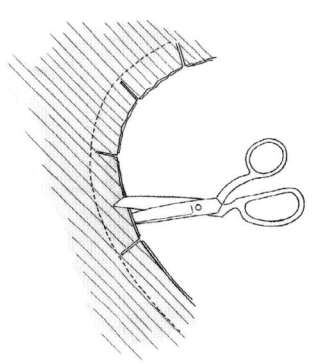

clipping: Cut short snips into the seam allowance of inward curves—working with only the tips of the scissors—to help them lie flat. Cut up to, but not through, the stitching.

types of seams

There are many types of seams you can use to join two pieces of fabric. Your choice depends on the fabric characteristics, the construction requirements, and the finished effect you would like to achieve.

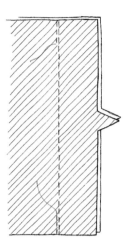

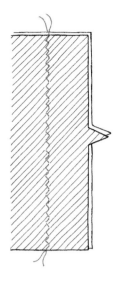

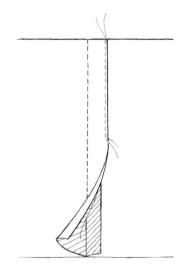

plain seam: This is the type of seam you'll use most often. With right sides together, stitch 5/8" (1.6 cm) from the edge. Backstitch two or three stitches at the beginning and end of the seam. Press the seam flat and then press it open.

narrow zigzag: This stitch prevents puckers by building stretch into the seam. It is effective with loose weaves and stretch fabrics. Set the machine for a narrow zigzag stitch and sew as you would a plain seam.

flat-fell seam: This style of seam adds strength to the construction. With wrong sides together, sew a 3/4" (1.9 cm) seam. Press the seam allowances to one side. Trim the lower seam allowance to 1/8" (3 mm). Press under 1/4" (6 mm) of the upper seam allowance, and pin it down, concealing the trimmed edge. Edgestitch on the fold (see page 57).

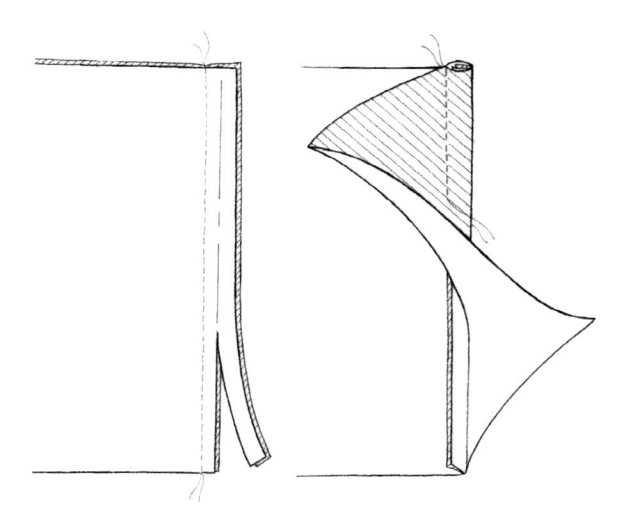

french seam: This type of seam is best for lightweight, sheer fabrics and visible seams. With wrong sides together, sew a ¼" (6 mm) seam. Trim the allowances to ⅛" (3 mm) and press to one side.

Fold the right sides together (enclosing the trimmed seam), with the stitching line on the fold. Stitch ¼" (6 mm) from the folded edge. Press the seam to one side.

seaming a straight edge and a curve: Staystitch just inside the seam line of the straight edge (see page 57). Clip into the seam allowance up to, but not through, the stitching. Pin the pieces right sides together, with the clipped edge on top, matching any marks. Clips will spread so the edges match. Stitch, with the clipped edge on top, keeping the bottom layer flat. Press the seam open on a tailor's ham (see page 22).

To keep seams from shifting, pin or hand-baste, or use a walking (even-feed) presser foot (page 12).

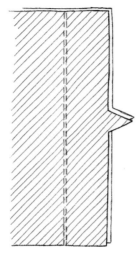

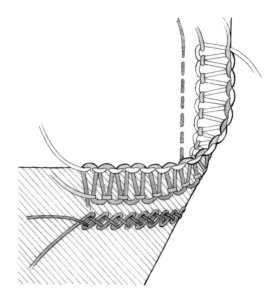

reinforced plain seam: This seam is especially effective on heavy, loosely woven fabrics. Sew a plain seam and then sew another line of stitching $^{1}/_{8}$" (3 mm) away, inside the seam allowance. Press both seam allowances together to one side.

4-thread or 5-thread overlock stitch: This stitch is suited to most types of seams, especially exposed seams. Stitch the seam with a serger (overlock machine), trimming the seam allowances and overcasting both raw edges together at the same time.

seam finishes

For a neat and professional finish, you should finish all your seams—unless the garment is lined. Finished seams also add durability to garments you will launder regularly. French and flat-fell seams (pages 61 and 62) enclose the raw edges, so they don't require further finishing.

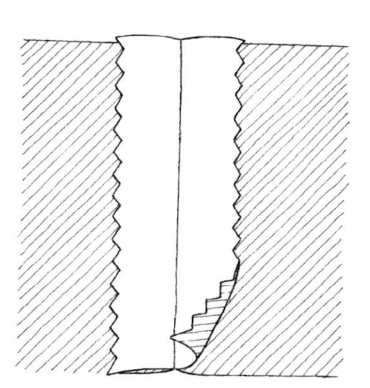

pinked edge: Working with pinking shears, cut a sawtooth edge along each seam allowance. A pinked edge is the simplest type of seam finish, although it does not entirely eliminate raveling.

stitch and pink: Press the seam open and stitch ¼" (6 mm) from the edge of each seam allowance. Cut the edge with pinking shears. This finish is more effective than pinking alone.

zigzag: Press the seam open. Set the machine to stitch a wide, medium-length zigzag. Stitch along the edge of each seam allowance so the stitches abut the raw edge to prevent raveling. For lightweight fabrics, zigzag the seam allowances together and press to one side.

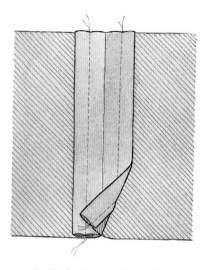 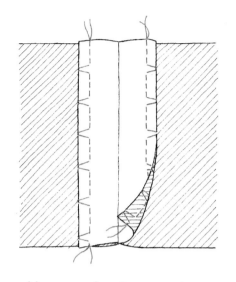 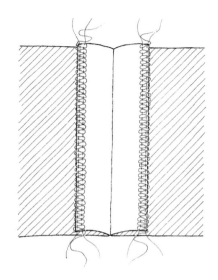

turn and stitch: Turn under each seam allowance edge ⅛" to ¼" (3 to 6 mm), and press. Stitch through the seam allowance to catch the folded edge.

machine overedge: Press open the seam and set your machine to a built-in stitch that combines straight and zigzag stitches. Stitch along the edges of the seam allowances.

overlock: Any two-, three-, or four-thread overlock stitch, made with a serger (or overlock machine, see page 15), produces a professional-looking finish.

hand-sewing

Sewing by hand is easy. It's the best method when mending small or hard-to-reach areas (such as narrow sleeves or one layer of several fabric layers), or when the pattern or design of the fabric requires careful matching.

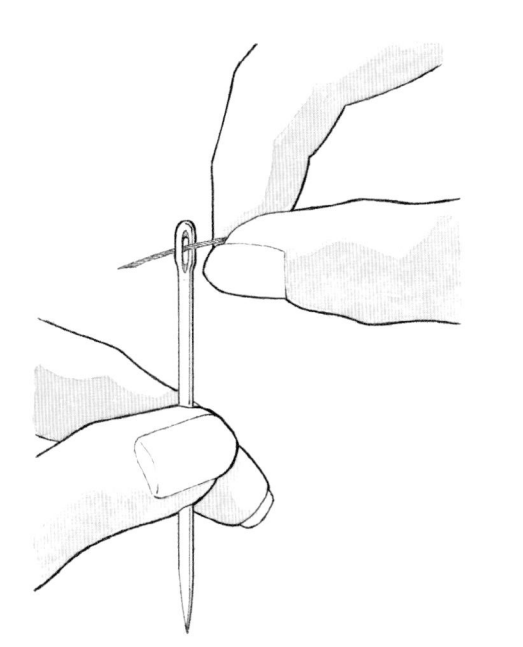

Sewing Tips

- When reattaching buttons or snaps, use a double strand of thread. For sewing seams or basting, use a single strand. Cut the thread 18" to 22" (45.5 to 56 cm) long. A longer strand will fray or tangle as you work.

- If you are sewing with a single thread, knot only one end of the thread.

- If you are sewing with a double thread (buttons, snaps), knot both ends together.

- Keep hand stitches close to together—from 12 to 15 stitches per inch (2.5 cm).

- When you can, bury or hide the thread knot between two layers of fabric, as shown below.

Threading a Needle

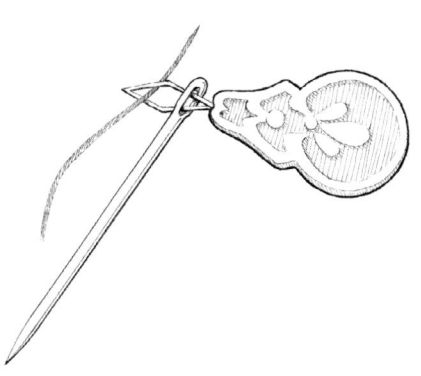

by hand: Cut the thread at an angle to make it easier to thread through the eye of the needle. Hold the thread between your thumb and forefinger, about 1/4" (6 mm) from the cut end. Push the thread through the eye of the needle. Wet or twist the thread end if you have trouble inserting it.

with a needle threader: Slide the wire loop of the needle threader through the eye of the needle. Insert the thread through the wire loop and pull the wire and thread back through the needle eye. Slide the wire threader off the thread.

To prevent the thread from pulling out of the needle as you sew, hold the needle with its eye between your thumb and middle finger. Position your forefinger in front to steer the needle's point.

hand stitches

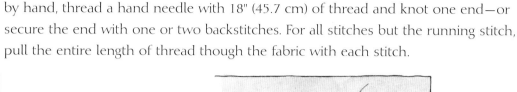

Hand sewing is sometimes quicker and more efficient than machine sewing—when you need to carefully match surface patterns, when the work area is small and tight, or when you don't want visible stitches on the right side. To stitch by hand, thread a hand needle with 18" (45.7 cm) of thread and knot one end—or secure the end with one or two backstitches. For all stitches but the running stitch, pull the entire length of thread though the fabric with each stitch.

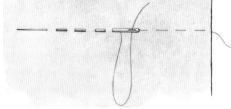

backstitch: This very strong stitch is used for seams. Bring the needle and thread to the right side of the fabric. Insert the needle 1/16" to 1/8" (1.6 to 3 mm) behind the point where the thread exited the fabric. Then bring the needle out through the fabric that same distance in front of that point. Repeat, inserting the needle into the previous exit point for each stitch.

running stitch: This stitch is used for seams. Insert the point of the needle in and out of the fabric several times before pulling the thread through, thus completing several stitches at a time. Keep the stitches and spaces between them small and even.

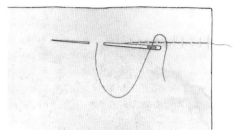

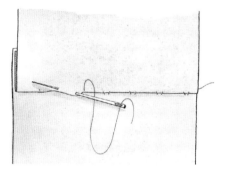

overcast stitch: This stitch is well suited for finishing edges. Form a series of close, evenly spaced, diagonal stitches 1/4" (6 mm) deep by passing the thread over and around the fabric edge.

slip stitch: This stitch is handy for hemming, closing openings, and joining two folded edges. When joining folded edges, insert the needle inside the fabric fold and bring it out through the folded edge. Insert the needle into the fold of the opposite edge and bring it out through the fold about 1/4" (6 mm) away. Alternate from edge to edge with each stitch. When hemming or closing openings, alternate stitches from one fabric surface to the other.

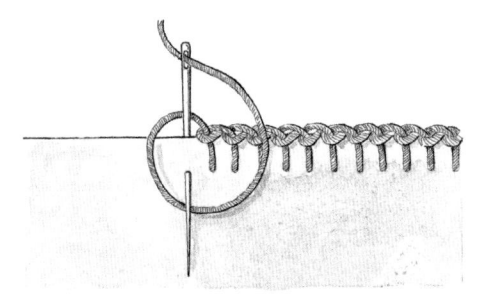

buttonhole stitch: This overedge stitch is used to make hand-sewn buttonholes or to finish other raw edges.

Insert the needle from the back to the front about 1/8" (3 mm) from the cut fabric edge. Wrap the thread under the eye of the needle and behind the point of the needle. Pull the needle through the thread so a loop forms along the fabric edge.

Repeat with closely spaced, even stitches along the cut fabric edge.

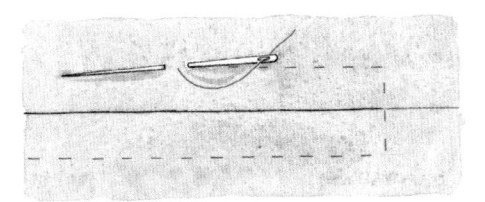

pick stitch: This stitch is a variation of the backstitch, perfect for inserting zippers by hand. Working from the right side of the fabric, secure the stitching with a backstitch.

Insert the needle behind the point at which the thread comes out of the fabric and bring it out 1/8" (3 mm) to 1/4" (6 mm) to the left of the same point. This stitching method leaves very small, evenly spaced stitches on the right side of the fabric.

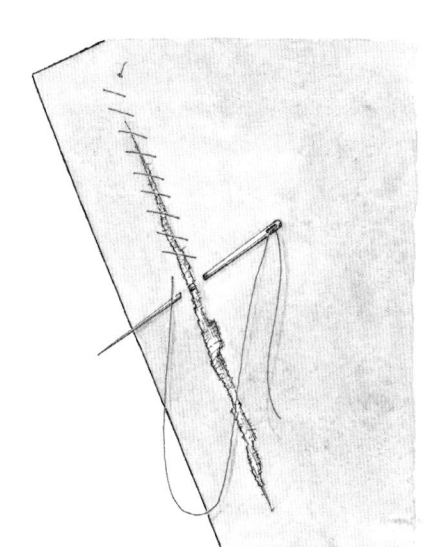

sloating stitch: This is a series of parallel stitches worked on the wrong side to repair tears in medium- to heavyweight fabrics. The stitches are invisible from the right side and look like small, slanted stitches on the wrong side.

Secure the stitch 1/2" (1.3 cm) before the tear with a small knot or two or three small backstitches. Working from top to bottom, insert the needle 1/16" (2 mm) from the torn edge and work it through the tear so it comes out 1/16" (2 mm) from the tear on the opposite side.

Repeat with the second stitch 1/16" (2 mm) below the first, never piercing the right side of the fabric, and only picking up a few threads on each side of the tear. Continue stitching to 1/2" (1.3 cm) beyond the end of the tear, backstitch to secure.

securing hand stitches

When you are hand-basting you don't need to secure the end of the thread because you will be removing the stitches. For all other types of hand-sewing, secure your stitches at the beginning and end of each seam.

Securing the Beginning of a Seam

tie a thread knot: Wrap the thread loosely around your index finger one or two times and hold the loop in place with your thumb. Twist the threads and roll the loop off by sliding your finger toward the base of your thumb. Pull the loop to form a knot.

backstitch: Form two or three small backstitches (see page 67) on the wrong side of the fabric that are invisible on the right side. Leave a small loop. Take another backstitch in the same place and run the needle through the thread loop, as shown in the drawing. Pull the thread tight.

backstitch: Backstitch as at the beginning of a seam, using two or three small backstitches (see page 67) on the wrong side of the fabric.

tie a thread knot: Form a thread loop at the end of the stitching on the wrong side, close to the fabric. Pull the needle through the loop, keeping the thread loop close to the fabric. Pull and tighten the knot.

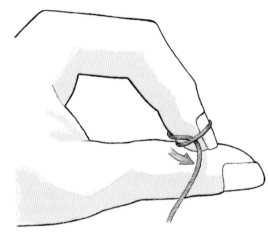

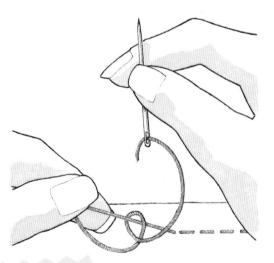

If the knot comes through the fabric, tie a second knot over the first one.

basting methods

Basting is a reliable way to hold fabric layers or fabric and trim together temporarily. Basting is especially helpful when working with slippery fabrics, matching plaids, and applying trims. Baste with thread of a contrasting color to make it easier to see the stitches when it's time to remove them.

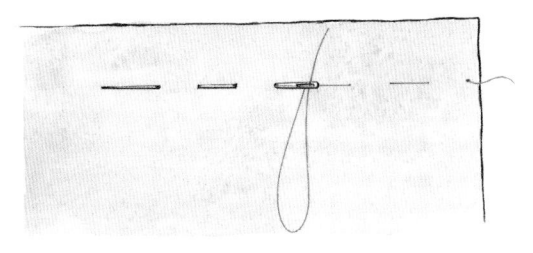

hand basting: This technique requires a long running stitch. Insert the needle in and out of the surface of the fabric to make several evenly spaced, ½" (1.3 cm) stitches. Pull the needle and thread through and repeat.

machine basting: This technique is effective when gathering. Adjust the machine-stitch length to the longest straight stitch, 3 to 6 stitches per inch (2.5 cm).

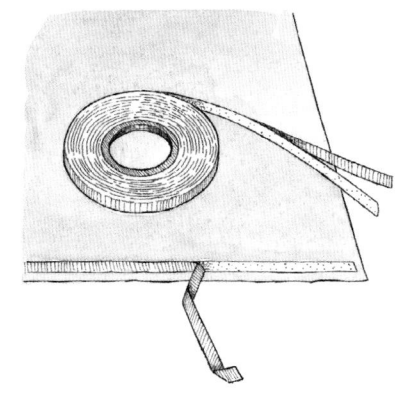

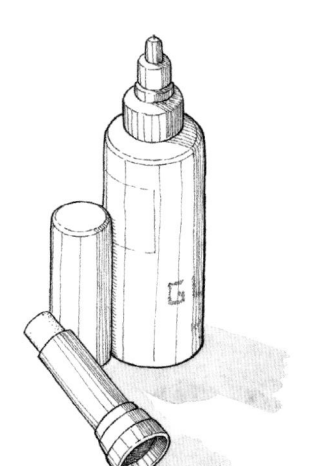

basting tape: This very narrow tape has adhesive on both sides with removable paper backing. Simply position the tape and press it in place with your fingers. Avoid stitching through it, as it will gum up your needle.

fabric glue: A glue stick or water-soluble glue, packaged in a tube applicator, temporarily holds fabric layers together to make it easier to sew the permanent stitches precisely.

machine-sewing

A sewing machine makes quick work of sewing garments and home décor as well as mending and repair jobs. No matter how basic your machine, it will enable you to make all sorts of neat, sturdy stitches. Familiarize yourself with your machine, and you won't dread working with it for stitching projects, darning or patching holes, altering items, and creating beautiful pieces.

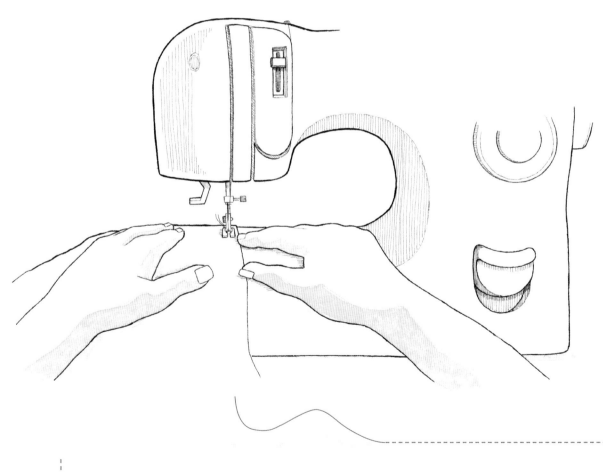

machine stitches

Most sewing machines have a variety of built-in stitches, but you can accomplish everything you need with straight and zigzag stitches. Straight stitches form the basis for most construction techniques in home décor sewing. The zigzag is invaluable for edge-finishing, applying trim, and mending.

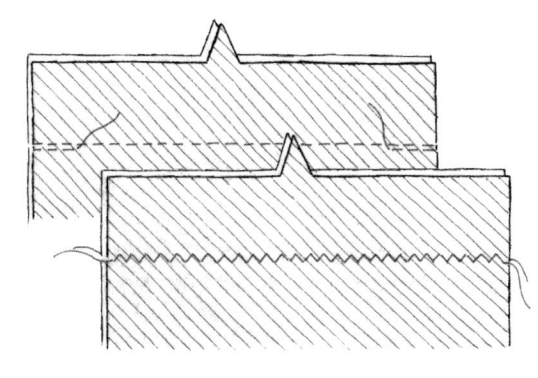

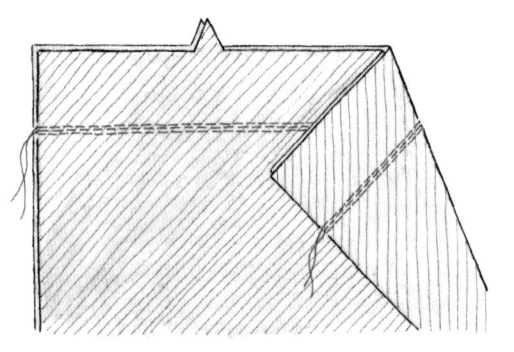

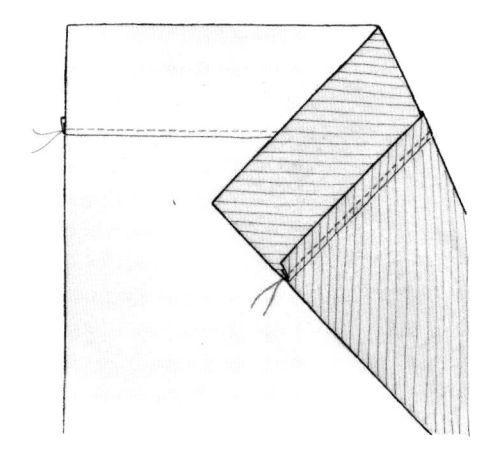

straight stitch: This basic stitch is perfect for most sewing. Choose the longest stitch for basting (see page 70) and a shorter stitch (8 to 12 stitches per inch [2.5 cm]) for regular sewing. Set the length of the stitch so that it matches the rest of the stitching. Be sure to backstitch to secure the beginning and end of the stitching.

zigzag stitch: This stitch is great for seaming stretch fabrics. It helps prevent puckers and broken stitches by building stretch into the seam. Choose a stitch length that is compatible with the weight of the fabric (longer stitches for heavy fabrics, shorter stitches for lightweight fabrics). The zigzag stitch is also commonly worked along the raw edges of fabric to clean-finish them.

straight stretch stitch: This specialty stitch is built into some sewing machines. Test the stitch on scrap fabric first, because it is difficult to rip out. It can have the appearance of three, very closely spaced, parallel rows of straight stitches (as shown in the drawing), or two forward stitches and one backward stitch.

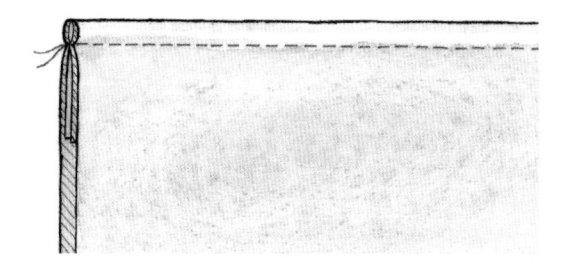

edge stitch: Edge stitching is topstitching that is close to the finished edge or seam line (1/16" to 1/8" [2 to 3 mm]). You can use a blind-stitch foot to ensure even stitching.

understitching: To prevent a lining from rolling to the right side of the decorator fabric, sew and press the seam allowance toward the lining. Trim the seam allowance that is closest to the decorator fabric. From the right side, stitch through the lining and seam allowances close to the seam line.

 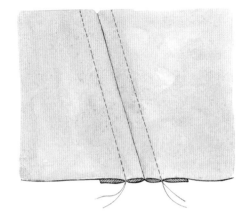 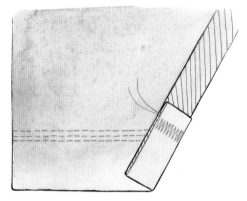

topstitching: Straight stitches are stitched on the right side of the fabric to emphasis a detail, to hold seam allowances in place, and/or to create design interest. Work with topstitching thread and a stitch length of 6 to 8 stitches per inch (2.5 cm).

single topstitched seam: Press both seam allowances toward one side of the seam. Stitch through all the layers $1/4$" to $3/8$" (6 mm to 1 cm) from the seam, catching the seam allowances underneath.

double topstitched seam: Press the seam open. Topstitch $1/4$" to $3/8$" (6 mm to 1 cm) from the seam line on each side, catching the seam allowances underneath. Stitch both sides in the same direction—working from the bottom of the item toward the top.

multiple rows of topstitching: Work with a twin or triple needle for perfectly parallel topstitching rows. The stitches will have some give, so this method is useful for sewing stretchy woven fabrics.

essential techniques

sewing darts

A dart adds dimension and shape to a flat piece of fabric, allowing the piece to mold to the body at the bust, waist, hips, or elbows. Different styles of darts are positioned in different areas of the garment, depending on the shaping needed. The single-pointed waist dart is the most common style.

1   Mark a single-pointed dart using the pattern as a guide (see pages 53 and 54). Fold the dart down the center, right sides together, matching the stitching lines. Pin.

2   Begin stitching at the wide end, backstitching at the start. Continue stitching toward the point, removing pins as you stitch.

3   Taper your stitching so the last two or three stitches are directly on the fold. Do not backstitch at the point. Leave long thread tails.

4   Press the dart flat up to the point. Then, working with a tailor's ham, press the dart to one side (as indicated in the pattern instructions). Do not press over the point.

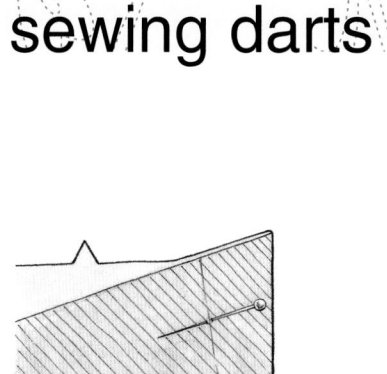

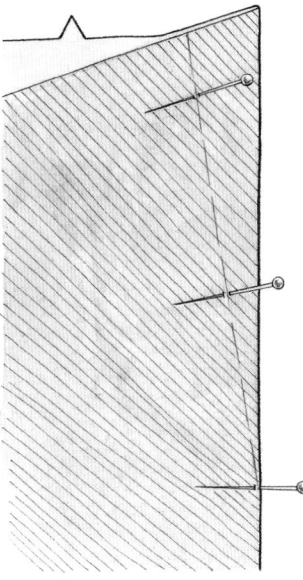

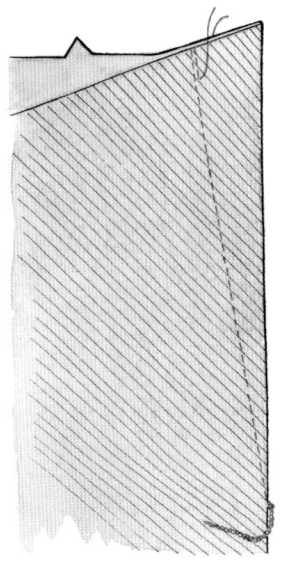

stitching & mitering corners

 The key to a perfectly shaped corner is the seam allowance. Reduce bulk by stitching and trimming the allowance or by mitering. Mitering—which is great for hemming and for the corners of patch pockets—joins two adjacent edges diagonally with a neat, flat finish.

Stitching

Stitch the seam, stopping two or three stitches from the corner. Turn the hand wheel toward you to make the last few stitches. To turn the corner, keep the needle in the fabric, raise the presser foot, and pivot the fabric. Lower the presser foot and continue stitching. Trim the fabric, cutting diagonally to remove the corner point.

Mitering

1 Press all seam allowances to the wrong side to crease the fabric. Open the allowances. Fold the corner diagonally so the crease marks line up at the seam lines, as shown in the drawing. Press the fold to create a stitching guide.

2 Open the fabric and refold, right sides together, bringing together the crease marks in the corner seam allowance. Stitch along the pressed diagonal fold.

3 Trim the corner seam allowance to 3/8" (1 cm) and press open.

4 Turn the seam allowances to the wrong side and press, forming a flat, mitered corner.

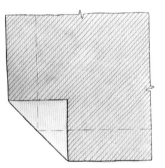

1

2

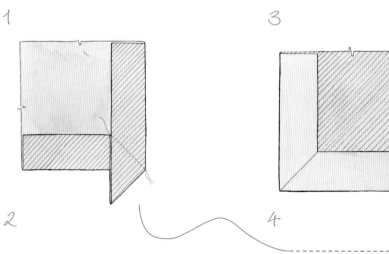

3

4

making bias binding

Bias tape, or binding encloses fabric edges for a neat, often decorative, finish. Because of the bias grain direction, the binding wraps around curves without puckering. You can purchase binding in an assortment of colors. Or, for a perfect match, you can easily make your own single-fold or double-fold binding.

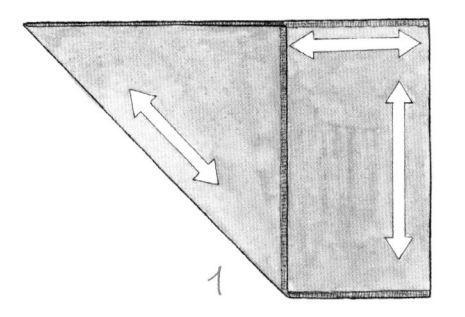

1   Fold the fabric diagonally so that one selvage is at a right angle to the other selvage. Press along the fold—the direction of the fabric grain at the fold is the bias grain. Cut along the pressed line. Set aside the triangle of fabric.

2   Multiply the desired finished width of the binding by four to determine how wide to cut the strips. For example, for a ¼" (6 mm) finished binding, you'll need strips 1" (2.5 cm) wide.

Beginning at the diagonal cut edge of the fabric, measure and mark parallel lines that are the desired cut width. After you have drawn the last strip, discard the triangular remnant—or save it as scrap.

3   Fold the fabric right sides together, matching selvages to form an irregular tube. Match the marked lines so that one strip of fabric extends beyond the tube on each side. Sew a ¼" (6 mm) seam and press it open. Starting at one end, work around the tube to cut a continuous strip along the marked line.

4   Press both long edges to the center of the tape, taking care not to distort the width of the strip. Press the strip in half again to create a double-fold bias tape.

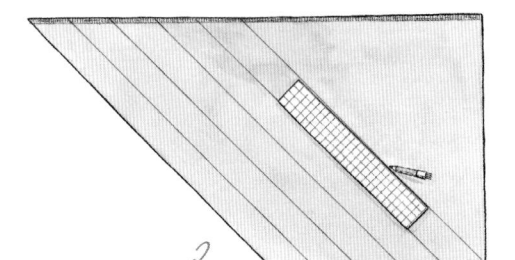

1

2

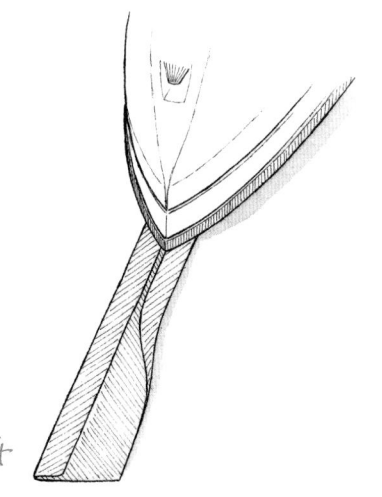

3

4

mitering bias trim

Bias trim provides a sturdy, decorative edge finish on placemats, tablecloths, curtains, and draperies. A mitered corner adds a smooth, neat finish.

1 Press open the bias tape. Beginning in the center of one side, stitch the right side of the bias tape to the wrong side of the fabric, aligning the edges. Slow the machine and pivot precisely at the corner. Continue stitching, pivoting at all corners.

2 Trim the seam allowance diagonally at each corner. Fold the bias tape so it forms a right angle and the fold aligns with the stitching. Finger-press the fold.

3 Unfold the bias tape so it extends over the seam. Stitch on the finger-pressed fold. Trim off the point at the corner.

4 Finger-press to open the mitered seam. Turn the bias tape to the right side and press. Topstitch the edge of the tape to encase the edge of the fabric.

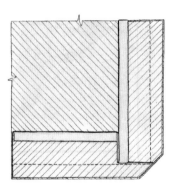

1

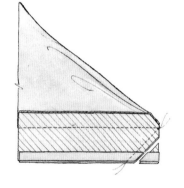

2

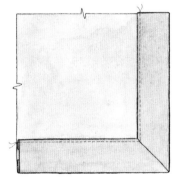

3

4

attaching trims

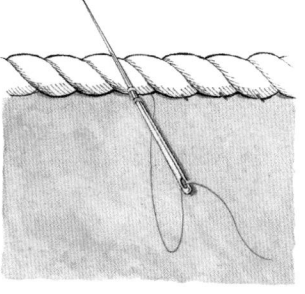

There are several ways to apply decorative trims, depending on the kind of trim you choose and the way in which you want to use it. Before you begin, mark placement lines for the trim with a water- or air-soluble pen. If pins will damage the trim or fabric, use a glue stick or fabric adhesive to temporarily hold the trim in place while you sew. There are several application methods, depending on the style of the trim and the way it is used.

hand-stitched trim: Raised trim must be attached by hand. Slipstitch (see page 67) the trim to the fabric with thread that is the same color as the fabric.

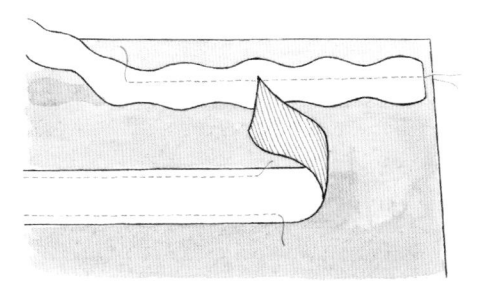

machine-stitched band trim: Secure the trim in place with basting tape or fabric adhesive. If the trim is less than 1/4" (6 mm) wide, machine-stitch down the center. If it is wider than 1/4" (6 mm), machine-stitch both long edges in the same direction.

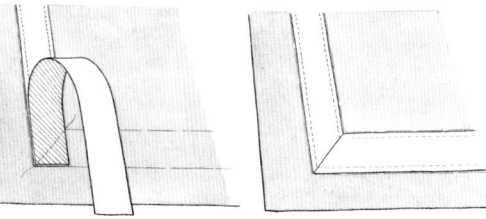

mitering trim: Pin the trim along the placement line until it reaches the corner. Topstitch both edges, stopping at the line. Fold the trim back on itself and finger-press. Fold the trim diagonally to form a right angle and align the edges with the placement lines.

Refold the trim back on itself and stitch directly through the diagonal crease. Fold the trim back down so it turns the corner neatly. Topstitch along both edges.

bias tape: Open the tape and, with right sides together, pin it to the fabric, matching cut edges. Stitch along the fold line closest to the raw edge.

Fold the binding up and over to encase the raw edge. On the right side of the fabric, edges-titch (see page 57) the binding in place. (This stitching will catch the underneath layer, which is slightly wider than the top layer.)

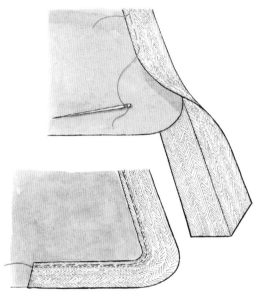

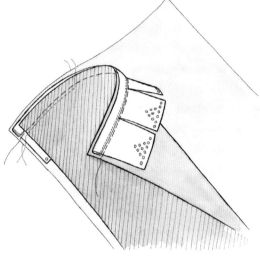

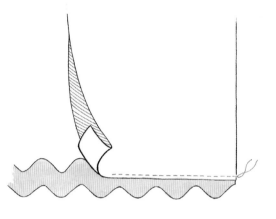

fold-over braid: With the narrower edge on the right side of the fabric, encase the raw edge with the braid. Hand-baste (see page 70) through all layers. Topstitch close to the inside edge.

edging in a seam: Working on the right side of the fabric, align the unfinished edge of the trim with the raw edge of the fabric, with seam lines matching. Baste. Pin the two fabric layers together with the trim in between. Stitch. Use a zipper foot if the trim doesn't lie flat.

edging along a finished edge: Position the wrong side of the folded or hemmed fabric edge on top of the edging and topstitch. Or sew the trim on the right side of the fabric and cover the seam with ribbon.

essential techniques

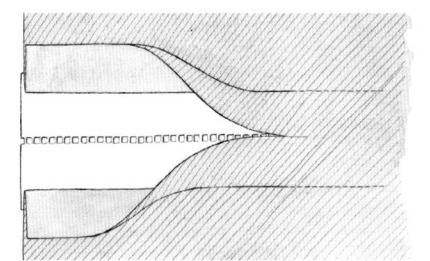

insertion trim: Pin or glue the trim to the right side of the fabric and top-stitch it along both straight edges (in the same direction). From the wrong side, cut the fabric down the center, between the two rows of stitching, to create seam allowances. Press the seam allowances away from each other, exposing the trim. Edgestitch though all layers close to the folds. Trim the seam allowances close to the edgestitching.

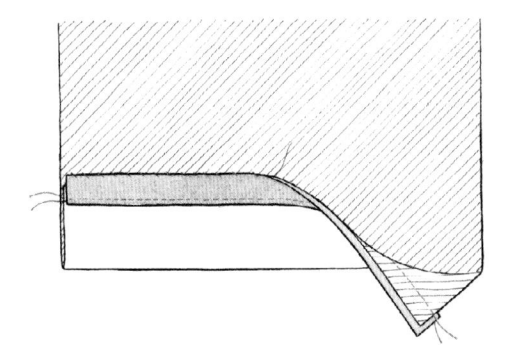

seam binding/seam tape: To hem loosely woven fabrics, stitch the edge of the tape or binding ¼" (6 mm) from the raw edge of the fabric. To clean-finish loosely woven seam allowances, press the tape or binding in half and wrap it over the raw edge. Edgestitch in place.

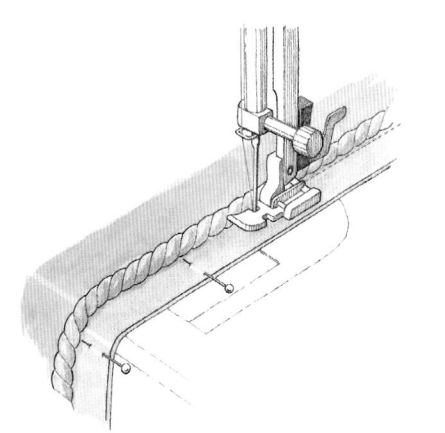

piping: Apply piping just as you would edging in a seam. Attach the zipper foot so you can stitch as close to the trim as possible. (To make your own piping, see page 86.)

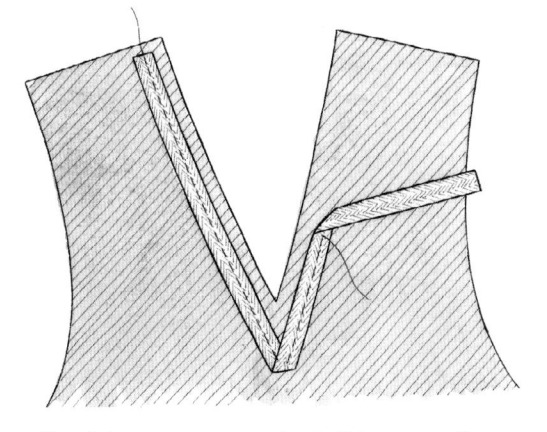

twill tape: To reinforce a seam, center twill tape over the seam line, inside the garment, and stitch it in place. To extend seam allowances, machine-stitch one edge of the tape to the raw edge of the fabric.

sewing elastic to fabric

You can sew lengths of elastic directly to the wrong side of the fabric to shape a garment at wrists, ankles, and waistlines. Choose woven or knitted elastic that is soft enough to wear close to your skin. Cut it slightly shorter than you need because it stretches during sewing. Sew with a stretch stitch or a zigzag stitch, which will stretch along with the elastic.

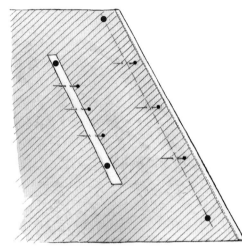

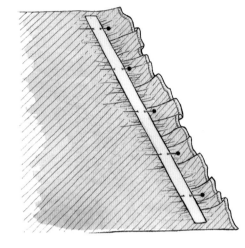

1 Finish the hem of the garment, if applicable. Mark the seam allowances at the sides of the garment piece. Fold the fabric between the marks into four equal sections. Mark the folds with pins. Fold the elastic into fourths and mark with pins the same way.

2 Pin the elastic to the wrong side of the garment, matching the three pins on the elastic and on the fabric. Add pins as needed to stretch the elastic across the entire length of fabric. Leave ½" (1.3 cm) of fabric free at each end for the seam allowance.

3 Stitch the elastic to the fabric, stretching the elastic between the pins. Hold the fabric taut with one hand behind the presser foot and the other in front. Let the feed dogs move the fabric as you sew.

inserting elastic in a casing

Elastic is sometimes inserted in a fabric tunnel called a casing. You can create a casing by folding and stitching the fabric at a garment edge. Or you can apply a band of tricot (sheer ribbon) or bias tape (see page 28) close to the garment edge—at the waistline of a dress, for example.

To determine how much elastic you need, wrap the elastic strip around your body and add 1" (2.5 cm) for finishing the ends. Braided and non-roll elastic won't twist inside the casing.

Edge Casing

1   Press the garment edge ½" (1.3 cm) to the wrong side. Fold the fabric again the desired amount to form the casing. Make the casing ¼" (6 mm) wider than the elastic for easy insertion.

2   Edgestitch close to the top fold. Edgestitch close to the bottom fold, leaving a 2" (5.1 cm) opening near one side seam.

3   Secure a safety pin to one end of the elastic and insert it into the casing opening. Push and pull the safety pin through the casing until it reaches the opening. Make sure that the opposite end of the elastic doesn't get pulled into the casing.

4   Feel along the casing to make sure the elastic is not twisted. Overlap the ends of the elastic and hand-stitch them together or machine-stitch with a zigzag stitch.

5   Stretch the elastic to pull the ends into the casing. Edgestitch the opening closed, being careful not to catch the elastic in the stitches.

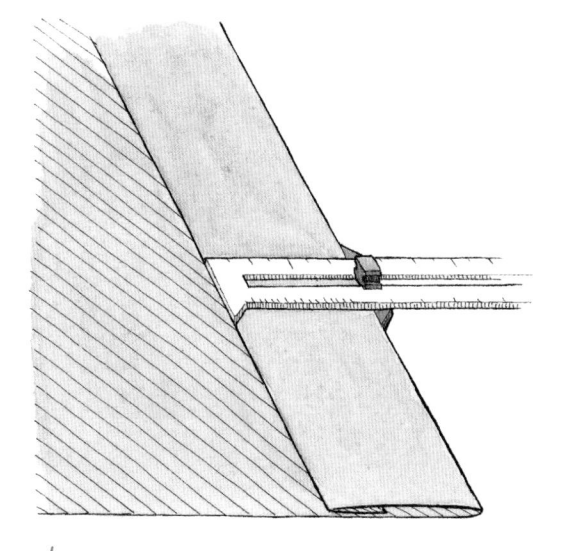

1

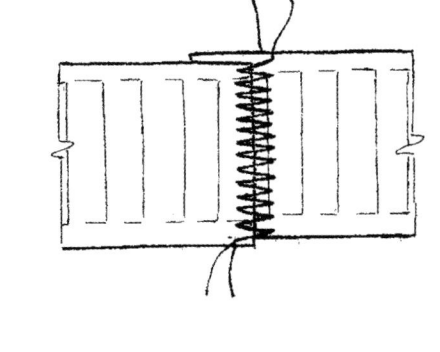

3

4

Applied Casing

1 Pin bias tape or a strip of tricot that is 1/4" (6 mm) wider than the elastic over the marked casing line. Press under the ends 1/4" (6 mm) and abut the folds. Stitch close to both long edges.

2 Insert the elastic and stitch the ends together as for the edge casing (page 82, steps 3 and 4). Ease the elastic back into the casing. Slipstitch the casing ends closed.

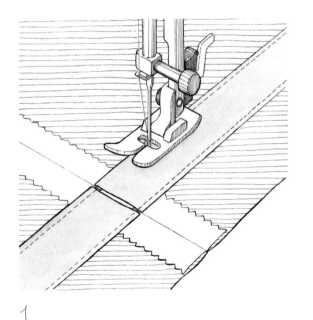

1

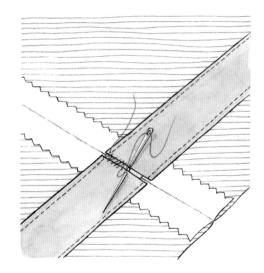

2

making welting

Welting creates a well-defined edge finish on many types of home décor items. You make welting by wrapping a strip of bias fabric around a filler cord. The cord can be either cotton or polyester and of various thicknesses.

The most common size welting for home décor sewing is ⁵/₃₂" (0.16 cm) in diameter. Cut a bias strip that is 1¹/₂" (3.8 cm) wide to cover a cord of that diameter. This size welting is appropriate for pillows, cushions, slipcovers, table runners, and placemats.

For welting thicker than ¹/₄" (6 mm) in diameter, wrap a piece of paper around the cord. Pin it close to the cord and trim the paper ¹/₂" (1.3 cm) from the pin. Measure the paper to determine the cut width of the bias strip. Attach thicker welting to large pillows, pillow shams, duvet covers and cover-lets—or to any other item for a bold effect.

1 Cut bias strips as you would for bias binding (page 76, steps 1 through 3). Allow extra length so you can overlap the ends and ease the welting around corners as you sew.

2 Attach the zipper foot or piping foot to your machine (page 12). Wrap the bias strip, right side out, around the cord, keeping the raw edges even. Stitch right next to the cord, gently stretching the fabric as you sew.

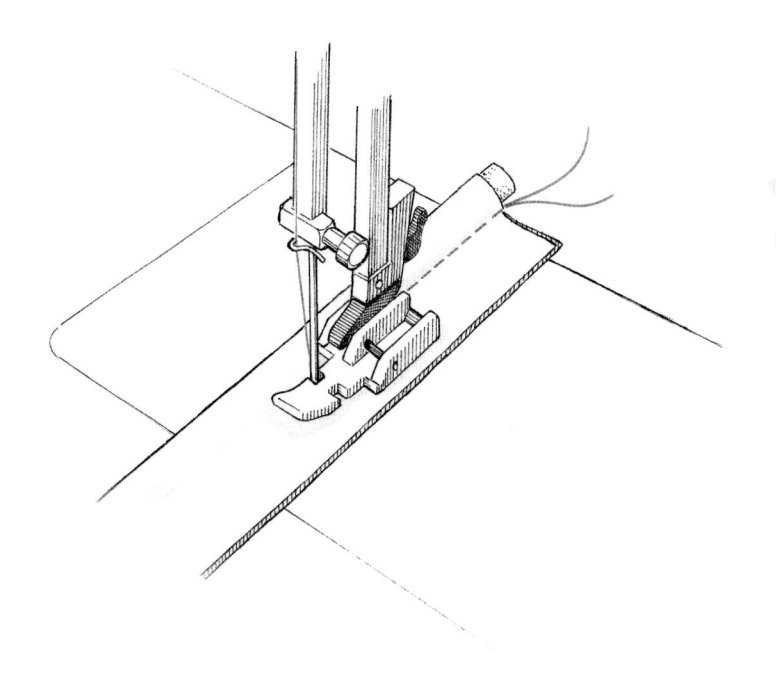

To avoid ripples in welting:
• pin or glue-baste the strip around the cord before stitching
• feed both layers of fabric evenly through the presser foot
• make sure the cord is not twisted within the fabric.

attaching welting

Welting reinforces the seams on pillows, cushions, slipcovers, tiebacks, tablecloths, and bedcovers while adding a decorative, finishing touch.

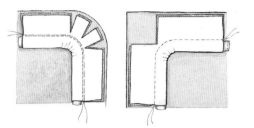

To ease welting around a curve, clip into the seam allowance up to the stitching several times. For sharp corners, cut once and trim away the seam allowance.

1. Place the welting on the right side of the fabric, aligning the edges of the seam allowances. Position it so the stitching will begin and end in the middle of one side of the pillow (not near a corner).

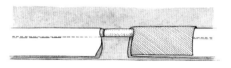

2. Machine-baste the welting just to the right of the seam line, leaving the first 2" (5.1 cm) and the last 2" (5.1 cm) of the welting free. Cut off the extra length, leaving a 1" (2. 5 cm) overlap.

3. With a seam ripper, remove 1" (2. 5 cm) of stitching on both ends of the welting. Pull back the fabric on one end and cut the cording so the ends abut.

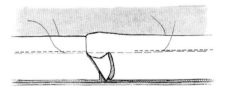

4. Fold under ½" (1.3 cm) of fabric on that same end. Then wrap the fabric around the other end of the cording for a smooth joining. Finish stitching the welting.

5. With the right sides together and the welting sandwiched between, sew together the two fabric pieces with a regular stitch length. Stitch directly over the basting stitches.

making piping

Piping is a bias fabric wrapped around a narrow polyester or cotton cord. You sew piping into a seam for a well-defined edge finish. You can purchase piping in an assortment of colors. For a perfect match, it's easy to make your own.

1   Cut bias strips as you would when making bias binding (page 76, steps 1 to 3). The width of the strip should be two times the seam allowance plus the circumference of the cord. Allow extra length so you can overlap the ends and ease the piping around corners as you sew.

2   Attach a zipper foot or piping foot to your machine. Wrap the bias strip, right side out, around the cord, keeping the raw edges even. Stitch right next to the cord, gently stretching the fabric as you sew.

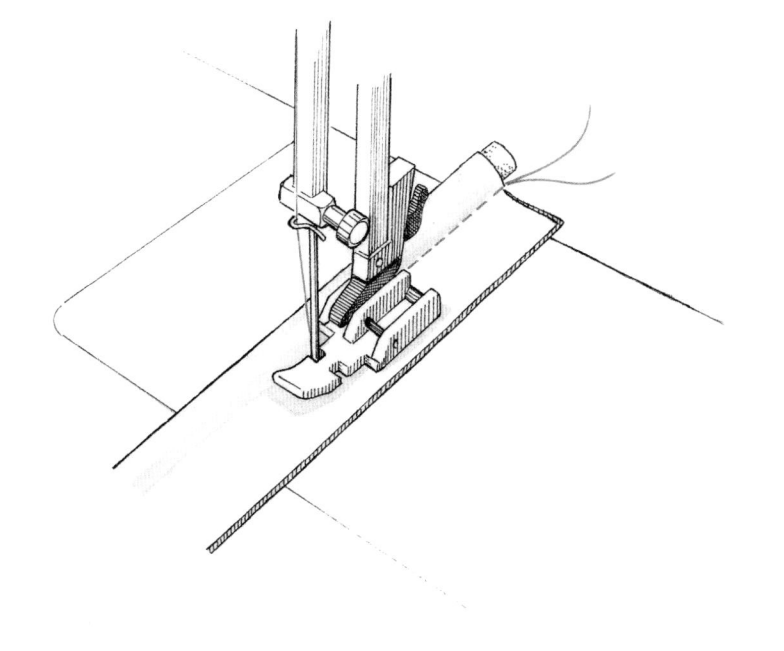

making fabric bows

Fabric bows are quick accents for window treatments, bedding, and pillows. Make a bow that ties and unties or a fixed bow with a permanent shape.

To determine the best size bow for your project—and how much fabric you'll need—tie a bow with fabric scrap, old ribbon, or a tape measure. Pin the bow in place to see how it looks and adjust as needed.

Untie the bow, measure the length, and add 1" (2.5 cm) for finishing the ends. Double the measurement and add 1" (2.5 cm) for the seam allowance. Cut a strip of fabric to your dimensions.

Tie Bow

1   Fold the strip in half lengthwise, right sides together. Stitch ½" (1.3 cm) from the long cut edges, leaving a 3" (7.6 cm) opening near the center.

2   Center the seam and press it open, working only with the tip of the iron.

3   Stitch across the ends on a diagonal and trim. Turn the fabric right side out through the opening and press. Slipstitch the opening closed (page 67).

4   Tie the bow and hand-stitch it in position—or weave the ends through your project and tie the bow in place.

Fixed Bow

1   Follow steps 1 to 3 at left. Tie the bow.

2   Cut a piece of fabric to make a knot cover. The fabric should be the same width as the bow fabric and 1" (2.5 cm) longer than the circumference of the knot.

3   Fold the fabric in half lengthwise, right sides together. Stitch ½" (1.3 cm) from the long edges. Turn the knot cover right side out, center the seam in the back, and press the ends to the inside.

Wrap the knot around the center of the bow and slipstitch the ends together in back (page 67). Stitch or glue the bow in place.

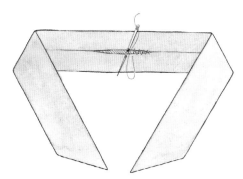

If your fabric needs more body, apply soft fusible interfacing (page 25) to the wrong side for a crisper bow.

making tassels

Tassels add elegance, whether stitched to the corners of a pillow, attached to a shade pull, or draped over a valance or swag. If you can't find the perfect tassels for your project, make your own with decorative cords, threads, and yarns.

1 Cut a piece of heavy cardboard the desired length of the tassel and about 3" (7.6 cm) wide. Wrap the yarns around the length of the cardboard until the bundle looks full (at least 100 times).

2 Thread a tapestry needle with a double strand of yarn. Slide the needle under the yarns at the top of the cardboard, remove the needle, and tie the bundle securely. Cut straight across the yarns at the opposite end and remove the cardboard.

3 Wrap a double length of yarn several times around the tassel, about 1 1/4" (3 cm) from the top, and tie it securely. Thread the tail onto the tapestry needle and bring the needle out at the top of the tassel. Work with the yarn tail to slipstitch the tassel to the fabric (page 67) or hand-sew two tassels to a length of cord— one at each end—to make a decorative tie.

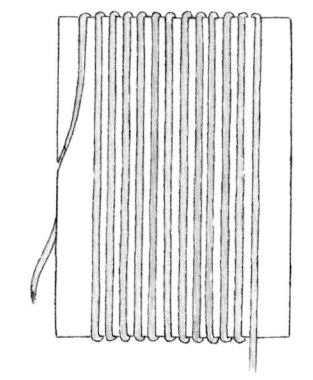
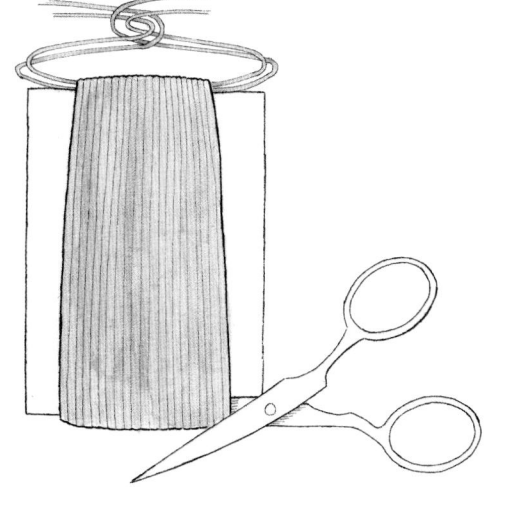

forming gathers

Gathers are a series of tiny, soft folds of fabric that create shaping. Usually, you'll add gathers to garments at waistlines, yokes, sleeve caps, cuffs, and necklines.

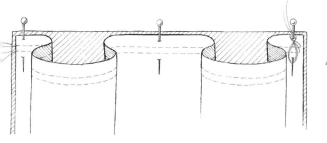

1   Set your machine to its longest straight stitch (the basting stitch). Loosen the upper thread tension slightly. Thread the bobbin with a contrasting color of thread for greater visibility.

2   On the right side of the fabric, stitch two parallel lines in the seam allowance: one just inside the stitching line and the other ¼" (6 mm) away. Leave long thread tails at both ends. If the fabric is long, divide the area to be gathered in half and break the basting stitches at the halfway mark.

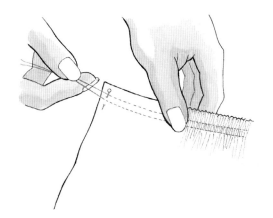

3   Pin the basted edge to its corresponding edge, right sides together. Match notches, seam lines, and markings. The piece with the basting stitches will be the longer piece. Secure the threads at one end by wrapping them around a straight pin to form a figure eight, as shown in the top drawing at left.

4   From the other end, pull the bobbin threads gently, sliding the fabric along the threads to distribute it evenly.

5   When the gathered piece "fits" the straight piece, pin the layers together at close intervals (about every ½" [1.3 cm]). As you work, adjust the gathers with a pin or with your fingernail so they are evenly distributed.

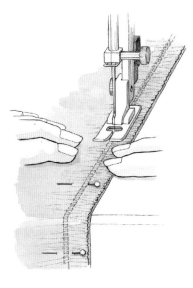

6   Change to a standard stitch length and normal upper-thread tension. With the gathered side up, machine-stitch a ⅝" (1.6 cm) seam. Remove pins as you sew—do not ever sew over pins! Hold the fabric taut with your fingertips on both sides of the needle to keep the gathers from shifting or pleating.

7   Open the garment and carefully press the seam allowances toward the flat, ungathered side with the tip of the iron. Do not press across the surface of the gathers or you will flatten them.

sewing ruffles

A ruffle is a strip of fabric that is gathered along one edge and attached to a flat piece of fabric—for example, on a skirt hem or the edge of a pillow. The visible edge is finished. The gathered raw edge is hidden in a seam or enclosed between two fabrics. Most ruffles are cut on the straight grain.

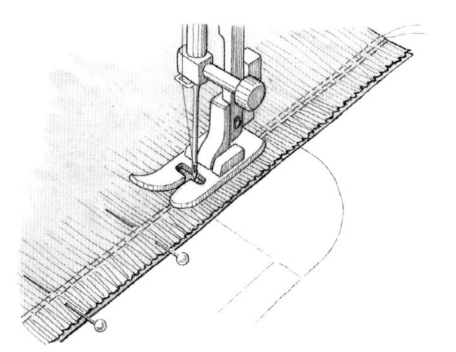

For a Hem Ruffle

1   Stitch the ruffle pieces together to form one long strip. Stitch a narrow hem on one long edge (see page 95). Press.

2   Sew two rows of basting stitches along the opposite long edge, just inside the seam line. Pull the threads to form gathers (see page 89).

3   Pin the ruffle with right sides together to the garment edge, aligning the raw edges and matching notches or dots. Adjust the gathers to distribute fullness evenly along the garment edge.

4   Stitch the ruffle in place. Remove the basting. Trim the seam allowances (see page 60). Zigzag-stitch or serge them together for a clean finish.

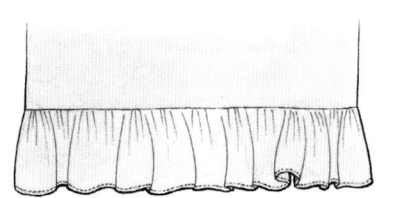

For an Enclosed Ruffle

1   Follow steps 1 to 3 above.

2   Stitch the ruffle to the first fabric, distributing the fullness evenly. Pin the second piece to the first, right sides together, with the ruffle in between. Stitch with the first piece up so you can use the existing stitching line as a guide.

3   Turn the pieces right side out. The ruffle will be along the outer edge.

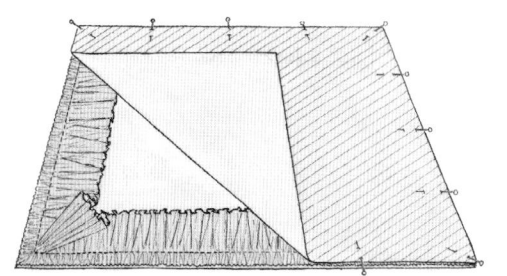

When applying a ruffle around corners, allow extra fullness at each corner so the ruffle lies flat.

sewing pleats

Pleats are fabric folds that are stitched in place. You can press them for a crisp, tailored look or let them hang in soft folds. They add dimension and visual interest to even the simplest valances and bed skirts.

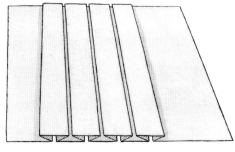

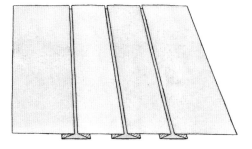

Make single pleats at corners, cluster them, or arrange them across a surface. You can also pleat large fabrics with heading tapes (page 187).

The best way to plan your pleats is to make a paper pattern. Cut a narrow piece of paper to the desired finish width. Add a $1/2$" (1.3 cm) seam allowance and the hardware return (if any) at each end. You need from 4" to 6" (10.2 to 15.2 cm) of fabric for each pleat, with $3\frac{1}{2}$" to 4" (8.9 to 10.2 cm) of fabric between each one.

Experiment to decide how many pleats you want, how wide they should be, and in which direction they will fold. Measure the width of the pleated pattern to determine yardage.

knife pleats: formed with a single fold line and placement line; folded pleats all face the same direction

box pleats: formed with two fold lines that fold to meet on the wrong side of the fabric; fabric pleats on the right side

inverted box pleats: same as box pleats, except folds meet on the right side of the fabric; pleat forms on the wrong side

Transfer the folds and placement lines from your paper pattern to the fabric with dressmaker's carbon paper and a tracing wheel.

Fold the fabric along each fold line to meet the placement line to form the pleat. Pin the entire length at regular intervals (knife pleats are shown in the drawing below). Baste across the seam allowance to hold the pleats in place. Stitch the pleated piece to the corresponding piece, as needed for the project.

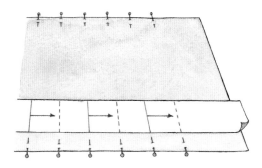

easing

Some areas of a garment need only subtle shaping, which you can create by "easing" the seam. Unlike a gathered seam, an eased seam does not have any visible folds. Easing allows for a comfortable fit and ease of movement at shoulders, back yokes, elbows, sleeve caps, and inseams.

1   Set the machine stitch length to approximately 10 stitches per inch (2.5 cm). Fine fabrics require a shorter stitch length. On the right side of the fabric, sew one row of stitching just inside the ⅝" (1.6 cm) stitching line for the required length of the eased area.

2   Pin the stitched edge to the corresponding piece of fabric so the edges and all markings align. Pull the bobbin thread gently to shorten the fabric and distribute the extra fabric fullness evenly. Pin every ¼" to ½" (6 mm to 1.3 cm) along the easing line.

3   With a long machine stitch, baste the seam. Ease the fullness without stitching any folds into the seam. (Be patient! This takes a little practice.) Check the seam from the right side of the fabric. If you see any puckers or folds, remove the basting stitches and try again.

4   When the basted seam is perfect, shorten the stitch length and sew the pieces together, stitching over the basting stitches.

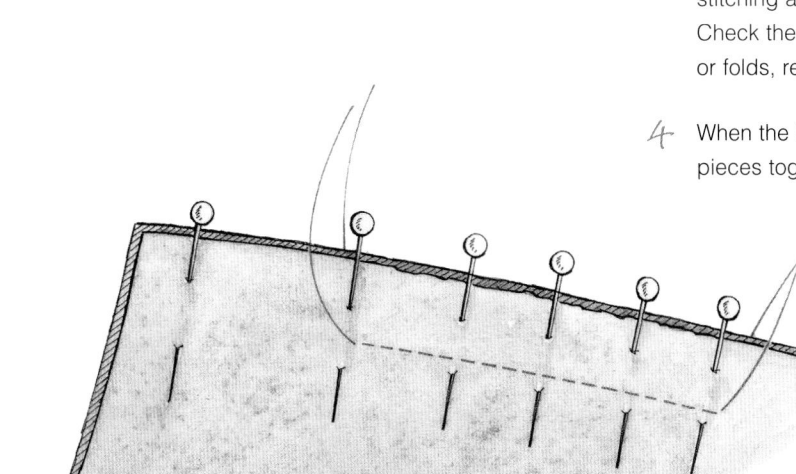

marking & preparing hems

You can stitch hems by machine or by hand. Some hems should be invisible on the right side of the garment, but others are meant to be seen. For a straight garment, the hem allowance can be up to 3" (7.6 cm) wide. For a flared garment, the hem is usually from 1½" to 2" (3.8 to 5.1 cm) wide. Sheer fabrics and lightweight knits almost always have narrow hems stitched by machine.

Marking a Hem

Put on the garment, with all the appropriate undergarments and accessories. Enlist the help of a friend to chalk or pin-mark the hem an even distance from the floor. Stand in one place while your helper moves around you, measuring with a yardstick (meterstick) and marking.

Pin up the entire hem to make sure you like the length. Make adjustments as needed.

Preparing to Hem

1. Trim seam allowances below the marked hemline to reduce bulk.

2. Fold up the hem along the marks and hand-baste it to the fabric, close to the fold. Measure and mark the desired hem depth from the fold. Add ¼" (6 mm) if you are clean-finishing the edge. Trim away the excess fabric.

3. If the hem is curved, stitch only ¼" (6 mm) from the raw edge with a long machine stitch. Pull up the bobbin thread every few inches to ease the fullness.

To Clean-Finish the Edge

If your fabric tends to ravel, you may want to clean-finish the edge before you hem.

- Turn under ¼" (6 mm) to the wrong side and press the fold. Machine-stitch.

- Machine-straight-stitch ¼" (6 mm) from the edge. Trim the edge with pinking shears.

- Zigzag or overcast the raw edge.

- Edgestitch a seam binding or hem tape to the right side of the garment edge, overlapping the short ends.

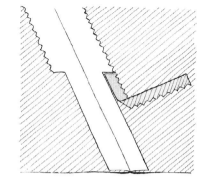

1

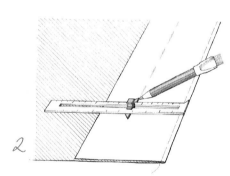

2

3

If your garment is cut on the bias, hang it on a hanger for 24 hours before marking the hem. The fabric will relax to its true length.

hemming methods

After you have marked and prepared the garment hem, you're ready to stitch the hem in place. You can hem in several ways, either by hand or machine. You can also fuse the hem on some fabrics. For hand and machine stitches, see pages 57, 58, and 67.

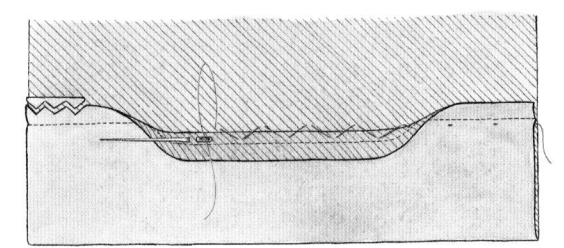

Hemming by Hand

hand blindstitch: Fold back the top edge of the hem. Take a tiny stitch in and out of the garment fabric. Take the next stitch ¼" (6 mm) away within the top fold of the hem. Continue, keeping stitches small and ¼" (6 mm) apart. The stitches will be hidden between the layers of fabric.

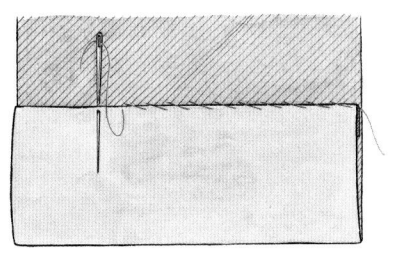

slant stitch: Take a tiny stitch in and out of the garment, and bring the needle through the edge of the hem. Repeat, evenly spacing and slanting the stitches. If your fabric ravels, pink the edge before hemming.

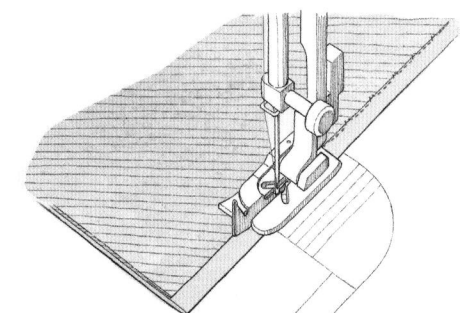

Hemming by Machine

machine blindstitch: (Refer to your owner's manual for machine settings.) Place the hem allowance facedown on the machine bed and fold back the rest of the fabric, leaving about ¼" (6 mm) of the hem edge extending beyond the fold. Align the fold against the guide in the foot. Stitch along the hem, close to the fold, catching only one or two threads of the garment with each left-hand stitch. Open the fabric and press the hem flat.

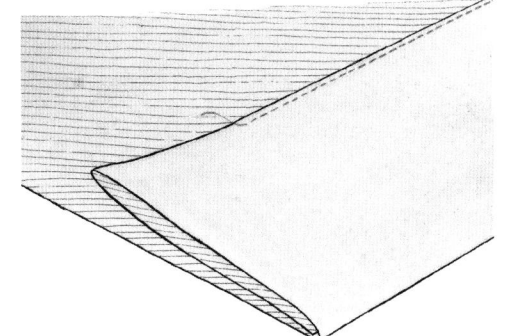

double-fold hem: Press one-half of the hem allowance to the wrong side of the fabric. Fold the remaining half to enclose the raw edge and press. To make a 2" (5.1 cm) double-fold hem, for example, you will fold 2" (5.1 cm) of the 4" (10.2 cm) hem allowance each time. Pin the folded edge in place. Stitch close to the inner folded edge through all layers.

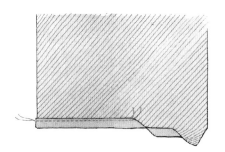

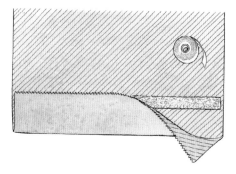

machine topstitch: Fold the hem to the desired width. Finish the edge of woven fabrics by turning under the garment edge ¼" (6 mm). Press. Topstitch close to the pressed edge. You can also add a second row of stitching ¼" (6 mm) away from the first.

twin needle: Hems stitched with a twin needle (see page 10) will stretch a little—so they are great for knit garments. Stitch on the right side of the fabric, catching the underside of the upper edge of the hem allowance. (You may need to buy a twin needle for your machine.)

narrow hem: A narrow hem is great for sheer and silky fabrics. Trim the hem allowance to ½" (1.3 cm). Press under ¼" (6 mm) and then ¼" (6 mm) again. Machine-stitch close to the inner fold. This style hem is also suitable for bias-cut garments.

Fusing

fused hem: Hemming with fusible web is a good method for hemming lightweight woven fabrics. Test the web on scrap fabric before applying to your garment. Clean-finish the raw edge of the fabric for a neater appearance (see page 93). Insert a strip of the fusible web between the hem and the garment. Steam-press, following the manufacturer's instructions.

When hand-stitching or machine blindstitching a hem, catch only one thread of the garment fabric in each stitch for a truly invisible hem.

essential techniques

zippers

Zippers make it easy to put on and take off clothes. All zippers open and close through the action of a self-locking slider and pull tab. There are three types of zippers, distinguished by their teeth: a polyester interlocking coil, molded plastic teeth, and stamped metal teeth. All of these teeth styles are attached to a fabric (usually polyester) tape.

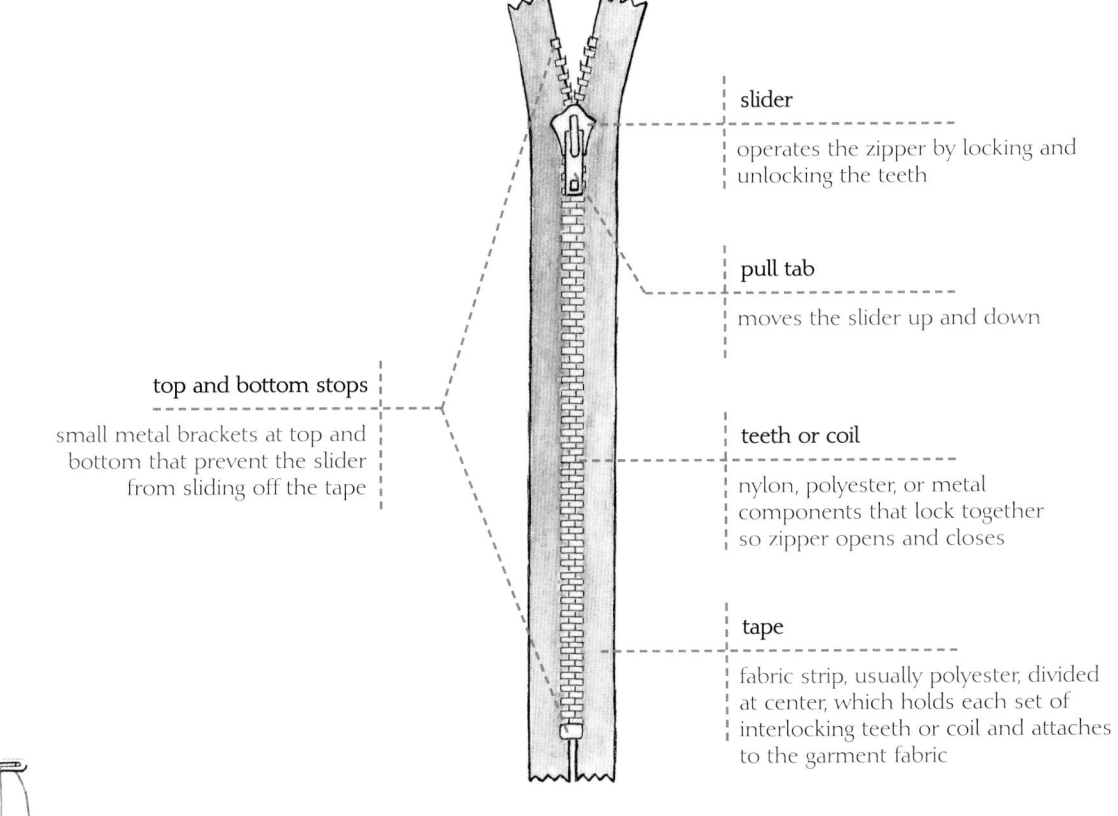

slider

operates the zipper by locking and unlocking the teeth

pull tab

moves the slider up and down

top and bottom stops

small metal brackets at top and bottom that prevent the slider from sliding off the tape

teeth or coil

nylon, polyester, or metal components that lock together so zipper opens and closes

tape

fabric strip, usually polyester, divided at center, which holds each set of interlocking teeth or coil and attaches to the garment fabric

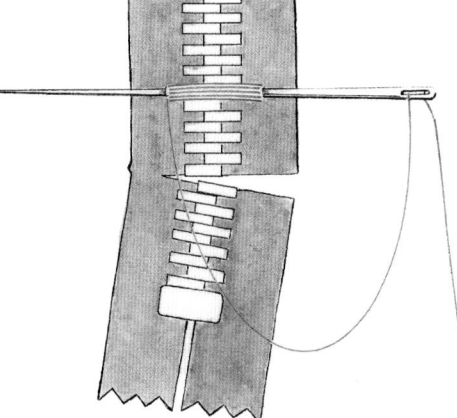

Shortening a Zipper

If you can't find the right length zipper, buy a longer one and shorten it. Close the zipper and mark the desired length. Straight-stitch several times back and forth over the coil or teeth at the mark. Trim the zipper ½" (1.3 cm) below the stitches.

closed bottom zipper

separating zipper

two-way separating zipper

invisible zipper

trouser zipper

Type	Construction	Characteristics	Uses
closed bottom	coil	4" to 22" (10.2 to 55.9 cm) long; lightweight, flexible, heat resistant	dresses, skirts, pants, sportswear, home décor
closed bottom	molded	4" to 22" (10.2 to 55.9 cm) long; medium-weight, large teeth, decorative, meant to be visible	dresses, jackets, sportswear
closed bottom	stamped metal	4" to 22" (10.2 to 55.9 cm) long; medium- to heavyweight, sturdy, teeth are usually enameled to match tape color	pants, sportswear, work clothes
separating	coil	12" to 48" (30.5 to 122 cm) long; lightweight, flexible, less bulky than metal or molded teeth	handknit sweaters, childrenswear, lightweight jackets
separating	molded	12" to 48" (30.5 to 122 cm) long; medium- to heavyweight, durable, sporty	jackets, sweaters, sportswear
separating	stamped metal	12" to 48" (30.5 to 122 cm) long; medium- to heavyweight	jackets and home decorating items
two-way separating	molded and stamped metal	12" to 48" (30.5 to 122 cm) long; medium- to heavyweight, two pull tabs (so garment can be zipped from top or bottom)	heavy jackets, ski parkas, action sportswear
invisible	coil	9" to 22" (22.9 to 55.9 cm) long; special insertion so it is invisible from right side of garment; requires special presser foot	dresses, skirts, pants, home décor
brass jeans or trousers zippers	stamped metal	6" to 9" (15.2 to 22.9 cm) long; slider has locking feature, slightly wider tape for fly-front insertion	jeans, work pants, skirts (any fly-front design)

essential techniques

inserting a zipper

There are several types of zippers (see pages 96 to 97), and each style is inserted into the garment in a slightly different way. The two most common ways zippers are inserted are with centered and lapped positioning. With a little patience and some tried-and-true tips, adding zippers can be a breeze.

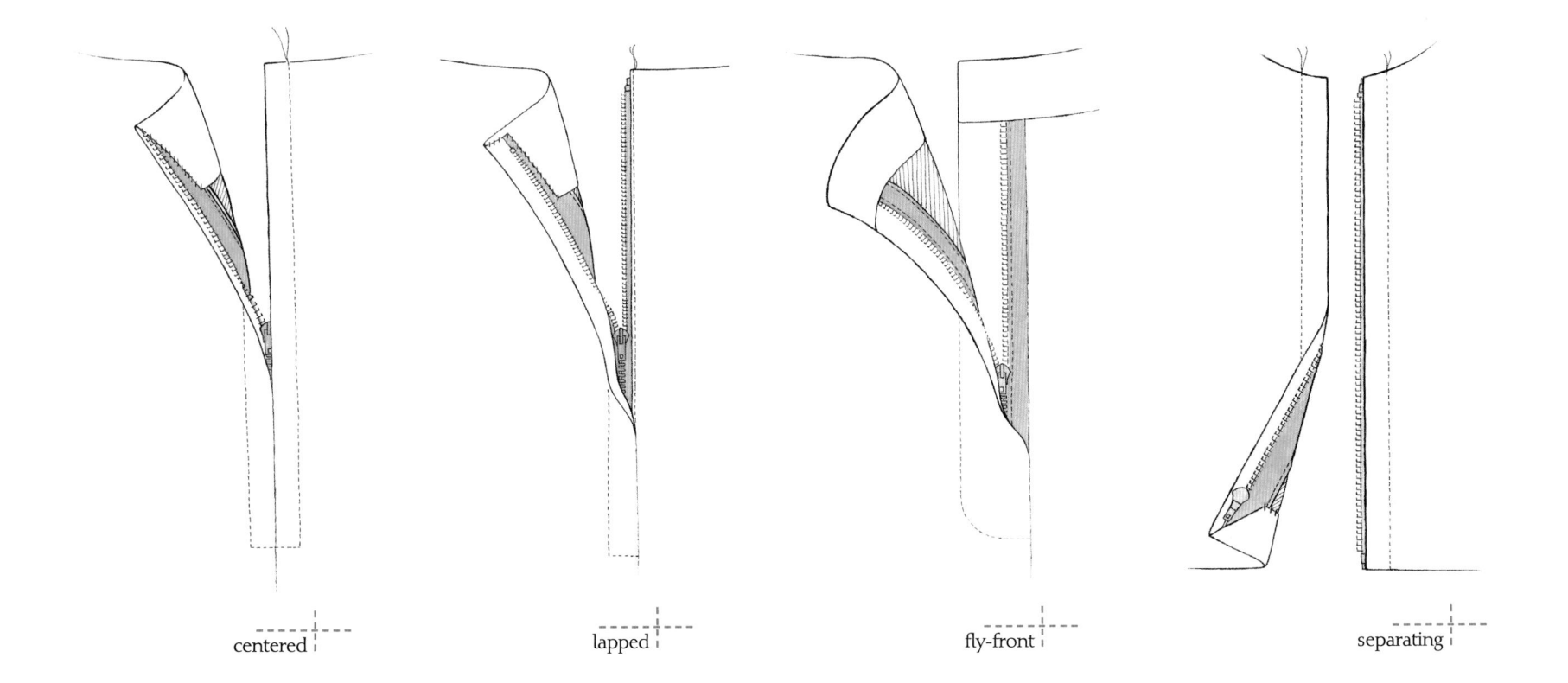

centered   lapped   fly-front   separating

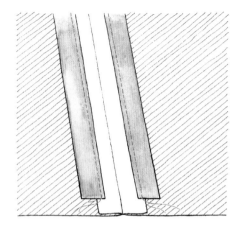

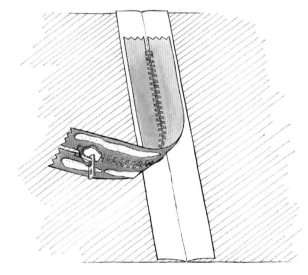

Preparing the Seam

It helps to have a little extra room in the seam allowances, so when you cut out the pattern, cut the zipper seam allowances to ¾" (1.9 cm) instead of the usual ⅝" (1.6 cm). Clean-finish the raw edges before installing the zipper. You can extend narrow seam allowances by stitching seam binding to the raw edges. When working with stretch fabric, stabilize the zipper area by fusing a narrow strip of interfacing to the wrong side of each seam allowance.

Before Inserting the Zipper

Remove the zipper from the package and press out the folds with a cool iron. Attach a zipper foot to your machine and adjust the needle position or foot position so the needle will be between the foot and the zipper teeth. Basting tape or fabric glue will temporarily hold the zipper in place on the seam to make it easier to stitch.

When sewing a zipper, flip up the pull tab to stitch past it more easily.

inserting a lapped zipper

Lapped zipper construction conceals the zipper and is most often used at side seams or at the center backs of dresses, skirts, and pants. (If the zipper is in a curved side seam, use a coil zipper, which is more flexible, and press it on a tailor's ham.)

1 Follow step 1 for the centered zipper construction (page 102). Attach the zipper foot and adjust so it is to the right of the needle. Open the zipper and place it facedown on the right-hand side of the seam allowance (with the open end facing you). Position the zipper coil directly over the seam line and the top stop 1" (2.5 cm) below the cut edge. Flip up the tab. Pin, glue, or hand-baste the zipper tape to the seam allowance only.

2 Machine-baste from the bottom to the top of the zipper, as close to the edge of the coil as possible.

3 Close the zipper, turn the zipper faceup, and flip up the pull tab. Smooth the fabric away from the zipper, forming a narrow fold between the coil and the seam. Adjust the zipper foot to the left of the needle and, starting at the bottom of the zipper, stitch through the folded seam allowance and the zipper tape, as close to the edge of the fold as possible.

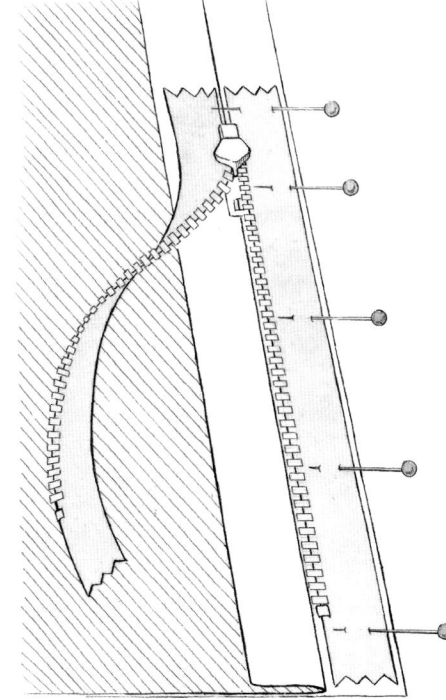

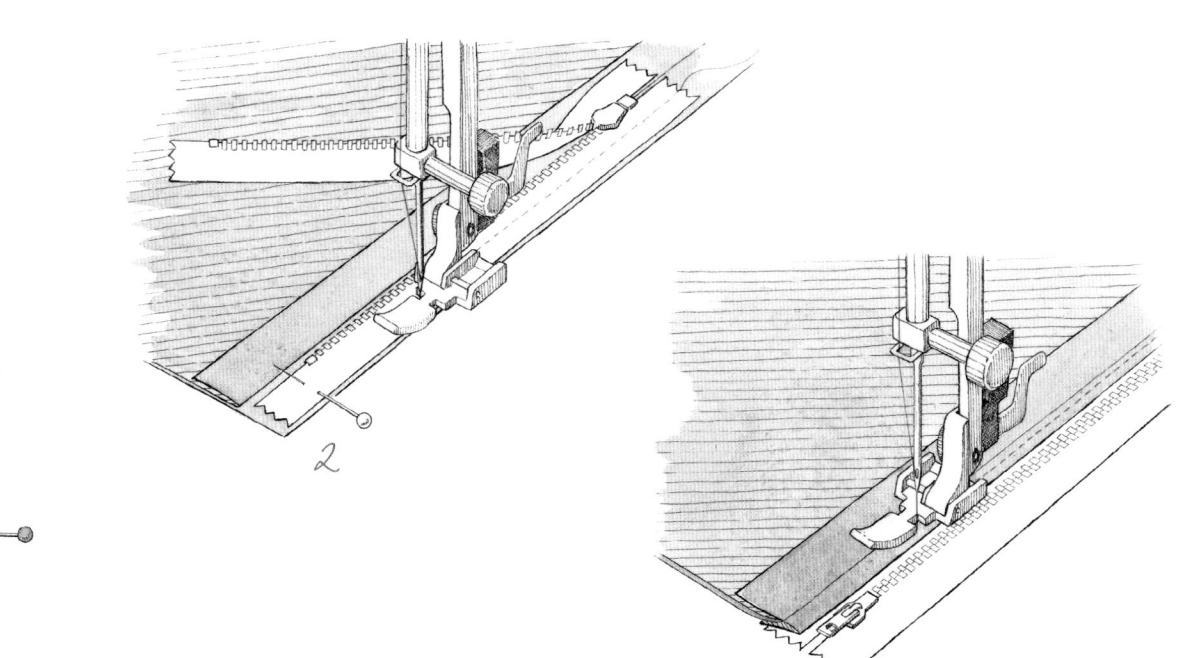

4 Turn the garment to the right side and spread the fabric as flat as possible. Mark the bottom of the zipper with a pin. Place ½" (1.3 cm) wide clear tape along the right side of the seam to act as a topstitching guide. Starting at the seam line at the bottom of the zipper, topstitch across the bottom and up the outside edge of the tape.

5 Remove the tape. Pull the thread tails to the wrong side and knot them. Remove the basting stitches and press. Press on a tailor's ham if the seam is curved.

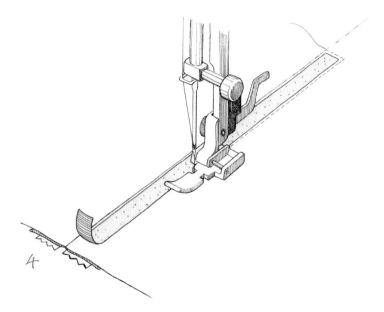

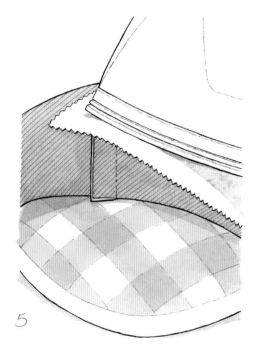

inserting a centered zipper

Centered zippers are typically sewn in home décor items and in the center front or center back of a garment.

1 Machine-baste the zipper opening closed. Clip the basting stitches every 2" (5.1 cm) so they can be easily removed later. Press the seam open. Finish the seam allowance edges with pinking or zigzag stitches (see page 64).

2 Use a glue stick or basting tape to position the zipper facedown on the wrong side of the garment. Center the teeth over the seam line and position the top stop 1" (2.5 cm) below the cut edge. Flip up the pull tab.

3 Place a pin below the bottom stop on the right side of the garment. Center a piece of ½" (1.3 cm) wide clear tape over the seam to act as a stitching guide. (Do not use tape on napped or delicate fabrics.) Remove the pin.

4 Attach the zipper foot and adjust so it is to the right of the needle. Begin stitching at the seam at the bottom of the tape. Stitch across the bottom of the zipper, pivot at the edge of the tape, and stitch up the side, using the edge of the tape as a guide.

5 Adjust the zipper foot to the left of the needle. Again begin stitching at the seam at the bottom of the tape. Stitch up the opposite side of the zipper.

6 Pull the thread tails to the wrong side and knot them at the bottom of the zipper. Remove the basting stitches and press with a press cloth.

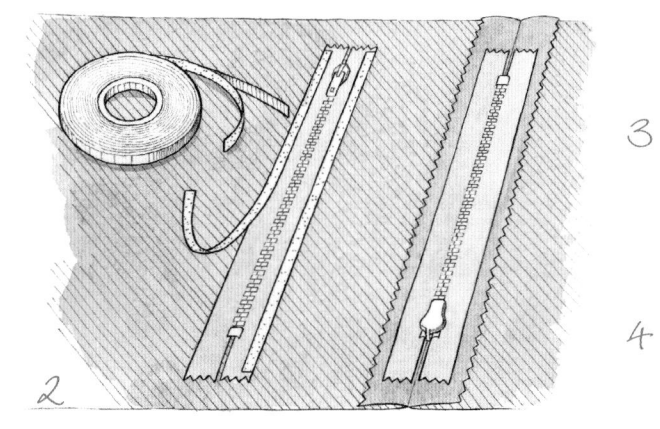

2

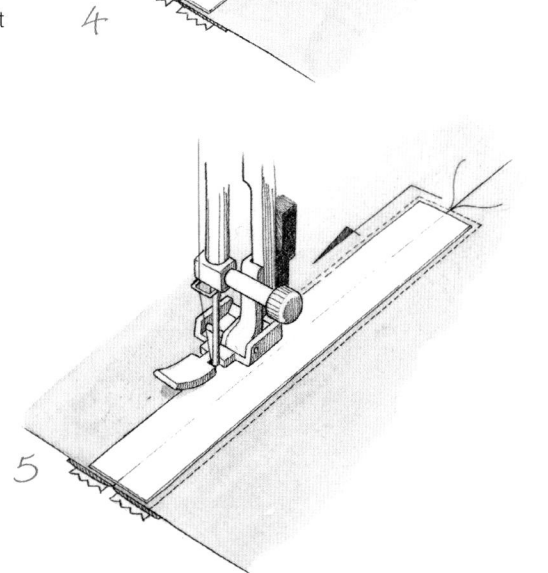

4

5

buttons & fasteners

Buttons and fasteners are a fun way to personalize your sewing projects—and they're functional, too. Buttons are made in three basic styles, and just about every type of material: plastic, mother-of-pearl, rhinestone, crystal, gemstone, glass, wood, leather, horn, bone, stone, ivory, porcelain, ceramic, and clay. For more about attaching buttons and fasteners, see pages 105 and 108 to 109).

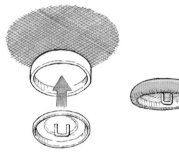

Sew-through buttons are mostly flat and have two or four holes. They are best for thin fabrics, blouses, shirts, dresses, pants, and skirts. If you add a thread shank (page 109), you can attach these flat buttons to heavier fabrics.

Fabric-covered buttons are sold in kits that include tops, bottoms, and shanks with assembly instructions. Cover the buttons with the fabric of your choice.

Shank buttons have a "neck" that lifts them up from the surface of the fabric. They are used on medium- to heavy-weight fabrics, for jackets, coats, denim garments, and sweaters.

Button size indicates the diameter of the button. Buttons can be as tiny as 1/4" (6 mm) and as large as 2" (5.1 cm).

essential techniques

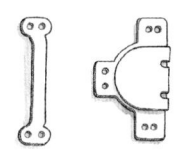

Toggles consist of a cord loop and button-like bar. This type of fastener is effective on lapped closings for a sporty look.

Hook-and-loop tapes (such as Velcro) have two halves. One half has soft loops, the other half has stiff hooks. The two halves cling together for a secure closure. Varieties include sew-in, fusible, or adhesive-backed tapes.

Hooks and eyes come in several shapes and styles. This two-part fastener is used on waistbands and at the top of zipper plackets for a neat overlap.

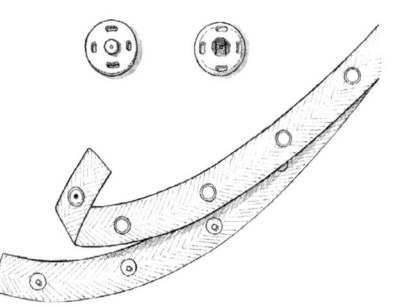

Frogs are a decorative closure consisting of a pair of loops and a ball button. Those made of cording or braid add unique style.

Snaps are another type of two-part fastener. The interlocking parts are a ball and a socket. Styles include individual sew-on snaps and continuous snap tape, shown above. Gripper snaps, generally in bright colors, are a decorative-style snap for the outside of a garment.

attaching fasteners

There are many other fasteners—beyond the basic button—for keeping garments closed. Make sure the weight and size of the fastener is compatible with the weight of your fabric.

toggles and frogs: Slipstitch these fasteners faceup, with the loop extending over the garment edge. Take small invisible slipstitches (see page 67) around the trim.

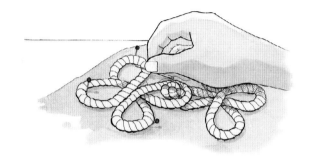

snaps: Position the ball half on the wrong side of the overlap, close to the edge. Stitch through each hole through the facing only so the thread doesn't show on the right side. Knot the thread. Mark the position for the snap socket on the right side of the underlap and attach. Sew through all layers.

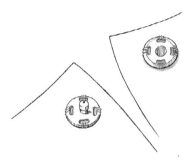

hook-and-loop tape: This style fastener is applied to overlapping edges. Position the hook tape on the right side of the underlap. Edgestitch around the perimeter. Align the loop tape on the wrong side of the overlap. Edgestitch around the perimeter.

hooks and eyes: Sew the hook to the wrong side of the overlap, without stitching through to the right side. Stitch several times over each hole. Close the garment. Mark the position of the end of the hook on the right side of the underlap. Sew the eye at the mark.

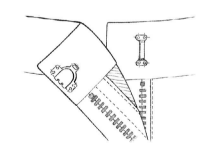

essential techniques

buttonhole tips

Computerized machines make automatic, one-step buttonholes in several styles—but you can make quality buttonholes on any type of machine with a simple zigzag stitch. Use a wide zigzag stitch for heavier fabrics and a narrow one for lightweight fabrics. To prevent the buttonhole from gaping or puckering, stabilize it with similar color interfacing. If the fabric is sheer or lightweight, use a tear-away stabilizer so you can remove it later. For button styles, see page 103.

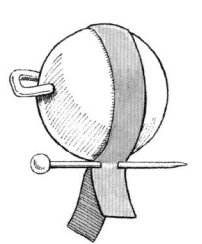

What Makes a Good Buttonhole?

• The thread and garment color match.

• The button weight is compatible with the weight of the fabric, thread, and interfacing/stabilizer.

• Each buttonhole lies smooth and flat without puckering.

• Interfacing or stabilizer is not visible, but simply supports the stitches.

• All the buttonholes are evenly spaced.

• All the buttonholes are the same length and width.

• The buttonholes are 1/8" (3 mm) longer than the button.

To Determine Buttonhole Length

flat button: Measure the diameter and thickness of the button. Add 1/8" (3 mm) to these numbers.

shank button: Pin a thin strip of paper around the button. Slide the button out and measure between the pin marks. Add 1/8" (3 mm) to this number.

For extra stability, apply a patch of fusible web to the wrong side of the buttonhole area.

making buttonholes

Horizontal buttonholes—perpendicular to the garment edge—are best for jackets and coats. Vertical buttonholes—parallel to the edge—are used on plackets, shirt bands, and with small buttons.

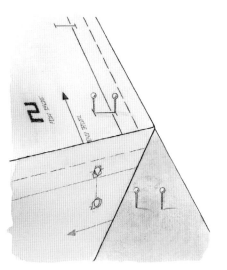

How to Make a Buttonhole

1. Place the pattern tissue over the garment, aligning the pattern seam line with the garment opening. Insert pins to mark the position of the buttonholes on the right side of the garment.

2. Carefully remove the pattern. Mark the buttonhole positions with pins, hand-basting, or a fabric-marking pen (see page 20).

3. To make a four-step buttonhole, start with a full bobbin, new needle, and buttonhole foot. Lower the foot over the center marking. Stitch three or four stitches across the end to form the first bar tack (the stitching at one end of the buttonhole).

4. Stitch down one side to the other marked end. Stitch three or four wider stitches to form the bar tack on the other end of the buttonhole.

5. Stitch up the opposite side, stopping at the bar tack. Make one or two small stitches in place to secure the threads.

6. Insert pins across the buttonhole, just inside each bar tack so you won't cut through them when you open the buttonhole. With small, sharp scissors or a seam ripper, carefully cut the fabric between the lines of stitching.

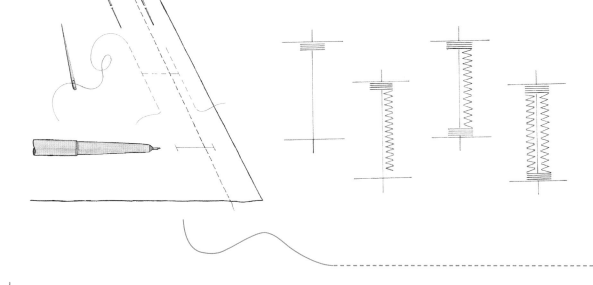

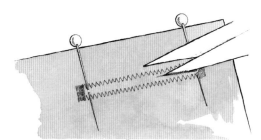

essential techniques

sewing on buttons

Make sure you position buttons in the right locations so the garment closes correctly and lies flat. Mark their positions carefully on the right side of the garment. Lap the buttonholes over the button area, measuring to the amount indicated by the pattern. Push a pin through the buttonhole ⅛" (3 mm) from the end to mark the button location. Hand-stitch with a doubled length of all-purpose thread for light- and medium-weight fabrics and a doubled length of heavy-duty thread for heavier fabrics.

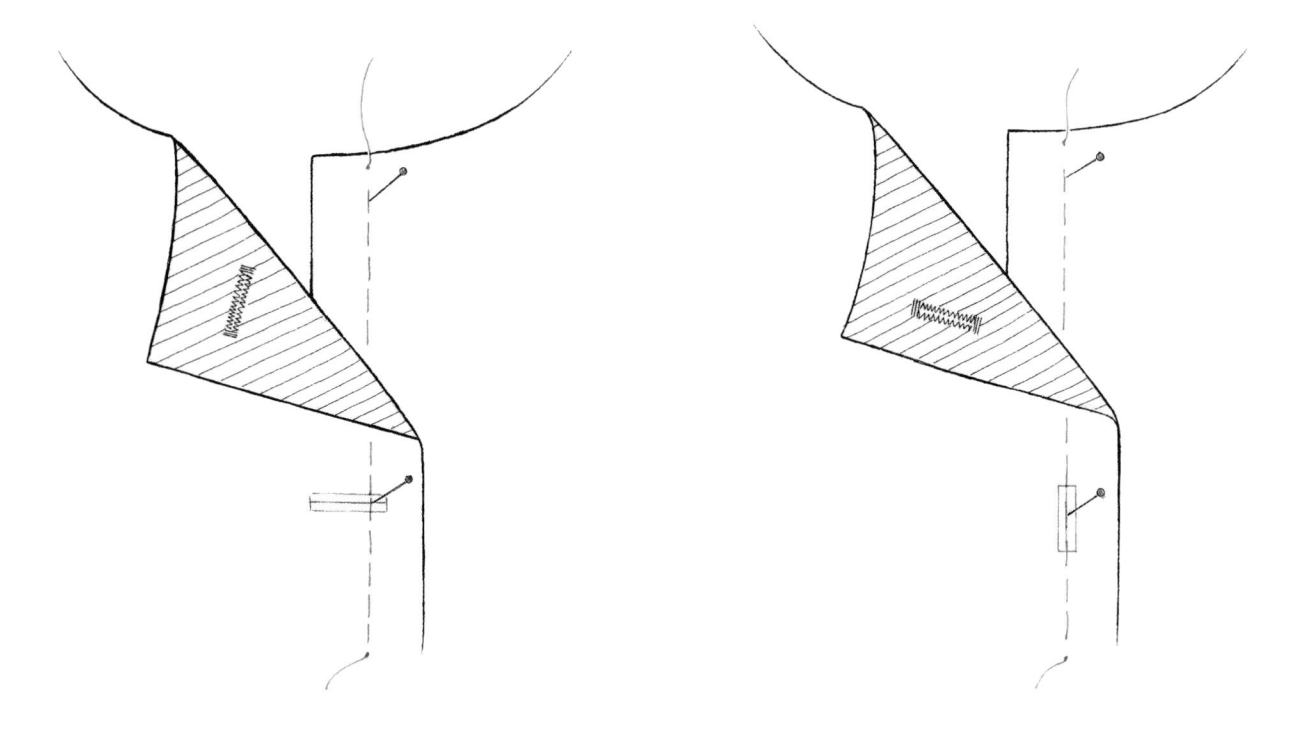

Nothing is easier than sewing on a button. Just thread a needle. Work with a double strand of thread, about 20" (50.7 cm) long. For lightweight fabrics, use all-purpose thread. Heavy-duty thread or buttonhole twist, a special heavyweight thread, is great for heavier fabrics.

Flat Button

(for lightweight fabrics and nonfunctioning buttons)

Thread the needle and knot the ends together. Bring the needle up from the wrong side of the fabric and through one hole of the button. Bring it back down through the opposite hole and the fabric.

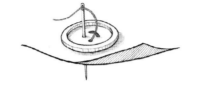

Repeat several times. If there are four holes, stitch through the other two holes the same way.

Knot the thread on the wrong side of the garment.

Shank Button

(for medium- to heavyweight fabrics)

Thread the needle and knot the ends. Position the button with the shank perpendicular to the fabric.

Bring the needle up from the wrong side of the fabric, through the hole in the shank, and back down through the fabric. Sew several stitches through the shank and fabric.

Take two or three tiny stitches on the wrong side of the fabric to secure. Knot the ends.

Flat Button with Thread Shank

(for medium- to heavyweight fabrics)

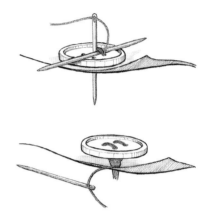

Thread the needle and knot the ends. Bring the needle up from the wrong side of the fabric and insert it through one hole of the button.

Lay a toothpick across the top of the button. Bring the needle down through the opposite hole, over the toothpick. Take about six stitches. If there are four holes, do the same for the other two holes.

Remove the toothpick and lift the button away from the fabric. Bring the needle out between the button and the fabric surface. Wind the thread around the stitches to create a thread shank.

Take two or three tiny stitches on the wrong side of the fabric to secure and knot the ends.

reinforcing buttons

Buttons pop off for many reasons. If a garment has gotten a little snug, sew the new button a little closer to the edge. If the button is at a stress point, such as the bust or waist, sew a backer button (any small, flat button) to the inside of the garment, behind the fashion button. You can also add backer buttons to closures on heavy fabrics.

Adding a Backer Button

sew-through buttons: Choose a backer button with the same number of holes as the fashion button. Line up the holes and sew on both buttons at the same time.

Follow the steps for attaching a flat button with a thread shank (see page 109). If you have a hard time holding both buttons in place, stick a pin through one set of holes while you sew the other set.

shank buttons: Choose a backer button that has two holes. Position the button on the wrong side of the fabric and sew two small stitches through it. Bring the needle to the right side and through the hole in the button shank, as shown in the drawing.

Continue sewing through the shank hole and backer button holes until both buttons are secure. Wrap the thread around and under the backer button and make a knot.

Sewing an Interior Button

It takes a little extra care to sew buttons to the inside of the garment or item—because you don't want the stitches to show on the right side of the fabric. So, as you stitch, do not bring the needle through the fabric. Instead, just pick up a couple of fabric threads on the wrong side with each stitch.

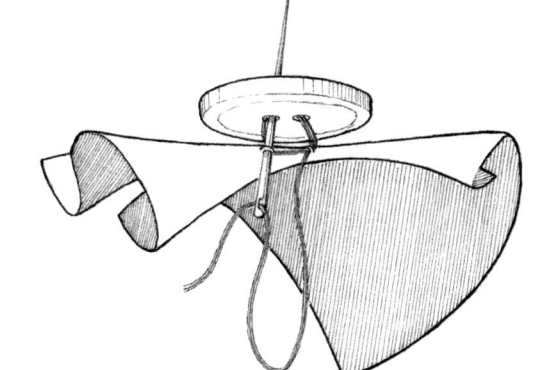

When you're working on a lightweight fabric, sew a small patch of fabric or seam binding behind the button instead of a backer button.

working
with
fabrics

woven fabrics

Most fabrics are woven. There are several weave patterns, created by the interlacing of lengthwise (warp) and crosswise (weft) yarns. If the yarn strands are dyed before weaving, the fabric has consistent color on both sides. If not, the fabric is printed to create a patterned right side and a mottled or solid-color wrong side.

plain weave: Plain-weave fabrics are flat, smooth, and easy to sew. They wrinkle but do not ravel excessively. They don't drape well and are difficult to ease. Muslin, taffeta, percale, and wool challis are plain-weave fabrics.

satin weave: Satin-weave fabrics have a characteristic surface sheen because the warp yarns float over several weft yarns. The fabrics have a lustrous surface, snag easily, and are marred by pins and needles. They ravel excessively and slip during stitching. Antique satin, charmeuse, crepe-back satin, and sateen are all satin-weave fabrics.

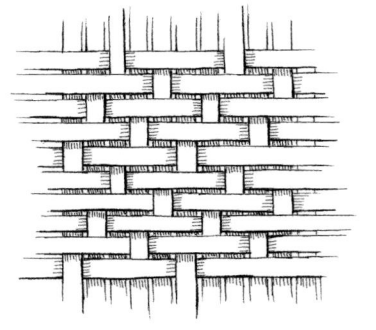

rib weave: Rib weave is a variation of plain weave, with one yarn thicker than the other. The fabric tends to slip during stitching and is weaker than plain weave. Rib-weave fabrics, which include poplin, faille, and ottoman, may require a "with nap" layout.

twill weave: Twill-weave fabrics appear to have diagonal lines on the surface. These sometimes-bulky fabrics are strong, durable, heavy, and wrinkle resistant. They tend to fray, abrade at edges, and may require a "with nap" layout. Denim, serge, ticking, and gabardine have a twill-weave structure.

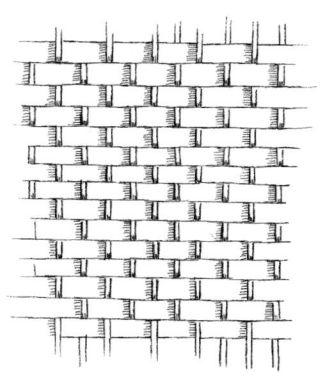

knit fabrics

Knit fabrics are formed by a series of interlocking loops. Although they may differ in their weight, texture, and fiber content, all knits are stretchy, comfortable, wrinkle resistant, and easy to sew. Most should be sewn with stitches that stretch with the fabric (see page 120). Cut edges don't ravel, so seam allowances usually don't need to be finished. Some knits may shrink, depending on their fiber content. Some might require a "with nap" layout.

single knits: Single knits are made with a single set of needles so there are knit stitches on front, purl stitches on back. These fabrics are stretchy and best suited for close-fitting garments with few construction details. Crosswise-cut edges can run, and lengthwise-cut edges can curl.

double knits: Double-knit fabrics are made with two sets of needles, so the fabric has the same knit structure and appearance on both sides. Double knits are stable, with very little stretch, so they hold their shape well.

stable knits: Stable knit fabrics have limited stretch or none at all. They are generally not suitable for "knits only" patterns. Garments made with stable knits don't need stretch seams. The fabric won't curl at the edges or ravel.

moderate and two-way: Moderate-stretch knits stretch lengthwise but not crosswise. Two-way stretch knits stretch both lengthwise and crosswise, which makes them suitable for active sportswear. Garments made with moderate-stretch or two-way-stretch knit fabric need to have stretch seams (see page 120).

Knit Characteristics

☐ elastic

☐ comfortable fit

☐ wrinkle resistant

☐ easy to sew

cotton

Most cotton fabrics are easy to sew—great for beginners and expert sewers, too. Cotton is the most popular fiber in the world. It comes from the seedpod of the cotton plant. The fiber can be knit or woven and is manufactured in many different weights and weaves.

Characteristics	Care Requirements	Types of Cotton Fabric
• very absorbent • comfortable to wear year-round • easy to launder, but soils easily • dyes well, retains color • strong, durable • very flammable • resists abrasion, pilling, and damage from moths • wrinkles easily • tendency to shrink • exposure to sunlight weakens fibers	• Cotton can be laundered at high water temperature with soap and water. • Fibers tend to pick up dirt, so should be washed frequently. • Cotton shrinks more in hot water than cold, so unless garment is very soiled, wash in cold water. • Loose weaves shrink more than tight weaves, so should be dry-cleaned.	• **batiste:** soft and lightweight; suitable for lingerie, blouses, baby dresses • **broadcloth:** light to medium weight; suitable for sportswear, shirts, pajamas • **corduroy:** pile fabric, very durable; suitable for pants, casual sportswear • **denim:** strong, durable fabric; suitable for jeans and work pants • **flannel:** very soft with slight nap on one or both sides • **lace:** textured fabric with open pattern • **muslin:** inexpensive fabric; often used for crafts and sample garments • **sateen:** shiny and lustrous; often used for formalwear

linen

Linen fibers are obtained from the stem of the flax plant. The fabric is luxurious, but expensive to produce, and wrinkles easily. It is also two times as strong as 100 percent cotton and five times as strong as 100 percent wool! Traditionally a warm-weather fabric, linen is ideal for summer dresses, shirts, and slacks.

Characteristics	Care Requirements	Types of Linen Fabric
<ul><li>absorbent and cool in warm weather</li><li>natural luster</li><li>quick-drying</li><li>retains shape well</li><li>sheds surface dirt, stain resistant</li><li>yellows with age</li><li>wrinkles easily</li><li>frays easily</li><li>shrinks</li><li>poor elasticity</li><li>develops shine if pressed without a press cloth</li></ul>	<ul><li>Dry-clean linen garments because they wrinkle and lose their trademark crispness in the wash.</li><li>If you intend to wash the finished item, preshrink it in the washing machine before cutting.</li><li>If you intend to dry-clean, steam-press the fabric before cutting.</li><li>Machine-wash in gentle cycle and cool water and dry on a regular heat setting.</li><li>Remove from dryer while still damp and immediately press on the wrong side, or with a press cloth, at a high temperature.</li></ul>	<ul><li>**damask:** reversible with elaborate designs woven into the cloth</li><li>**handkerchief linen:** very lightweight; ideal for lingerie, baby clothes, dresses, and blouses</li><li>**lawn:** very fine, lightweight, and closely woven; suitable for fine lingerie, dresses, and collars</li><li>**linen:** any weight of strong, lustrous, and absorbent fabric made from the flax plant</li></ul>

silk

Silk is sometimes called the queen of fibers. It has a soft hand (tactile quality), beautiful drape, and unique luster. Silkworms produce silk as they spin their cocoons, and the fiber is cultivated mostly in Asia and China. It takes about 600 silkworm cocoons to make enough fabric for a shirt.

Silk fibers are knitted and woven into lightweight fabrics, such as crepe de chine, suitable for eveningwear, and crisp fabrics suitable for tailored jackets. Light, slippery silks benefit from special sewing techniques (see page 122).

Characteristics	Care Requirements	Types of Silk Fabric
• natural luster • absorbent and cool in warm weather • insulating in cold weather • strong and long lasting • resilient, doesn't wrinkle easily • resists shrinking and stretching • dyes well; some bold colors fade or lose dye when washed • may stain with perspiration and water • expensive • difficult to care for • sometimes requires special sewing techniques	• Dry-clean silk garments with loose weaves, bold colors, heavy weight, and a lot of tailoring or construction details. • Hand-wash small, lightweight garments in warm water with mild detergent. Roll the garment in a towel to remove excess water and lay out on a second towel to dry. • Iron the garment on the wrong side while it's still damp, using a press cloth. • To test washability, prewash a small scrap. After it dries, check to make sure the color, texture, and luster didn't change. • Never spot-clean silk; water may leave a permanent mark.	• **charmeuse:** soft with lustrous face and dull back; drapes well • **chiffon:** lightweight and transparent; suitable for eveningwear • **crepe de chine:** light to medium weight; suitable for dresses, blouses, lingerie, and eveningwear • **doupioni:** uneven surface with yarn slubs, ravels easily; suitable for suits and dresses • **peau de soie:** dull surface, satin weave; suitable for bridal gowns and eveningwear • **shantung:** dull or lustrous finish with irregular yarns and surface slubs; suitable for suits, dresses, slacks, and blouses • **taffeta:** smooth and crisp, with characteristic rustle as it moves; suitable for dresses and eveningwear

wool

Wool comes from the fleece of sheep and lambs. More specialized fabrics come from angora, cashmere goat, camel, alpaca, llama, and vicuña. Wool has a medium luster and is manufactured in all weights, for all types of garments. It is easy to sew and care for.

There are two basic types of wool fibers. Woolens are soft with a fuzzy texture. The more expensive, lightweight worsteds are smooth, strong, and lustrous and they wear and press well.

Characteristics	Care Requirements	Types of Wool Fabric
• long lasting • easy-care finishes • absorbent • stain and moisture repellent • resilient (stretches up to 35 percent when dry and 50 percent when wet) • comfortable in all kinds of weather • shrinks and felts when washed • susceptible to insect damage • coarse fibers may irritate skin • expensive • wrinkle resistant • develops shine if pressed without a press cloth	• Dry-clean. Wool does not need to be laundered as frequently as other fabrics. • Brush and hang wool garments immediately after wearing. • Sponge the garment periodically to remove surface dirt. • Treat stains immediately with a mild solution of soap and water. • Launder washable wools (check the end of the bolt) in cool water with mild detergent and lay flat to dry to retain shape. • Press with a press cloth to avoid shine.	• **blanket cloth:** heavily napped for warmth; suitable for coats, jackets, and bathrobes • **bouclé:** loops or curls on the surface; suitable for dresses and suits • **challis:** great drapability, gathers well, often printed; suitable for dresses, skirts, and scarves • **crepe:** dull, crinkled surface in variety of weights; suitable for dresses, skirts, and slacks • **flannel:** lightly napped surface; great for slacks, jackets, and suits • **gabardine:** firm, twill-weave, worsted wool; durable; suitable for slacks, suits, dresses, and jackets • **serge:** worsted wool; suitable for tailored suits and trousers • **tweed:** rough with slubs and nubs on the surface; yarn-dyed tweed has flecked appearance; suitable for jackets, slacks, and skirts • **wool jersey:** comfortable, lightweight knit fabric that drapes well; suitable for sportswear and dresses

rayon, acetate & triacetate

Rayon, acetate, and triacetate are made from plant cellulose (cotton waste, wood pulp) that is pushed through spinnerettes (metal plates with tiny holes). Variations in the process produce three distinct fiber types. The fabrics resemble cotton, linen, wool, and silk. Sewing ease depends on the weave and surface of the actual fabric.

Rayon Characteristics	Acetate Characteristics	Triacetate Characteristics	Care Requirements	Types of Fabrics
• drapes beautifully • absorbent and cool • soft, comfortable to wear • easy to dye • blends well with other fibers • loses strength when wet • ravels easily • shrinks, poor shape retention • poor resiliency, wrinkles easily • fades from exposure to light	• high luster • drapes well • resists mildew and mold • poor resiliency, wrinkles easily • subject to abrasion • sensitive to high heat, melts	• drapes well • high luster • poor durability and elasticity • wrinkle resistant • can be permanently heat-set, good pleat and crease retention • often blended with cotton and rayon	• Dry-clean rayon and acetate or hand-wash with mild detergent and water. Remove excess water by rolling the garment in a towel and then dry on a plastic hanger. Press on the wrong side with press cloth while the fabric is damp. • Hand-wash or machine-wash triacetate and air- or machine-dry.	• **challis (rayon):** soft, firm fabric, often printed with small, overall design; suitable for dresses, skirts, and scarves • **faille (acetate):** flat rib surface; dressy fabric for dresses, jackets, and coats • **satin (rayon or acetate):** firmly woven with smooth surface; suitable for eveningwear and bridal gowns • **taffeta (rayon or acetate):** smooth and crisp, rustles as it moves; suitable for eveningwear • **velour (triacetate):** thick, short pile; suitable for robes and active sportswear

synthetic fibers

This group of fibers includes acrylic, nylon, polyester, and spandex. They are completely synthetic and are made from combined molecules of carbon, hydrogen, nitrogen, and oxygen. Because of modern production methods and special finishes, all of these fibers compete well—and are often blended—with natural fibers.

Microfibers, are finer versions of the man-made fibers, most often polyester. They can be one hundred times finer than human hair and one-half the diameter of fine silk fibers. They produce very soft, luxurious fabrics with easy-care properties.

Acrylic Types and Characteristics	Nylon Types and Characteristics	Polyester Types and Characteristics	Spandex Types and Characteristics	Care Requirements
(fake fur, fleece, knits, pile fabrics, some sheers) • soft, warm, and lightweight • developed as a substitute for wool • wrinkle resistant • nonabsorbent, but quick drying • moth, mold, and mildew resistant • prone to pilling • shrinks • can be heat-set into permanent pleats and creases	*(plisse, sheers, velvet, microfiber)* • very strong, resistant to wear and tear • elastic • water repellent • colorfast, easy to dye • tends to cause skipped stitches and puckered seams • pills and frays easily • can be damaged by hot iron • wrinkle resistant	*(almost any fabric type, either 100 percent polyester or blended with other fibers)* • crisp, resilient, and wrinkle resistant • good elasticity, good shape retention • easy to launder by machine, wash and wear • moth, mold, and mildew resistant • tends to cause skipped stitches and puckered seams • dulls needles and scissors • damaged by high heat • poor absorbency • pills and attracts lint • accepts dye well, colorfast • blends well with natural fibers	*(blended with other fibers to add elasticity)* • extremely elastic, stretches more than 500 percent without breaking • adds stretch to other fibers • improves fit, comfort, and shape retention in foundation garments and exercise clothing • tends to cause skipped stitches and puckered seams • easily damaged by high heat • requires special sewing techniques	• Synthetic fabrics can be machine-washed and machine-dried at low temperature. • These fabrics have a fairly low melting point, so press carefully. • Launder blended fabrics according to the care requirements of each of the fiber types. (For instance, a silk and polyester blend might need to be hand-washed to avoid water-staining the silk fibers.)

sewing stretch fabrics

The term "stretch fabrics" refers to stretch-woven fabrics, single knits, some double knits, and bias-cut fabrics (see page 113). The seams in these elastic fabrics need to stretch with the fabric, or they may pucker and stitches might break, so they need to be sewn with stitches that stretch, too. If you must sew stretch fabrics with a straight stitch, hold the fabric taut—don't pull it. Stop occasionally and, with the needle in the fabric, raise the presser foot to relax the fabric. Sew a second line of stitching 1/8" (3 mm) from the first.

narrow zigzag: Every machine can sew this style of stitch. Set the stitch width to a very narrow setting and the stitch length equal to the stitch width.

straight stretch stitch: This specialty stitch looks like three parallel rows of straight stitches. To create it, the machine stitches back and forth in a straight line.

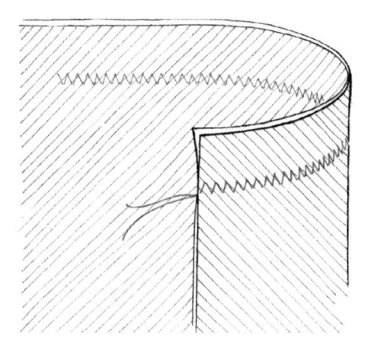

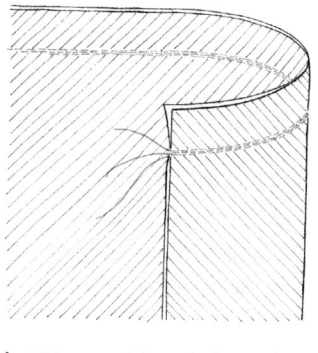

overedge stitch: This specialty stretch stitch locks over the edge of the fabric so it stitches and finishes a seam in one pass.

twin-needle stitch: This specialty stitch requires a twin needle. The right side of the fabric has two parallel rows of stitching. On the wrong side, the bobbin thread follows a zigzag pattern.

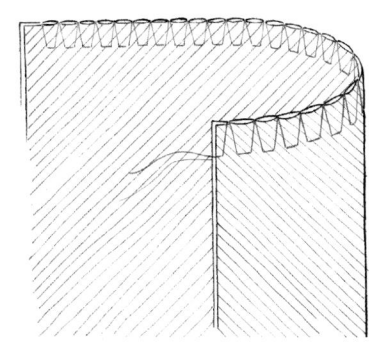

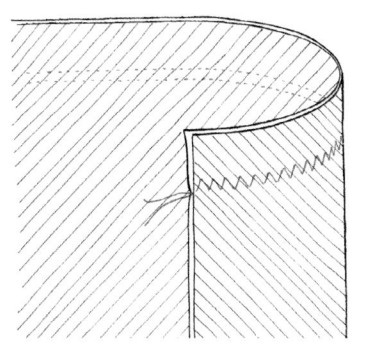

- Prewash or dry-clean the fabric, following the care instructions.
- Gently press out any creases.
- Lay out the pattern on the fabric so the most stretch wraps around the body. Follow the "with nap" layout.
- If both sides of the fabric look the same, mark one side of each cut piece as the right side with chalk or a small piece of tape.
- Stitch with a ballpoint needle, polyester thread, and a stretch stitch.
- Press carefully—don't slide the iron—to avoid stretching the fabric.
- To stabilize but not restrict the knit, apply fusible knit interfacing to collars, cuffs, pockets, plackets, and facings.

Commercial patterns that call for knit fabrics usually have a stretch gauge on the back. To test a knit, fold it crosswise and hold it up to the gauge. If it stretches to the indicated point, the fabric has enough stretch for that pattern.

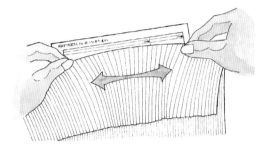

If the seam allowances tend to curl, sew a second row of stitching and trim the seam allowance close to the second row.

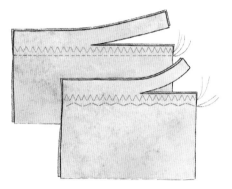

When stitching buttonholes in a stretch fabric, stitch in the direction of the least stretch. Stabilize the wrong side of the fabric first with fusible interfacing.

sewing slippery fabrics

The key to sewing slippery fabrics—silk, polyester, rayon, and acetate— is to avoid overhandling them. These delicate fabrics mar easily. Set the stitch length to between ten and fifteen stitches per inch (2.5 cm) and hold the fabric taut while stitching. You might need to loosen the thread tension and lighten the presser foot pressure slightly. Make a practice seam with a scrap piece of your fabric. Stitch with a straight-stitch presser foot or an even-feed foot (page 12) to keep the fabric from creeping.

If the fabric does creep or slip, baste the seam first by hand or use basting tape to hold the fabric in place (see page 70). Sew with plain, straight-stitch seams. If the fabric ravels, pink the seam allowances or apply liquid fray pre-venter to the edges. If the fabric is sheer, make French seams (page 62).

- Prewash the fabric, lining, (and interfacing, if necessary) following the fabric care instructions. Before laying out the pattern, fold the fabric right side out so the wrong sides are together.

- Follow the "with nap" layout to avoid shading variations in the finished garment.

- Use extra-fine pins or fabric weights to hold the paper pattern in place. Place pins in the seam allowances.

- If the fabric is very slippery, place tissue paper under it. Pin through the paper pattern, fabric, and tissue paper.

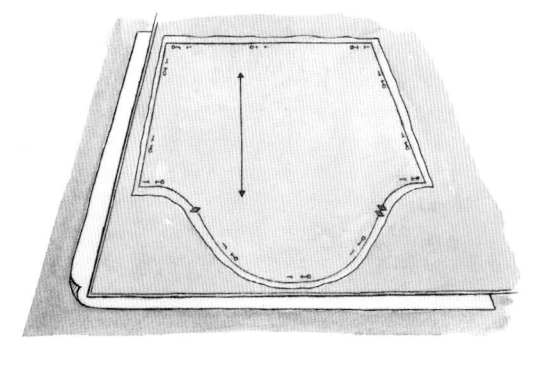

- Cut pieces with a rotary cutter to prevent the fabric from shifting.

- You can also cut with bent-handled dressmaker's shears (page 19)—one blade rests on the cutting surface. Scissors with serrated blades help grip the slippery fabric while cutting, trimming, and grading.

To find the right iron temperature for a slippery fabric, press a scrap piece of the fabric first, beginning with the iron on a low setting. Raise the temperature slowly, as needed. Use another fabric scrap for a press cloth, right side down. Don't press too hard. If the fabric is very lightweight, seam allowance edges might be visible on the right side. To avoid this, press the seams on a seam roll or slip a sheet of paper between the seam allowance and the fabric.

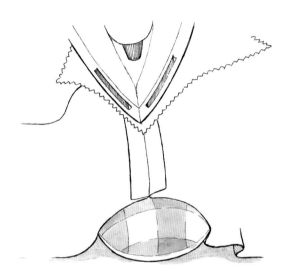

For better control when cutting slippery fabrics, cover the cutting surface with a sheet or flannel-backed vinyl tablecloth (flannel side up).

sewing sheer & lace fabrics

Sheer fabrics can be a sewing challenge. They are transparent, somewhat fragile, and have a tendency to creep. They are also beautiful and elegant, so don't let the challenges hold you back! Crisp sheers—organza, voile, organdy, and handkerchief linen—are easier to cut and sew than soft sheers and are fine for tailored items, such as shirts. Soft sheers—batiste, eyelet, chiffon, and georgette—and open weaves, such as net and lace, are better for loosely fitted garments with fewer tailored details.

Because all the seams in a sheer or lace fabric are visible from the outside, they should be narrow and neat. French seams and flat-fell seams (see pages 58 and 59) are best for these fabrics. Use short stitches (12 to 18 stitches per inch [2.5 cm]), a straight-stitch presser foot, and a straight-stitch throat plate (if you have them). Otherwise, work with a general-purpose presser foot. If the fabric still slips, try an even-feed foot (see page 12).

- Prewash the fabric, following the fabric care instructions.

- Before laying out the pattern, fold the fabric right side out, so the less slippery wrong sides are together.

- Follow the "with nap" layout if the fabric has a sheen or pattern.

- For laces and fabrics with a definite pattern, match pieces at the seams (see page 128).

- To prevent the fabric from being pulled through the throat plate at the beginning of a seam, place a small piece of stabilizer under the fabric at the beginning of the seam. Start sewing on the stabilizer and then stitch onto the fabric.

- Set the iron on a low temperature setting and increase only as needed.

- Hold both thread ends as you take the first few stitches so they don't tangle.

- Apply liquid fray preventer to the cut edges if they fray.

- Instead of backstitching, shorten the stitch at the beginning and end of the seam or knot the threads.

- To prevent puckers, place tear-away stabilizer or tissue paper under the fabric and stitch through all layers. Remove the paper carefully so you don't distort the stitches.

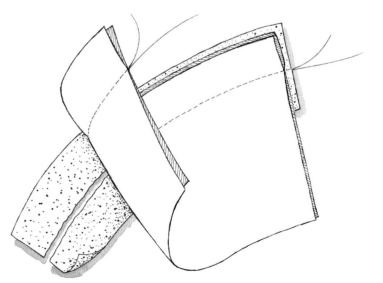

sewing textured fabrics

Rich surface textures add extra interest and dimension to your projects. You can choose fabrics with multicolor or single-color designs woven right into the structure or fabrics with a three-dimensional, looped, brushed, or plush surface. Each requires special layout and sewing considerations.

Fabrics with surface texture have nap—the raised fibers on the surface that have a natural up and down direction. On pile fabrics, such as corduroy or velvet, you can feel the nap. Fleece, faux fur, suede, leather, brushed cotton, some knits, terry, and velveteen are all napped fabrics. Lay out and cut all the pieces for your project in the same direction to avoid uneven shading.

Rub your hand along the surface of the fabric. If the fabric feels rough, the nap is running in the opposite direction—you are rubbing "against" the nap. If the fabric feels smooth, you are rubbing "with" the nap. In this direction, the fabric surface is also lighter and shinier.

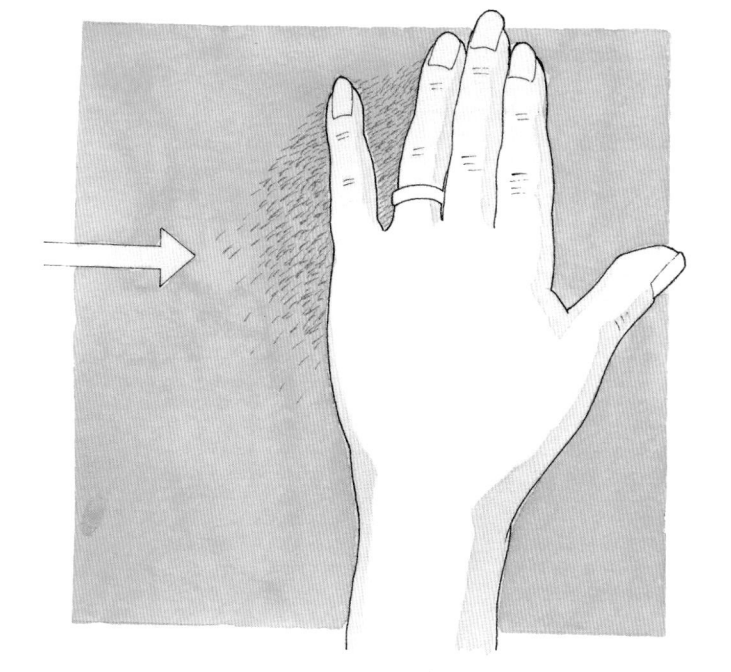

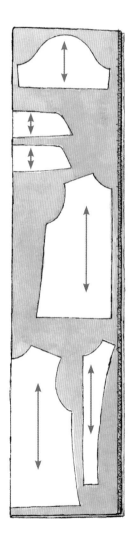

- It is sometimes easier to cut napped (especially pile) fabric in a single layer, as you would for striped fabrics (see pages 130 and 131). Make sure to flip the pattern pieces when you lay out the second set, so that you have both right and left sides.

- Stitch with a standard, straight seam. For heavier fabrics, use longer stitches—about 5 to 8 stitches per inch (2.5 cm).

- Hold the fabric taut when stitching, and whenever possible, stitch in the same direction as the nap.

- For fabrics that ravel, overedge-stitch or pink the edges (pages 64 and 65).

- Avoid seam finishes that add bulk.

- To press, place the fabric facedown on a needleboard, terry towel, or a piece of the same fabric, so you don't crush the pile.

It is important to cut all the pattern pieces in the same direction, or "with the nap." Deciding which direction to place the pattern pieces is a matter of personal taste. Either way is fine as long as you are consistent.

To reduce bulk on heavy pile fabrics, such as faux fur, trim away the extra fibers from the seam allowances.

sewing striped, plaid & print fabrics

Plaids, stripes, and prints are strong visual patterns, so it is important to match them at prominent seams. If you are careful laying and cutting out the pattern, the seams will be almost invisible. You need to buy extra fabric, 1/4 to 1/2 yard (0.25 to 0.5 m), depending on the size of the pattern repeat (the distance from one bar of the plaid or stripe to the next identical bar or from one large motif to another). The larger the repeat, the more extra fabric you need.

Small-scale and overall prints do not require pattern matching, so they are easier to lay out and cut. Lay out fabrics with a border print (a prominent design along the selvage) so the pattern falls at a center front opening or runs along the garment hem. Choose simple style garments and avoid any pattern that says it is not suitable for plaids or stripes.

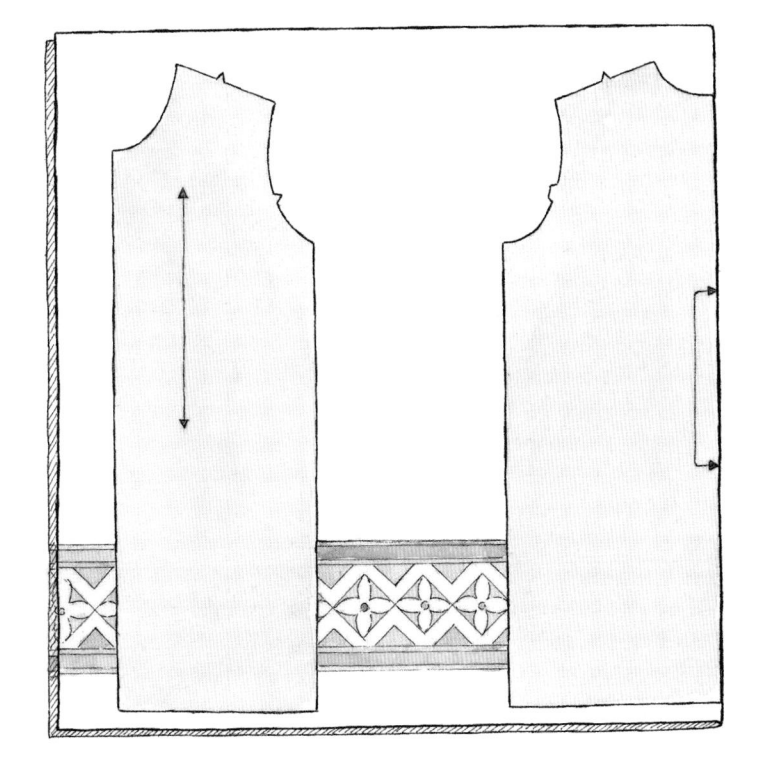

To keep seams from shifting while sewing:
- pin frequently
- hand-baste or use basting tape
- use a walking foot

You'll need extra fabric if you are making large items—such as window treatments or bedding—with plaid, stripe, or print fabrics. The design repeats at regular intervals across the surface of the fabric, so you'll need to carefully join fabric widths so you don't interrupt the pattern.

The distance between one motif and the same point on the next identical motif is called a *pattern repeat*. The repeat is often marked on the selvage of the fabric. Add the length of the repeat to your yardage for each piece you need to cut.

Layout Guidelines

Stripes	Plaids	Checks	Small Overall Prints	Medium Overall Prints	Large Prints	Geometric Prints
• center or balance dominant stripe in small items • match horizontal stripes • continue stripe sequence, uninterrupted, across seams	• center or balance dominant bars in small items • match pattern both vertically and horizontally • cut woven plaids by following a bar in the plaid • make sure printed plaids are on the grain (page 49)	• match pattern both vertically and horizontally • cut woven checks by following one bar in the check • make sure printed checks are on the grain (page 49)	• don't need to match at seams • may be directional	• match at seams for large items • balance design for small items	• match at seams for large items • center dominant motif in small items (pillows, cushions) • may need extra fabric for multiple, identical small items	• match at seams, as for plaids and checks • balance placement of design for small items

Matching Stripes, Plaids and Prints

1   Place two fabric widths right sides together, aligning the selvages. Fold back the upper selvage 1" (2.5 cm) and shift the pieces slightly up or down until the pattern matches exactly. Press the fold line.

2   Keeping the layers in place, unfold the pressed selvage and pin the fabric widths together, inserting the pins in the fold line. Turn the fabric over and check the match from the right side.

3   Stitch the seam, following the fold line and removing pins as you come to them. Check the match from the right side and make adjustments if necessary.

4   Trim away the selvages, leaving 1/2" (1.3 cm) seam allowances. Trim the upper and lower edges of the fabric panel evenly to the desired cut length.

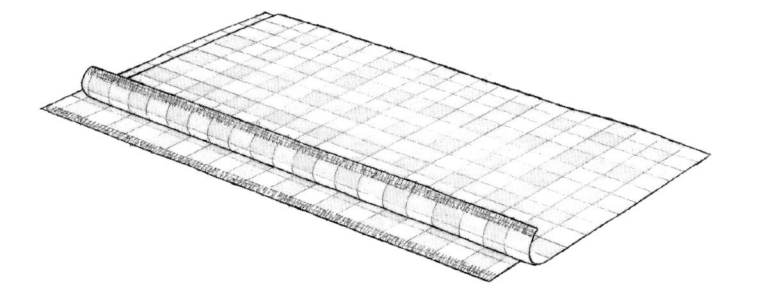

1

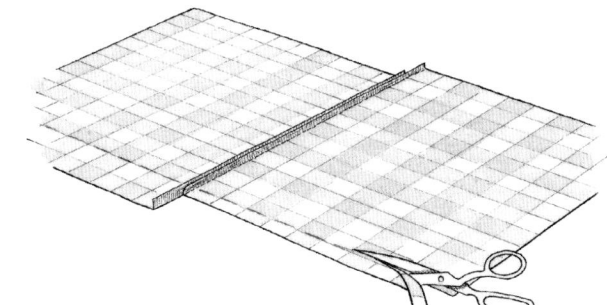

4

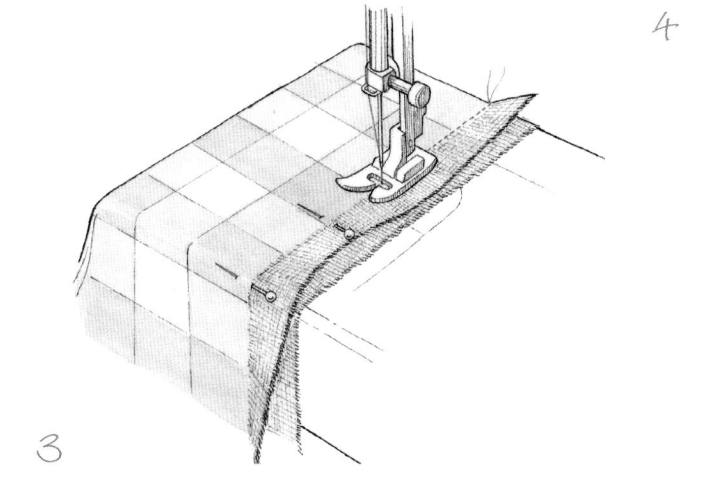

3

Roll out your length of fabric and stand back to find the dominant design motif, stripe, or bar. Sometimes you may see an unexpected secondary pattern.

Laying Out Pattern Pieces

Open the fabric in a single layer, right side up. Trace pattern pieces that need both a right and a left side. If a piece is to be cut on the fold, abut the right and left pieces together, as shown in the drawing below, at left.

Center the front and back pattern pieces on a prominent color bar or motif. Carefully align the side seam notches. Match the pattern pieces at stitching lines, not cutting lines.

Center the sleeve on the same prominent color bar or motif as the front and back. Align the front armhole notches of the sleeve and the garment front.

Position smaller pieces, such as yokes, plackets, or patch pockets, on the true bias (45 degrees to the grain) or position them so the plaid, stripe, or print motifs will match the larger garment pieces.

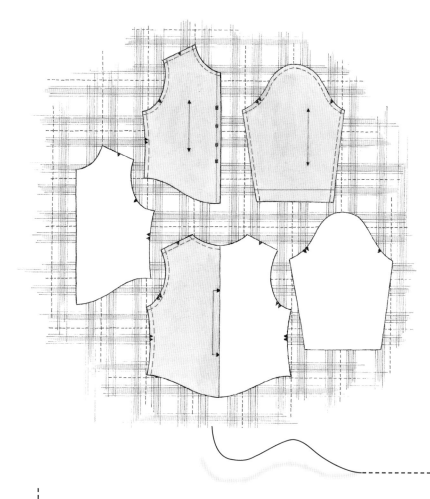
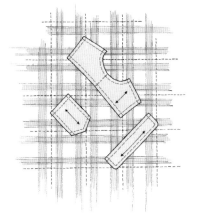

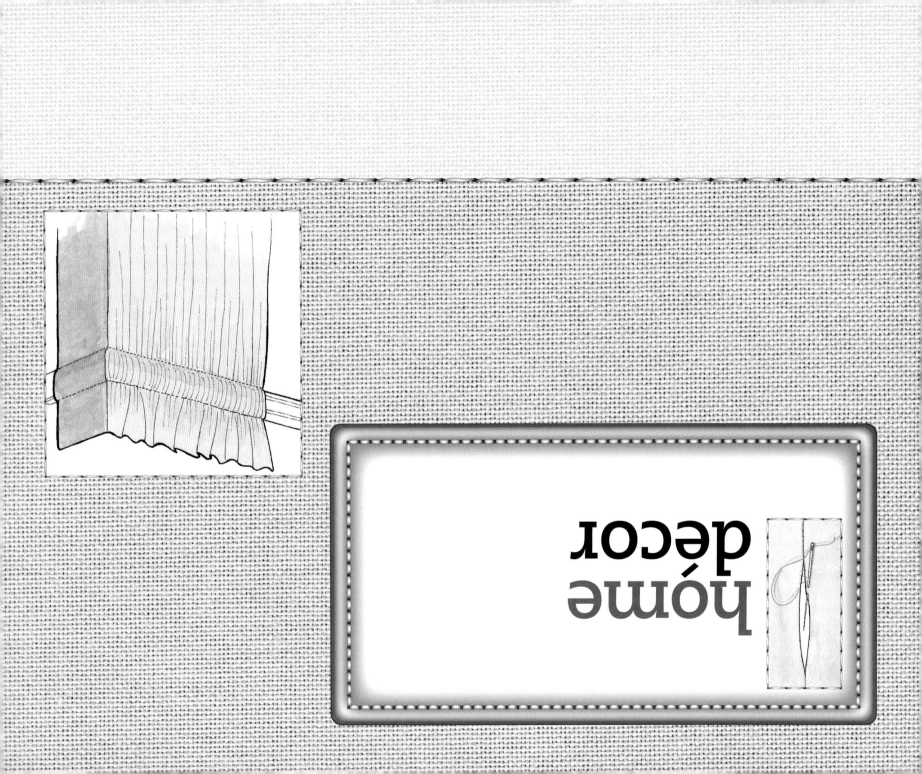

home décor

choosing the right fabric

Here's an at-a-glance guide that will help you choose fabrics for your home decorating projects. For specific care instructions, always check the labels on the fabric tubes—fiber content may affect the care requirements.

Fabric	Weight	Formal/Informal	Common Uses	Durable	Care
Antique Satin	Heavy	Formal	Draperies, upholstery, cushions, tablecloth	Yes	Dry-clean
Batiste	Light	Formal/informal	Under curtains, casual curtains, balloon shades	No	Machine wash
Broadcloth	Light to medium	Informal	Curtains, soft shades, bed linens, pillows, cushions, table linens, shower curtains	Yes	Machine wash
Brocade	Heavy	Formal	Draperies, bedcovers, pillows, cushions, tablecloth	Yes	Dry-clean
Calico	Light to medium	Informal	Curtains, pillows, table linens	Yes	Machine wash
Chintz	Medium to heavy	Formal/informal	Curtains, draperies, upholstery, shower curtains, cushions, Roman shades	Yes	Dry-clean
Damask	Medium	Formal	Draperies, upholstery, bedcovers, tablecloths	Yes	Machine wash or dry-clean
Dimity	Light	Formal	Under curtains, soft shades	No	Machine wash
Duck	Heavy	Informal	Draperies, slipcovers, Roman shades	Yes	Machine wash or dry-clean
Gingham	Light	Informal	Curtains, soft shades, tablecloths, napkins	Yes	Machine wash
Lace	Light	Formal	Curtains, tablecloth	Varies	Machine-wash or dry-clean
Lawn	Light	Formal	Curtains, under curtains, pillows, napkins	Yes	Machine wash

Fabric	Weight	Formal/Informal	Common Uses	Durable	Care
Matelasse	Heavy	Formal	Draperies, upholstery	Yes	Dry-clean
Moiré	Light to medium	Formal	Draperies, curtains, tablecloths	Yes	Machine-wash or dry-clean
Muslin	Light	Informal	Curtains, table linens, linings	No	Machine-wash
Organdy	Light	Formal/informal	Curtains, under curtains	No	Machine-wash
Percale	Medium	Informal	Curtains, bed linens, table linens	Yes	Machine-wash
Sateen	Light to medium	Formal	Curtains, bed linens, table linens, draperies	Yes	Machine-wash
Satin	Medium to heavy	Formal	Draperies, curtains, pillows, bed linens, Roman shades, upholstery	Yes	Machine-wash or dry-clean
Shantung	Light to medium	Formal	Draperies, curtains	Yes	Dry-clean
Suede cloth	Heavy	Formal/informal	Cushions, draperies, upholstery	Yes	Dry-clean
Taffeta	Light to medium	Formal	Draperies	Yes	Machine-wash or dry-clean
Velvet	Medium to heavy	Formal	Draperies, upholstery	No	Dry-clean
Voile	Light	Informal	Curtains, under curtains, balloon shades	No	Machine-wash

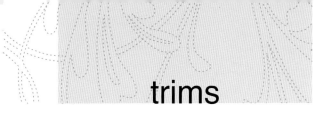

trims

Trims are the creative extras that give your projects a designer's touch and a custom finish. When selecting trims, make sure they have the same care requirements as the decorator fabric. It is easiest to categorize trims by the way they are applied to the fabric.

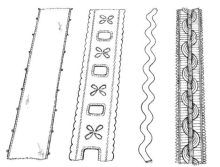

applied trims: band trim, beading, braid, gimp, ribbon, or any trim that is finished on both sides and sewn by hand or machine to the right side of the fabric

bias binding & fold-over braid: decorative and functional trims that encase raw edges; can be purchased ready-made or made from bias strips of fabric (page 76)

edgings: flat or gathered trim with one decorative edge (the unfinished edge is caught in a seam or hem); includes eyelet, fringe, lace, and ruffles

welting: fabric-covered cording or decorative cord attached to a braided tape; adds decorative accent to outer edges of a project and strengthens the seams

tassels: decorative elements in assorted styles and sizes

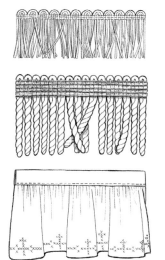

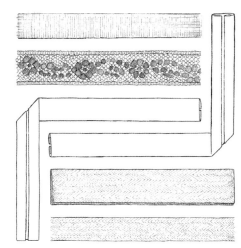

cutting the fabric

You can sew home décor items without paper patterns, especially large items like draperies and tablecloths—but, if you prefer, you can find patterns with step-by-step instructions for anything you want to make. In either case, the key to home décor sewing is careful measuring and cutting.

Prepare the Fabric for Cutting

Work on a large, flat surface so you can lay out the fabric straight and smooth. For most home décor projects, the fabric is cut in a single layer, with the right side up. This layout makes it easy to position and match design motifs.

If the fabric is directional, either because of surface nap or a one-way design (or if you're not sure), mark the top of the fabric and place all pattern pieces or cut all measured pieces in the same direction. If you are using a commercial pattern, follow the layout guide, taking care to match stripes, plaids, and prints (page 130).

If you are cutting full fabric widths that need to match, cut the first panel and lay it on the remaining fabric, right side up. Shift the cut panel to perfectly align with the stripe, prints, or plaid on the fabric beneath it. Cut the second panel. Repeat for each of the matching panels.

For smaller square or rectangular items—pillows, placemats, table runners—mark the cutting lines directly on the fabric with measuring and marking tools or make your own pattern.

Make your own patterns for seat cushions and pillows with translucent paper, so you can easily position any design motifs.

piecing fabric widths

Many home décor items require large expanses of fabric. Although most decorator fabric is available in wide widths—up to 120" (3 m)—you may sometimes need to piece fabric to create a panel that is wide enough for your project.

A center seam detracts from the appearance of any type of item. When piecing, arrange the fabric so there is one full-width center panel and two partial-width side panels.

To make the panels, work with two full widths of fabric. Cut one of the full-width fabrics in half. Stitch one half to each side of the other fabric, with ½" (1.3 cm) seam allowances. Zigzag or overlock the seam allowances together, and press them away from the center panel. Very large projects—like curtains and draperies—may need several whole widths and/or half-widths of fabric.

If the fabric is striped or plaid or has a large printed pattern or motif, you will need extra fabric so that you can match the design at the joining seams (page 130). Include an extra pattern repeat in your yardage calculations for each width of fabric you ll need.

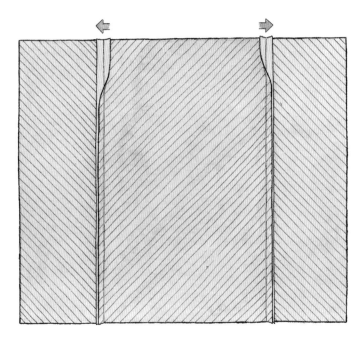

Before piecing fabric pieces, trim away the selvages — they will cause the stitched seam to pucker.

selecting a pillow style

Pick a pillow style, shop the remnant table for a fabulous find, and voilà—you've got a quick and easy way to give your home a new look! There are basically two pillow styles, knife-edge and boxed, but there are hundreds of variations in size, shape, and decorative detail, which is what makes pillows such a versatile and inspiring home accent.

Knife-Edge Pillows

A knife-edge pillow is the simplest style of pillow to make. It is thick in the center and flatter toward the edges and is filled with a standard pillow form or loose polyester fiberfill. Most throw pillows (for a chair or sofa) are knife-edge pillows. Common variations are the flanged pillow, which has a self-fabric border, and the ruffled pillow, which has a fabric or lace ruffle around the edge.

Boxed Pillows

Boxed pillows have a foam interior that makes them firm and uniformly thick—great for seat cushions. You can cut the foam to fit the contours of a chair or sofa. Most boxed pillows are made in three pieces: a top, a bottom, and a boxing strip. The boxing strip joins the top and bottom pieces along the edges.

Another style of boxed pillow—the bolster—is a cylinder-shaped pillow, often tossed on a bed or other bedroom furniture. The round ends are sewn to a wide center cylinder and often embellished with welting (page 84) or ruffles (page 90).

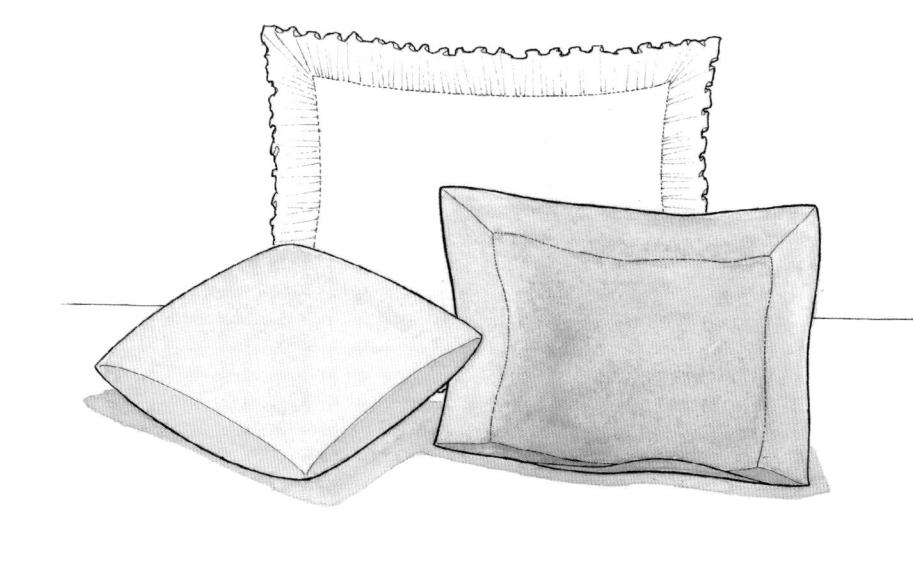

fabric choices

For decorative pillows, there's really no limit to your fabric choices. Be as creative as you'd like. For functional pillows, there are two important considerations: the amount of wear and tear the pillows or cushions will get and how often they will need to be laundered.

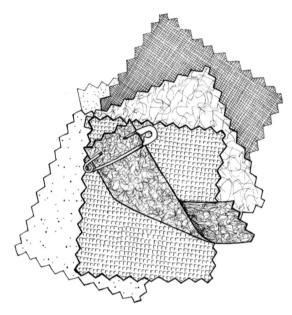

For pillows and seat cushions that will endure heavy wear, choose a durable, washable, and comfortable fabric. Closely woven fabrics retain their shape better than loose weaves and hold up better, too. Decorator fabrics are generally stronger, wider, and heavier than garment fabrics.

Popular pillow fabrics include polished cotton, antique satin, chintz, velveteen, corduroy, poplin, sailcloth, tapestry, ticking, and most microfibers (pages 133 to 134).

A pillow in a beautiful fabric adds charm to any room. You don't need much, so you have the perfect opportunity to splurge on slightly more expensive fabrics without blowing your budget. Shop the remnant counters and save good-size scraps from your sewing projects.

Create a lacy, decorative pillow with any loosely woven fabric. Cover the pillow form with a colored lining that will peek through the open weave.

pillow forms & fillings

The type of pillow form or filling you use determines the shape and firmness of the pillow.

down and/or feathers: encased in fabric covers of various sizes; expensive but very luxurious

polyester fiberfill: loose puffs of fiber sold by the ounce, particularly useful for odd-shaped pillows; machine washable, inexpensive, nonallergenic, does not deteriorate or mat with age

polyester fiberfill forms: polyester fiberfill encased in fabric; available as square, rectangular, and round knifed-edge inserts or bolster shapes in many sizes; inexpensive, nonallergenic, resilient

polyurethane foam: sold in sheets from 1/2" to 5" (1.3 to 12.7 cm) thick; can be cut into any shape for cushions; also available in shredded or chip form (which is difficult to work with and forms lumps)

closures

If you are making a decorative pillow that won't require washing, simply slipstitch the pillow closed. If you are making a pillow that will be laundered or dry-cleaned, you need to be able to remove the form or filling inside.

The closure can be an intentional design element—for example, an overlap closure with decorative buttons—or it can be an inconspicuous zipper hidden in a seam.

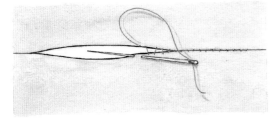

slipstitched: Leave an opening in the seam to insert the pillow form or filling. Slipstitch (page 67) the opening closed. If the pillow needs cleaning, remove the slipstitching, remove the stuffing, and clean the pillow cover. After restuffing, slipstitch to close. This method is best for decorative pillows that don't require frequent laundering.

overlap back: The pillow back is made of two separate pieces that overlap by 4" to 6" (10.2 cm to 15.2 cm). The overlap conceals the pillow form and provides an opening so you can insert and remove the pillow form easily. This style of closure is often found on bed pillow shams.

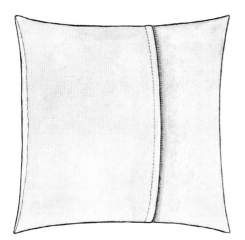

overlap with buttons: This closure is a 1" (2.5 cm) overlap closure reinforced with a series of button-holes and buttons. Add decorative touches if the closure is on the pillow front. Keep it simple if it's on the pillow back.

overlap with hook-and-loop tape: This closure is a 1" (2.5 cm) overlap closure positioned on the pillow back and reinforced with hook-and-loop tape.

zipper: To position a zipper in the middle of a boxing strip (page 146) or in the center of the pillow back, choose a centered zipper application (page 102). To insert the zipper in a seam, choose a lapped application (page 100).

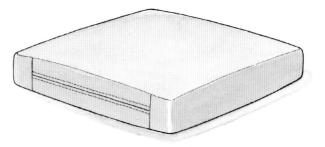

fabric requirements

Measure the pillow form to determine how much fabric you need. Use those measurements and the guidelines below to help you cut the pieces. For most pillow sizes, the pieces will fit side by side on one width of fabric. If you want an extra-plump pillow, cut the pieces to the exact measurements of the pillow form so the cover fits tightly.

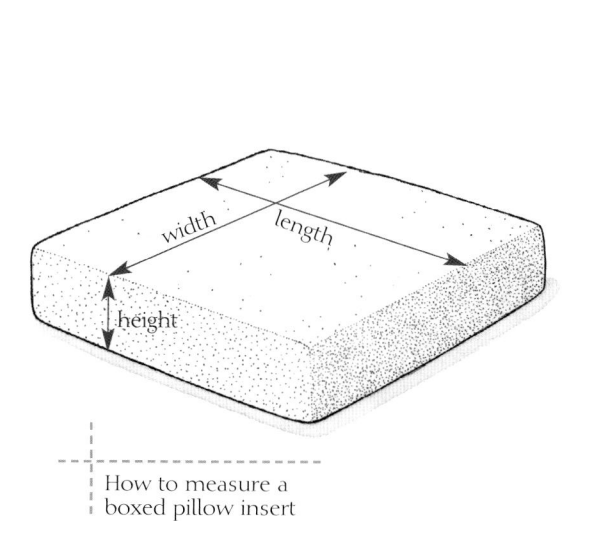

How to measure a knife-edge pillow form

How to measure a boxed pillow insert

Pillow Style	Closure Style	How to Cut
knife-edge	slipstitch	• Cut the front and back pieces 1" (2.5 cm) longer and wider than the finished size.
knife-edge	overlap	• Cut the front 1" (2.5 cm) longer and wider than the finished size. • To create a 4" (10.2 cm) overlap, cut two back pieces, each 1" (2.5 cm) longer than the finished size and equal in width to half the finished size plus 5" (12.7 cm).
knife-edge	zipper (in center back)	• Use a zipper 2" (5.1 cm) shorter than the width of the pillow back. • Cut the front 1" (2.5 cm) longer and wider than the finished size. • Cut the back 1¼" (3.2 cm) longer than the pillow front and the same width as the pillow front—allows for ⅝" (1.6 cm) zipper seam allowances.
boxed	slipstitch	• Cut the front and back pieces 1" (2.5 cm) longer and wider than the finished size. • Cut boxing strip 1" (2.5 cm) longer than the finished perimeter and 1" (2.5 cm) wider than the finished depth.
boxed	zipper	• Cut the front and back pieces 1" (2.5 cm) longer and wider than the finished size. • Cut one boxing strip piece 1" (2.5 cm) longer and wider than three sides of the pillow. • Cut the zipper boxing strip 1" (2.5 cm) longer and 2¼" (5.7 cm) wider than the finished pillow depth.

sewing a knife-edge pillow

The basic knife-edge pillow with a slipstitched opening is one of the easiest pillows to make. This style is best for decorative pillows that won't need frequent cleaning. Follow the same directions if you want to make your own pillow forms, too.

Shape the Corners

To eliminate floppy corners on your pillow, round or taper them before sewing. To round the corners, fold the fabric in quarters and mark a new stitching line, using a plate as a guide. To taper the corners, make marks on each side, 1/2" (1.3 cm) and 4" (10.7 cm) from each corner. Connect the lines and trim off the tapered slivers of fabric. Shape the corners as desired (page 143).

If you plan to sew tassels onto the pillow corner (page 135), keep the corners square.

Slipstitched Closure

1. Cut the pillow front and back pieces, following the guidelines. Reshape the corners as desired.

2. Pin the front and back right sides together. Stitch a 1/2" (1.3 cm) seam around the outer edge, leaving an opening on one side that is large enough to insert the filling or pillow form.

3. If the fabric is bulky, trim the corners diagonally. Press the seam flat to embed the stitches. Turn the pillow cover right side out.

4. Insert the pillow form or fiberfill. Finger-press the seam allowances of the opening to the inside. Slipstitch (page 67) the opening closed.

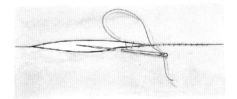

If you are making a knife-edge pillow that will need to be washed or dry-cleaned occasionally, make a cover with an overlap closure or a zipper.

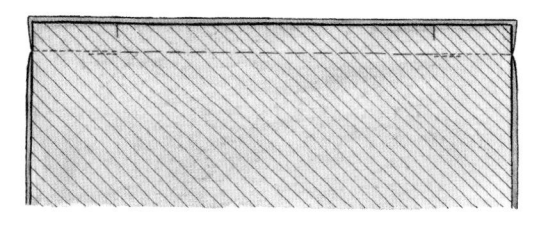

Overlap Closure

1. Cut the pillow front and two back pieces, following the guidelines on page 142.

2. Turn under ½" (1.3 cm) along the length of one back piece. Press. Turn under ½" (1.3 cm) again and press. Stitch close to the inner fold, forming a double-fold hem. Repeat for one edge of the other back piece.

3. Lay the pillow front right side up. Place one back piece on top, right sides together and cut edges even. Place the second back piece on top so the cut edges are even and the hemmed edges overlap. Pin the outer edges together.

4. Stitch a ½" (1.3 cm) seam around the outer edge. Trim corners diagonally. Turn the pillow cover right side out.

5. Add buttonholes and buttons, if desired (pages 107 to 109). Insert the pillow form.

Zipper Closure

1. Cut the pillow front and back pieces, following the guidelines on page 142.

2. Fold the pillow back in half across the longer direction, right sides together. Cut on the fold and then pin the pieces together along the cut edges.

3. Lay the zipper over the fabric and mark the ends of the zipper coil on the fabric. Stitch a ⅝" (1.6 cm) seam so it is easier to insert the zipper. Stitch to the first marking, backstitch two to three stitches, and then baste to the second marking. Backstitch two to three stitches again and then stitch to the end of the seam as shown in the bottom drawing at left. Backstitch to finish.

4. Press the seam open. Install a centered zipper within the basted area (page 102).

5. Open the zipper partway. Stitch the pillow front and back, right sides together. If the fabric is bulky, trim the corners diagonally. Turn the pillow cover right side out. Insert the pillow form.

sewing a boxed pillow

Box pillows often have welting in the seams for greater definition and stability. See pages 84 to 85 for instructions on making and attaching welting. You can make a bolster with these same techniques.

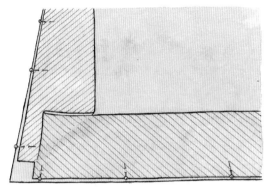

Slipstitch Closure

1. Cut the pillow front and back pieces, following the guidelines on page 142.

2. Baste welting (if you'd like to add it) along the seam line on the right side of the pillow top and bottom (page 85).

3. Pin the short ends of the boxing strip, right sides together, and stitch. Press open the seam.

4. Position the strip around the pillow form, with the seam in the center back. Snip to mark both sides of the strip at each corner.

5. Pin the boxing strip to the pillow top, with right sides together, raw edges even, and corner markings aligned with pillow corners.

6. Stitch a seam, shortening your stitches on either side of each corner. Take one or two diagonal stitches as you turn the corners.

7. Repeat for the pillow bottom, leaving an opening to insert the pillow form.

8. Turn the pillow cover right side out and press. Insert the pillow form, and slipstitch the opening closed (page 67).

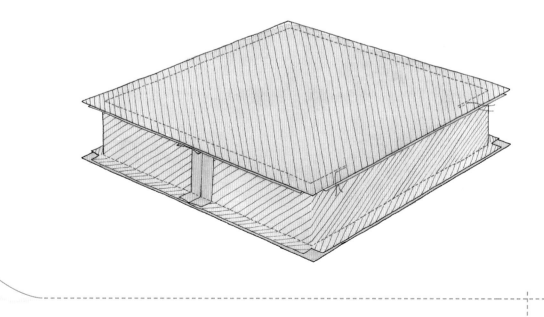

Zipper Closure

1. Cut the pillow pieces, following the guidelines on page 142. Cut the zipper boxing strip in half, matching long edges. Pin together the cut edges.

2. Center the zipper along the pinned edge and mark the ends of the zipper coil on the fabric for zipper placement.

3. Stitch a 5/8" seam along the pinned edge. Stitch to the first marking, backstitch two or three stitches, and then baste to the second marking. Backstitch two or three stitches again and then stitch to the end of the seam. Backstitch. The zipper will be sewn into the basted area (page 144).

4. Press the seam open. Install a centered zipper (page 102).

5. Pin the short ends of the boxing strip to the short ends of the zippered boxing strip, right sides together. Stitch. Press open the seams.

6. Position the strip around the pillow form, with the zipper in the center of one side. Snip into the seam allowance on both sides of the boxing strip to mark each corner.

7. Baste welting (if desired) along the seam line of the pillow top and bottom (page 85).

8. Pin the boxing strip to the pillow top, with right sides together, raw edges even, and corner markings aligned with the corners of the pillow top (see top drawing on page 145). Stitch a seam, shortening your stitches on either side of the corners. Take one or two diagonal stitches as you turn the corners.

9. Open the zipper slightly and repeat step 8 for the pillow bottom piece. Turn the cover right side out through the zipper opening. Open the zipper the rest of the way and insert the pillow form through the zipper opening. Close the zipper.

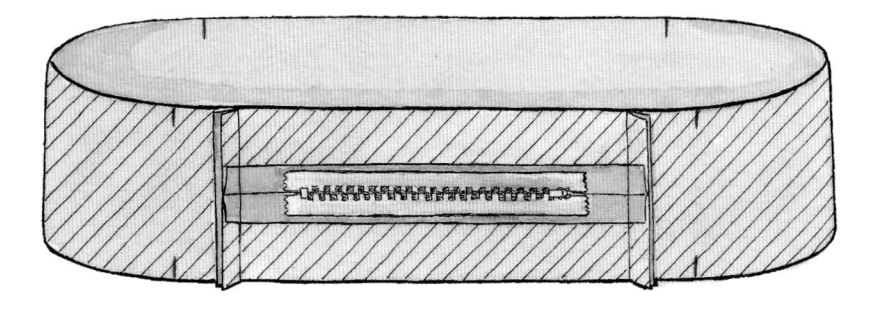

bedroom fashions & fabrics

One of the simplest rooms to redecorate is the bedroom. Start with fabulous bed linens to set the stage. Easy-care and easy-to-sew fabrics—such as polyester/cotton sheeting, sateen, and cotton flannel—are ideal for bedroom fashions.

If you are decorating a guest room, consider luxurious satin, antique linen, and lace fabrics for bed coverings. If the room has another use—as an office, for example—choose tailored bed linens. Fabrics should be durable, machine washable, and crease, wrinkle, and soil resistant.

bedspread: extends to the floor, with 12" to 15" (30.5 to 38.1 cm) of extra length to tuck under and wrap over pillows

comforter: drops 4" to 5" (10.2 to 12.7 cm) below the mattress on three sides; no additional pillow-tuck length; matched with dust ruffle and pillow shams; often reversible, with different fabrics on each side

coverlet: drops 4" to 5" (10.2 to 12.7 cm) below the mattress on three sides; 12" to 15" (30.5 to 38.1 cm) of extra length to tuck under and wrap over pillows

duvet cover: removable cover for a comforter or down duvet; matched with dust ruffle and pillow shams; easy to wash; quick, inexpensive way to redecorate a bed

dust ruffle or bed skirt: inserted between the mattress and box spring and drops to the floor; can be gathered or pleated

pillow shams: Knife-edge or flange pillow covers with decorative fronts and lapped closures at back

Try decorating with bed-sheet fabrics. They are available in coordinating patterns and colors—and are wide enough that you usually don't have to piece panels together.

measuring the bed

$\mathcal{M}$attresses have standard sizes, but the depth of the box spring and the mattress and the height of the bed frame may vary. Before you begin your project, measure the bed you have—with the sheets and blankets in place.

mattress width and length: Measure across the top of the bed from edge to edge.

mattress depth: Measure from the top edge to the bottom edge.

full drop: Measure from the top edge of the mattress to $1/2$" (1.3 cm) above the floor.

comforter or duvet drop: Measure from the top edge of the mattress to 3" to 5" (7.6 to 12.7 cm) below the bottom edge of the mattress (length depends on personal preference).

dust ruffle: Measure from the top edge of the box spring to $1/2$" (1.3 cm) above the floor (page 151).

Bed pillows come in standard sizes, but fullness (loft) varies, so you might want to measure each pillow to ensure the best-fitting pillow cover.

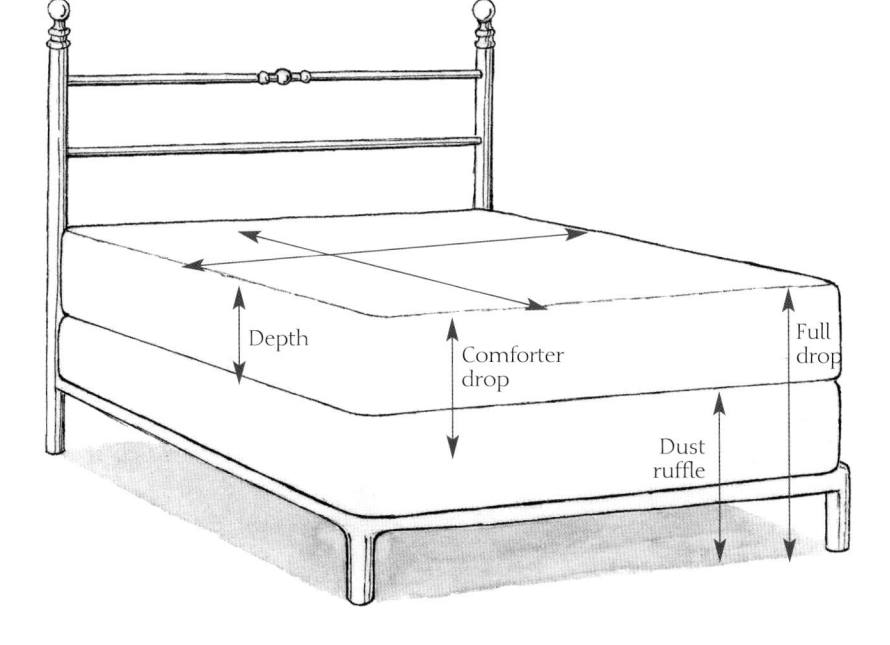

Standard Bed Pillow Sizes	
Name	**Size**
Standard	20" × 26" (50.8 × 66 cm)
Queen	20" × 30" (50.8 × 76.2 cm)
King	20" × 40" (50.8 × 101.6 cm)

fabric requirements for bed covers

Bed covers are large, so you usually need to piece fabrics—unless you work with sheeting, which is available in widths of 90" or 120" (229 or 305 cm). When piecing, try to avoid a center seam. It's much more attractive to have one wide center section with two narrower side sections (page 137).

Bedspreads and coverlets require only a top fabric. Comforter and duvet covers require a top and bottom fabric, and comforters also need a layer of batting.

The amount of fabric you need depends on the fabric width and the size of the bed covering—and on the pattern repeat, if there is one (page 137).

finished bed cover length = [bed length] + [desired drop length] + [12" to 15" (30.5 to 38.1 cm) for pillow tuck, if desired]

finished bed cover length = [bed width] + [two times desired drop length]

cut length = [finished bed cover length] + 4" (10.2 cm)

cut width = [finished bed cover width] + 4" (10.2 cm)

To determine how many widths of fabric you need, divide the cut width by the fabric width. Round up the number.

To determine the total length of fabric you need to buy, multiply the number of widths you need by the cut length.

sewing a duvet cover

1. Measure the duvet or comforter.

2. For the duvet front, add 1" (2.5 cm) to the finished width and to the finished length. For the duvet back, add 1" (2.5 cm) to the finished width and 2 1/2" (6.4 cm) to the finished length (to accommodate the zipper).

3. Cut the front and back pieces. If you need to piece the fabric, use a full width for the center and equal partial widths for the sides. When piecing, sew the front pieces together, using 1/2" (1.3 cm) seam allowances. Finish the seam allowances. Repeat for the back pieces.

4. Fold 16" (40.6 cm) of the back panel at the lower edge, right sides together. Press the fold. Lay the zipper over the fold and mark both ends of the zipper. Stitch a 3/4" (1.9 cm) wide seam, backstitch at the mark, and then baste to the other mark. Backstitch again and continue stitching to the end with a regular stitch length.

5. Cut the back apart on the fold. Press the seam open. Install a centered zipper (page 102).

6. Open the zipper partway. Pin the cover front to the cover back, right sides together. Trim the back to fit if necessary. Stitch around all sides with a 1/2" (1.3 cm) seam allowance.

7. Trim the seam allowances and corners. Finish the seam allowances together. Turn the duvet cover right side out. Press. Insert the duvet or comforter.

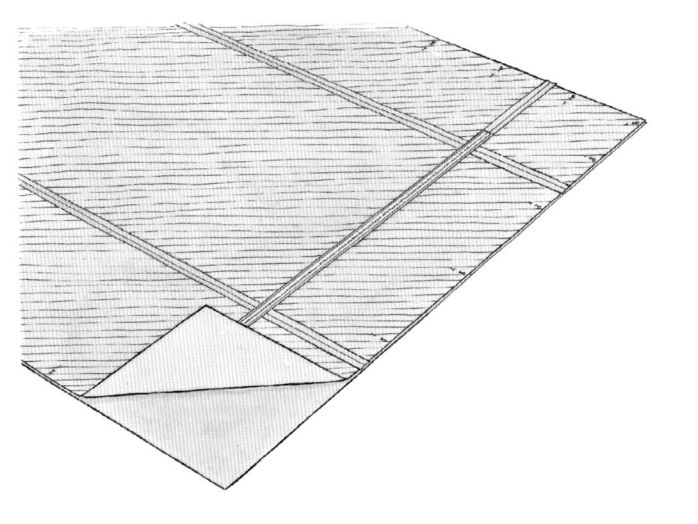

sewing a dust ruffle

Dust ruffles, or bed skirts, are pleated or gathered fabric panels that fall around the sides and foot of a bed. The skirt is often split at the corners to accommodate the legs of the footboard. Work with a fitted sheet or a piece of muslin to make the "deck." The dust ruffle is attached to the deck, which spans the width of the box spring.

For a gathered dust ruffle:

Cut length = [desired skirt drop] + [2½" (6.4 cm) for bottom hem and top seam allowance]

Cut width = [total measurement of two sides + measurement of foot of bed] x [2½ (for fullness)]

To determine how many panels you need to cut, divide the total skirt width (sideways) by the width of the fabric (minus selvages).

To determine the amount of fabric you need to buy, multiply the number of panels by the cut length.

1 Piece muslin as needed to make the deck (or put a fitted sheet on the box spring and mark a stitching line on the top edge with a fabric-marking pen).

2 Cut the dust ruffle pieces on the crosswise grain to save fabric. Piece as necessary to obtain desired width.

3 Hem the bottom edge and side ends of the ruffle with a 1" (2.5 cm) double-fold hem (page 94).

4 Gather the upper edge of the ruffle (page 89). Pin the dust ruffle to the sides and foot of the deck, right sides together.

5 Sew the skirt to the deck. Finish the seam allowances together.

6 Lay the deck between the mattress and box spring and arrange the ruffle around the perimeter of the bed.

bathroom fashions & fabrics

Update your bathroom in no time with a new shower curtain and coordinating bath towels (much easier than installing new plumbing!).

You can make a simple shower curtain, with grommets or buttonholes at the top, to hang from a rod with rings. Or you can design a decorative heading—with a rod pocket (pages 183 to 184), tabs (page 185), or heading tapes (page 187)—to add a design twist.

Make your shower curtain with a machine-washable fabric. You might want to choose a water-repellant fabric, such as ripstop nylon. If the fabric is not water-repellant, make a plastic curtain liner from waterproof nylon or vinyl. The decorative curtain hangs outside the bathtub or shower stall, and the plastic liner hangs inside to divert water into the drain.

You can hang the curtain and liner from the same rings, as long as the holes in each heading align. Or you can add a separate, smaller tension rod for the liner. The liner should be flat and span straight across the bathtub or shower stall so that it dries efficiently. The curtain itself can be decorative, with soft folds, gathering, or pleats.

To unify the room, choose bath towels that complement or contrast with the pattern or color of your shower curtain fabric. Stitch on washable ribbons and trims to add your own personal touch (page 155).

sewing a shower curtain

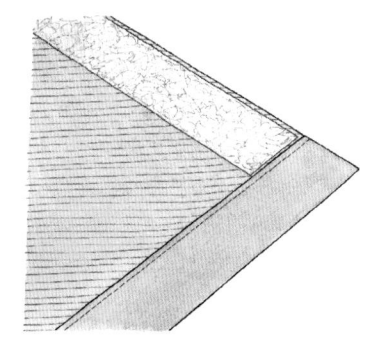

4

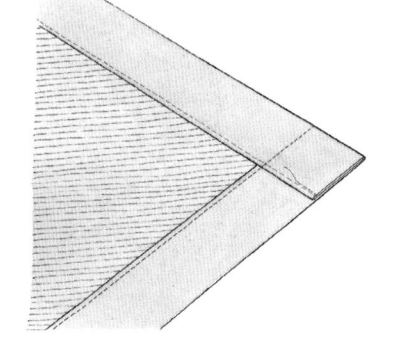

5

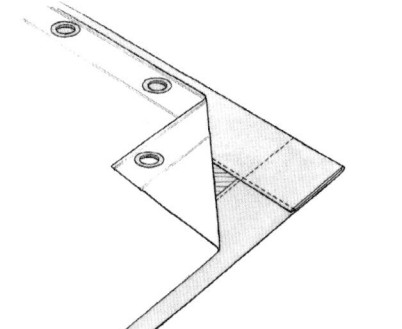

6

First, measure the width and length of the opening for your shower stall or bathtub area. To make the shower curtain, add 8" (20.3 cm) to the length measurement and 4" (10.2 cm) to the width measurement. The extra width and length allow for 1" (2.5 cm) double-fold hems at the sides and 2" (5.1 cm) double-fold hems at the top and bottom.

If your shower or bathtub opening is not standard size—72" × 72" (182.9 × 182.9 cm)—you may also need to make your own plastic liner (make the curtain from waterproof fabric).

Measure the distance from the bottom of the rod to well below the top edge of the tub or stall (but not completely to the floor). Also measure the width of the opening from side to side. To make the liner, cut a large sheet of plastic to those dimensions or trim a standard-size liner, as needed.

Ring Holes

Your curtain and liner will hang on rings supported by a rod. The rings pass through holes in the headings of the two fabrics. You can reinforce the holes with stitched buttonholes (page 107) or grommets.

Grommets are one-piece or two-piece metal rings. They come in several sizes, with a silver or brass finish. Grommets are installed with special tools, which are sold separately. Follow the manufacturer's instructions to apply them.

1   Cut fabric for the curtain to your desired size (or piece fabrics, if necessary, for width).

2   Sew 2" (5.1 cm) double-fold hems at the sides (page 94).

3   Sew a 2" (5.1 cm) double-fold hem at the bottom.

4   Fuse a 2" (5.1 cm) wide strip of fusible interfacing to the wrong side of the top edge to stabilize and reinforce the heading for the buttonholes or grommets.

5   Sew a 2" (5.1 cm) double-fold hem at the upper edge.

6   Cut a plastic liner, if necessary, or trim a standard liner to size.

7   Lay the liner over the curtain, with the top edge 1/4" (6 mm) below the top edge of the curtain. Mark hole positions by marking through the holes of the liner. If you are making your own liner, cut small holes at even intervals across the width of the liner. The holes should be placed approximately 6" (15.2 cm) apart—the first and last holes should be 3" (7.6 cm) from the finished side edge.

8   Apply grommets or make vertical buttonholes at the marks on the curtain fabric (page 107).

sewing bath towels

You have two options—and they're both easy. You can buy plain, inexpensive bath towels in the color or pattern of your choice and decorate them with laces, trims, or edgings. Or you can simply make your own towels.

Terry is the most popular bath-towel fabric. It has surface loops on both sides—or sometimes loops on one side and velour on the other. Terry is very absorbent, but tends to shrink, so prewash the fabric before sewing.

Decide on the style of towel you'd like to make. Find the standard measurements in the chart and add ½" (1.3 cm) on each side for the hem allowance. To hem, serge or zigzag-stitch the raw edges. Then fold the edges under ½" (1.3 cm) and topstitch along the fold.

Choose a complementary or contrasting trim. Keep the rest of your bathroom furnishings in mind as you choose colors and patterns. Glue the trim in position with fabric adhesive. Loosen the machine tension and lengthen the stitch length so the trim will lie flat on the surface of the towel.

Lap the folded or hemmed fabric edge over the edge of the trim. Topstitch the fabric to secure the trim. Or sew the trim on the right side of the fabric and cover the seam with a decorative ribbon.

Standard Towel Sizes

Style	Size
Washcloth	13" × 13" (33 × 33 cm)
Fingertip Towel	11" × 18" (27.9 × 45.7 cm)
Hand Towel	16" × 30" (40.6 × 76.2 cm)
Bath Towel	from 27" × 52" to 30" × 58" (from 68.6 × 132.1 cm to 76.2 × 147.3 cm)
Bath Sheet (a luxurious, larger size towel)	35" × 60" (88.9 × 152.4 cm)

If the toes of the presser foot get caught in the loops of terry fabric, wrap the foot with tape — or switch to a roller foot.

table fashions & fabrics

Dress up your dining room and brighten your kitchen with table linens of your own design. Tablecloths, placemats, table runners, and napkins don't require a lot of fabric, and they're quick and easy to make.

Cotton/polyester blends and medium-weight cottons with a crisp finish are perfect for everyday use. Linen and lace have a more formal look. Choose stain- and crease-resistant fabrics. Permanent-press fabrics can be machine-washed repeatedly without fading—a great benefit!

Tablecloth fabrics should have enough body to hang from the table without looking limp. Small, overall prints hide stains well (and the surface pattern doesn't require matching). If the table is small, however, be sure to keep the print small and avoid heavily napped fabrics, which can be overpowering.

Some tablecloths are wider than standard fabric widths. When necessary, piece fabrics with a French seam or serged seam, which are stronger than a standard seam. Never place the seam at the center of the tablecloth. Medium- or heavy-weight bed sheets are a good fabric source for casual tablecloths—and wide enough so they don't require piecing.

To keep outdoor tablecloths from blowing away, hand-stitch tassels, large buttons, jewelry charms, or beads as weights at the center edge of each side.

fabric requirements for tablecloths

You can sew a tablecloth to fit any size table. If your table is square, rectangular, or oval, measure its width and length. If your table is round, measure its diameter. *Drop* refers to the length of the tablecloth from the edge of the table to the hem. Place a bed sheet or an old tablecloth on the table and measure the drop to determine the desired length.

There are three standard drop lengths—each has its own look and best use:

short drop: 10" to 12" (25.4 to 30.5 cm); falls 1" to 2" (2.5 to 5.1 cm) above the chair seat; casual and perfect for everyday use

medium drop: 15" to 24" (38.1 to 61 cm); more formal

floor-length drop: 28" to 29" (71.1 to 73.7 cm); should fall 1" (2.5 cm) above the floor; for buffet and decorator tables

If you would like to add a ruffle along the lower edge of the tablecloth, subtract the desired depth of the ruffle from the drop measurement. Refer to page 161 to calculate your fabric requirements.

Refer to the chart below to determine what size to cut your tablecloth fabric. Choose the hem style that suits the weight of the fabric and the look you prefer—fine fabrics usually look better with a narrow hem (page 160).

Note that, in the calculations for the cut size of the fabric, the hem allowances are doubled—one allowance for each side of the tablecloth. Always cut the fabric on-grain (page 49).

Tablecloth Style	Hem Allowance and Style	Cut Size of Fabric
Round	1/2" (1.3 cm) for a 1/4" (6 mm) double-fold	width and length = table diameter + two times the drop + 1" (2.5 cm)
Square	1/2" (1.3 cm) for a 1/4" (6 mm) double-fold	width and length = table width + two times the drop + 1" (2.5 cm)
Square	21/2" (6.4 cm) for a 2" (5.1 cm) hem with 1/2" (1.3 cm) turn-under	width and length = table width + two times the drop + 5" (12.7 cm)
Rectangular	1/2" (1.3 cm) for a 1/4" (6 mm) double-fold	width = table width + two times the drop + 1" (2.5 cm) length = table length + two times the drop + 1" (2.5 cm)
Rectangular	21/2" (6.4 cm) for a 2" (5.1 cm) hem with 1/2" (1.3 cm) turn-under	width = table width + two times the drop + 5" (12.7 cm) length = table length + two times the drop + 5" (12.7 cm)
Oval	1/2" (1.3 cm) for a 1/4" (6 mm) double-fold	width = table width + two times the drop + 1" (2.5 cm) length = table length + two times the drop + 1" (2.5 cm)

If the cut width is narrower than the usable fabric width, buy fabric equal to the cut length of the tablecloth. If the cut width is wider than the usable fabric width, you need to buy two times the cut length of the fabric and sew two pieces together to obtain the cut width.

Just to be safe, always round calculations up to the next 1/8 yard (0.15 m). Buy extra fabric if you need to match a print or plaid.

shaping tablecloths

Once you've cut (or pieced) the fabric for your tablecloth, you may need to shape the lower edge before sewing. For a round tablecloth, or one with rounded corners, fold the fabric into quarters. Pin the layers together so they don't shift.

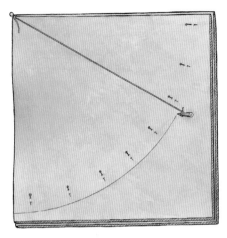

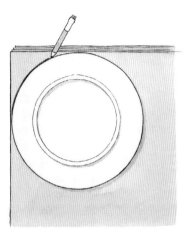

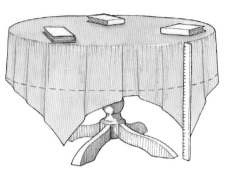

round tablecloth: Tie a piece of string around a marking pen. Cut the string so its length (from the pen) equals the radius (one-half the diameter) of the tabletop plus one drop and one hem allowance.

Pin the string end to the folded corner. Hold the string taut and mark the lower edge of the tablecloth. Cut through all layers along the marked line (or, if the fabric is heavy, mark and cut one layer at a time, using the edge of the previous layer as a guide).

square or rectangle tablecloth with round corners: Working with a marking pen and a dinner plate as a template, draw a smooth curve across the cut edges of the fabric opposite the fold. Cut along the marked line through all layers. If the fabric is heavy, cut one layer at a time, retracing the curve from each previous layer.

oval tablecloth: Center the fabric on the table and place small, heavy objects on top to keep the fabric from shifting. With a yardstick (meterstick), measure and mark the distance from the floor to the desired finished length. Mark the same measurement at regular intervals around the table. Cut the fabric 1/2" (1.3 cm) below the marked line for the hem allowance.

hemming tablecloths

After you've shaped the edges, all you have to do is hem the fabric, and your tablecloth is finished! There are several choices of hem styles. Other possible edge finishes for tablecloths include decorative trim (page 135), or fringes (page 164) and bias binding (page 76). If you'd like to add a ruffle, see page 90.

Serged Rolled

A serged rolled hem is very elegant, so it's perfect for fine, lightweight fabrics. For this style of hem, you'll need a serger that can convert to make a rolled hem. Refer to your serger manual for instructions.

Narrow Double-Fold Hem

1   Stitch ½" (1.3 cm) from the raw edge.

2   Press the raw edge to the wrong side so it meets the stitching line. Press the folded edge to the wrong side, enclosing the raw edge and rolling the stitching away from the right side of the fabric. Stitch close to the inner fold.

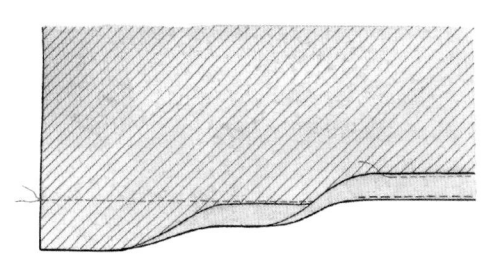

Curved Narrow Hem

1   Set the stitch length to 8 to 10 stitches per inch (2.5 cm). Stitch on the wrong side, ¼" (6 mm) from the raw edge.

2   Press the raw edge to the wrong side at the stitching line. Press the folded edge again to enclose the raw edge.

3   Gently pull the bobbin thread with a straight pin to ease the fabric fullness. Stitch close to the inner fold.

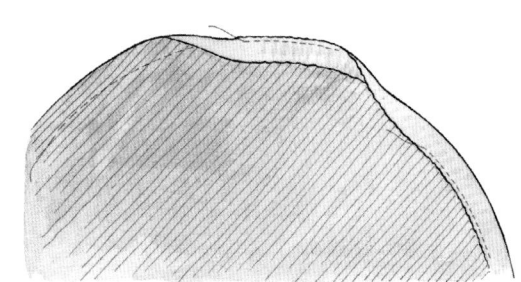

Wide Hem

1   On all sides, press under ½" (1.3 cm) and then another 2" (5.1 cm).

2   Miter all four corners (page 75). Stitch along the inner fold.

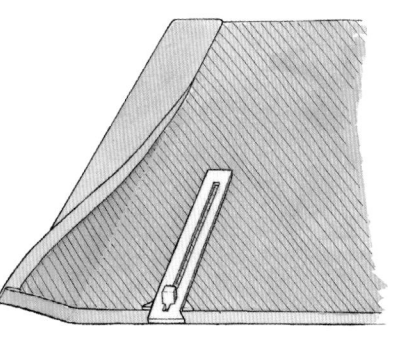

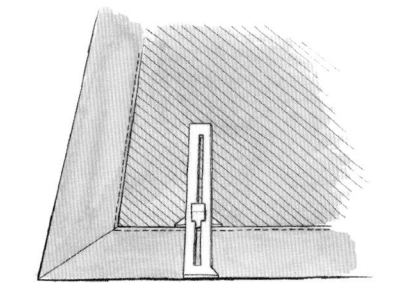

sewing a ruffled tablecloth

If you'd like to add a ruffle to the bottom edge of the tablecloth, first you'll need to determine how much fabric you'll need for the ruffle. You can create the ruffle with a fabric in a matching or complementary print or color. First decide on the size and style of tablecloth you would like to make (page 158).

1   Multiply the circumference or perimeter of the tablecloth (at the lower edge) by $2^1/2$ to allow for fabric fullness. This measurement is the total width of the ruffle.

2   Add 1" (2.5 cm) to the desired length, to allow $1/2$" (1.3 cm) for both the seam and hem allowances. This measurement is the cut length of the ruffle pieces.

3   Divide the total width needed by the usable fabric width (excluding selvages) to determine how many pieces you need to cut.

4   Multiply the number of pieces you need by the cut length to determine how much fabric you need for the ruffle.

5   Cut the ruffle pieces on the crosswise grain and sew the short edges to form a large circle.

6   Stitch a $1/2$" (1.3 cm) narrow, double-fold hem (page 94) along the lower edge.

7   Gather the ruffle and sew it to the lower edge of the tablecloth (page 90).

8   Serge or zigzag-stitch the seam allowances together. Press them toward the tablecloth fabric.

sewing placemats & table runners

Placemats and table runners add a lot of personality to your dining table, buffet, or breakfast bar. You won't need much fabric, so have some fun with tapestries, decorator prints, and seasonal fabrics. Quilted fabrics are great, too, because the layers protect the surface of the table.

Most placemats are rectangular—but you can round the corners (for a round table) or trim them diagonally to create an octagon. You can also round the ends of a table runner or cut them square or to a point. Shape placemats and table runners with the same techniques used for shaping tablecloths (page 159).

Increase your decorating options by making reversible placemats and table runners—simply line the main fabric with a complementary or contrasting decorator fabric. For extra body and durability, fuse a layer of interfacing to the lining. Cut table runners on the lengthwise grain to save fabric and avoid piecing. Make matching placemats with the remaining fabric.

As a finishing touch, you can hem the edges, encase them in bias binding, or add fringe, decorative stitching, or decorative trim. Be sure your trims and edgings are machine-washable, too!

Type of Item	Size
Placemats	18" × 12" and 16" × 14" (45.7 × 30.5 and 40.6 × 35.6 cm)
Table Runners	width: 12" to 18" (30.5 to 45.7 cm) length: [length of the table] + [8" to 12" (20.3 to 30.5 cm)]

Lined to the Edge

1. Cut a front and a back, each from a different decorator fabric, allowing for a ½" (1.3 cm) seam allowance all around.

2. Pin the pieces right sides together. Stitch a ½" (1.3 cm) seam around the outer edge, leaving a 5" (12.7 cm) opening for turning. Trim the seam allowances. Trim the corners diagonally.

3. Turn the placemat or runner right side out and press. Slipstitch the opening closed. Topstitch ¼" (6 mm) from the outer edge.

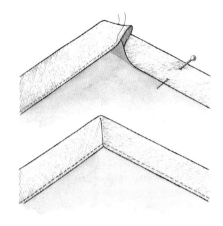

Bias Binding

1. Cut one piece of decorator fabric to the exact finished size—or cut two pieces if you are making a reversible placemat or runner.

2. Encase the outer edge in store-bought or custom-made double-fold bias tape (page 76).

3. At each corner, fold the excess binding diagonally and pin. Topstitch the adjacent side, taking care to catch the diagonal fold in the first few stitches. Repeat on all corners and sides.

Ribbon or Flat Trim

1. Cut the placemat 1" (2.5 cm) longer and wider than the desired finished size. Press ½" (1.3 cm) to the right side on all sides.

2. Cut trim equal to the perimeter of the placemat plus 2" (5 cm). Extend one end 1" (2.5 cm) beyond the edge of the placemat. Pin the trim along the folded edges of the mat.

3. At the first corner, fold the trim back on itself, then fold it diagonally to form a right angle (page 78). Finger-press and pin the fold. Continue pinning and folding at each corner.

4. To finish, fold the end of the trim to form a right angle over the first corner. Finger-press and cut away excess.

5. Remove pins and stitch on the fold lines to form miters. Trim seam allowances. Lay the trim on the placemat, aligning miters at each corner. Topstitch along both edges.

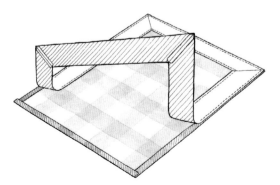

sewing napkins

Complete your custom-designed table setting with coordinating or contrasting napkins—folded simply or wrapped in a decorative ring. Choose a machine-washable fabric. Check that the grain is straight (page 49) so the napkins will be square.

Finish the edges as you would for a tablecloth, placemat, or runner—with decorative machine stitching, a serged rolled hem, a narrow double-fold hem, or fringe edges.

Napkins are typically 14" or 17" (35.6 or 43.2 cm) square.

Narrow Double-Fold Hem

1 Cut the napkins 1" (2.5 cm) larger in both directions than the desired finished size.

2 Follow the directions on pages 75 and 160 for making a narrow, double-fold hem with mitered corners.

Fringed Edge

1 Cut the napkins to the desired finished size. Make sure the fabric is cut on-grain (page 49).

2 Stitch ½" (1.3 cm) from the cut edges with short, narrow zigzag stitches. Stop stitching ½" (1.3 cm) from each corner, pivot, and continue the line of zigzag stitching.

3 Create fringe by pulling threads from the cut edge to the line of the stitching to create fringe. Repeat on each side. To make longer fringe, simply stitch farther from the cut edges in step 2.

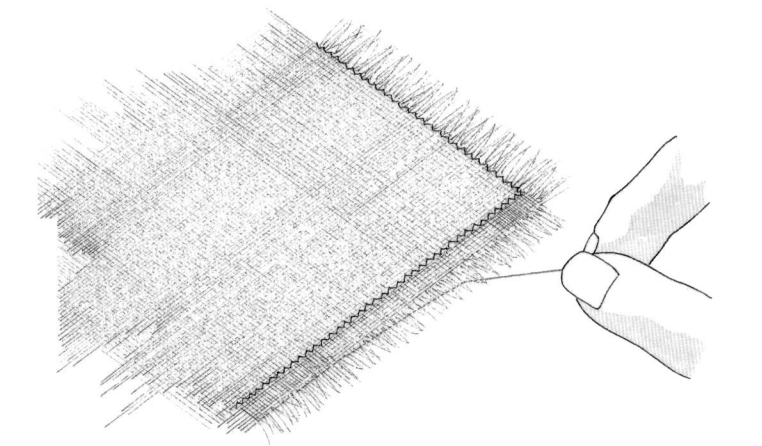

basic window treatments

Window treatments infuse a room with color, pattern, and personality. They also provide privacy, control light, conserve heat, minimize noise, and obscure or draw attention to a view.

Look through magazines, home décor catalogs, and decorating books to see what appeals to you—you'll be amazed at the possibilities. Choose the type that best suits your home (both the inside and outside) and your own personal style.

Window Treatment Style	Description	Fabric Suggestions
Curtains	• straight fabric panels that hang on the sides of the window, usually on stationary rods • usually unlined • many heading and length variations	• lightweight cottons and cotton/polyester blends; some fashion fabrics
Draperies	• long, straight fabric panels with pleated, smocked, or gathered headings • almost always lined • hang from drapery hooks, usually on traversing rods so they open and close	• medium- to heavy-weight cottons; formal fabrics, such as damask, toile, antique satin, brocade
Fabric Shades	• window covers, mounted inside or outside the window frame to filter or block light • can be flat, gathered, or pleated • raise from the bottom by pulling a cord	• firmly woven cloth for flat shades; soft, drapable fabric for gathered shades
Swags & Jabots	• swags are pleated or draped to hang across the top of the window • jabots hang down window sides and have an asymmetrical hemline • usually lined because reverse side shows	• soft, drapable fabrics, such as lace, silk, linen; choose attractive lining if fabric isn't reversible
Valances	• window toppers that hang alone or over curtains, draperies, or shades • variety of styles	• range of choices; depends on style and formality of room

formal window fashions

swags & jabots: traditionally used in formal rooms, often over sheer curtains or shades, but also used in casual rooms with appropriate fabrics

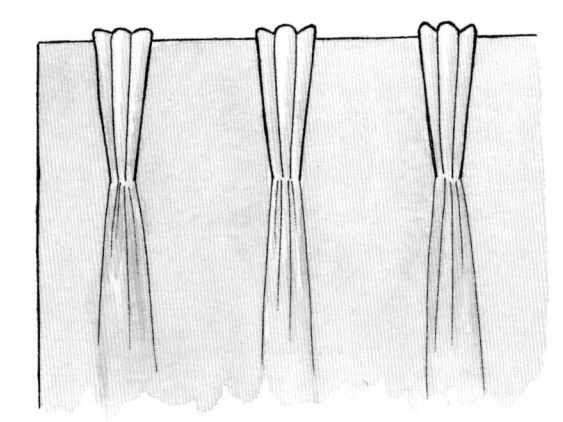

pleated draperies: suited to living rooms, dining rooms, master bedrooms; usually lined and floor-length; styles include traditional pinch pleats, goblet pleats (which pleat outward), and box pleats; smocked and shirred styles sewn with special heading tapes (page 187).

hourglass curtains: usually made of sheer fabrics for French or atrium doors.

rod-pocket curtains: formal or casual, depending on the fabric and hardware; can be floor-length, sill-length, or hung as valances

balloon shades: also called cloud shades; pleated or softly gathered panels, raised and lowered with a cord; short, stationary versions used as valances

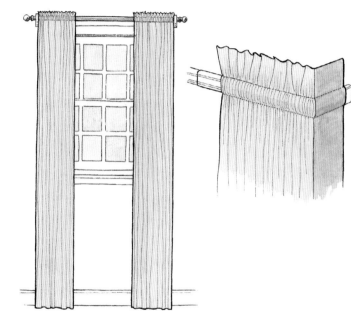

padded cornice: upholstered box that neatly finishes the top of any style window treatment; can also be used alone

casual window fashions

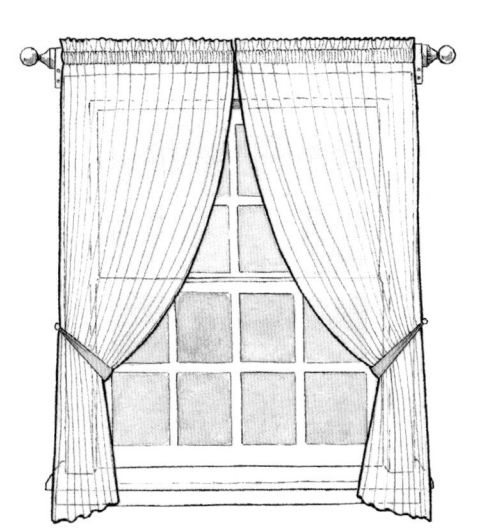

unlined curtain panels: simple lines; sometimes paired with a matching valance, which can conceal curtain hardware

contrast lining: helps the curtain hang smoothly, increases opacity, and adds a decorative accent

Roman shade: casual or formal, depending on the fabric; hangs straight but rises, forming soft folds, when pulled with cord

tab-top curtains: country-casual look, suitable for any room, particularly with decorative hardware

café curtains: cover the lower half of the window; perfect for the kitchen, bath, and bedroom, where privacy and sunlight are important; with or without a valance

stagecoach valance: stationary, flat fabric panel with a rolled or pleated lower edge and secured with fabric or ribbon ties

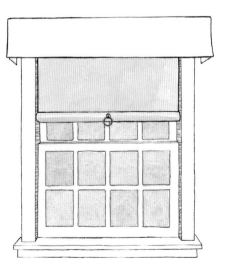

roller shades: block light and provide privacy; can be made from firmly woven fabric fused to shade backing; usually topped with a valance or pelmet (a valance that hangs from a wooden mounting board)

fabrics for window treatments

You can make great window treatments with almost any type of fabric. Decorator fabrics are more expensive than fashion fabrics, but they are usually also wider, heavier, and last longer. The average drapery lasts from eight to fifteen years, so buy the best fabric you can afford—you will certainly get your money's worth!

Lightweight and sheer fabrics are suitable for curtains, valances, balloon shades, and most gathered window treatments. Choose from batiste, dimity, dotted Swiss, eyelet, lace, lawn, marquisette, net, organdy, piqué, plissé, point d'esprit, and voile.

Lightweight fabrics (lined) and medium-weight fabrics work well for draperies, valances, Roman shades, swags and jabots, cornice and pelmet covers, tab-top curtains, and pleated curtains and draperies. Fabric choices include medium-weight cotton, linen, blends, open weaves with textured yarns, antique satin, brocade, chintz, damask, denim, moiré, poplin, satin, shantung, taffeta, and velvet.

Cotton sateen is a good choice for lining fabric. Remember to preshrink the lining fabric—and the main fabric, too—before cutting and sewing.

hardware for window treatments

The hardware that you'll use to hang the window treatment is as important as the window treatment itself. You can choose from among a variety of basic and decorative rods, hooks, rings, clips, grommets, and more. Each type of installation functions in a unique way and creates its own look, too.

Regardless of the type you choose, secure the hardware to the wall, ceiling, or window frame before you measure to determine the finished size of your window treatment and the amount of fabric you'll need.

Basic Curtain Rods

Simple, metal curtain rods work well for rod-pocket window treatments as the fabric conceals the rod. These rods are functional, not decorative. Most don't allow you to open and close the window treatment.

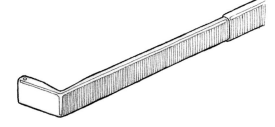

conventional, or standard, curtain rods: 1" (2.5 cm) wide in metal or clear acrylic (for sheer and lace fabrics); vary in length and in the distance they protrude from the wall; should be completely covered by the window treatment

double curtain rod brackets: hold two conventional rods (included in purchase), so you can hang a valance directly over a curtain or drapery

sash rods: flat or round rods with very shallow brackets that protrude only $1/4$" (6 mm); often used on doors or windows with sheer fabric panels

spring tension rods: positioned inside the window frame; adjust to varying widths and stay in place without brackets

traverse rods: allow window treatments to open and close with the pull of a cord; two-way traverse rod opens from the center; one-way rod opens from the side

wide, flat curtain rods: $2^{1}/_{2}$" or $4^{1}/_{2}$" (6.4 or 11.4 cm) wide; create a strong visual effect

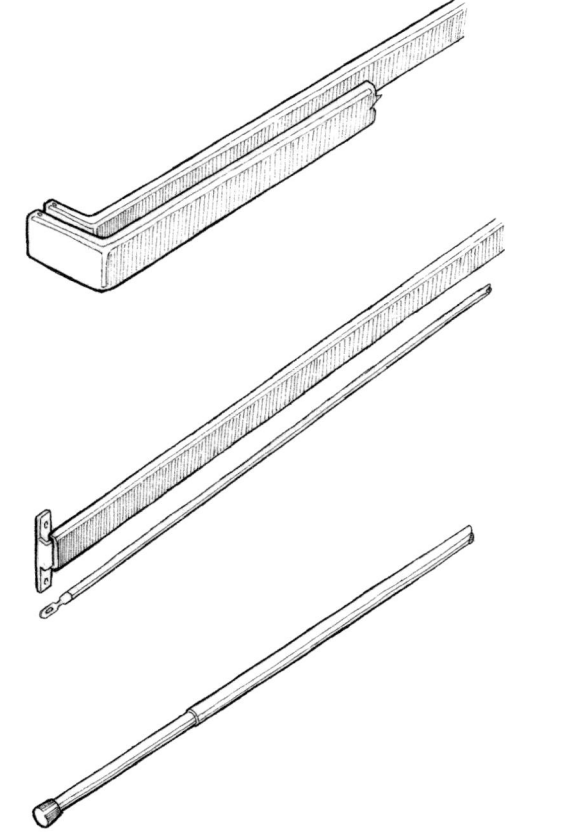

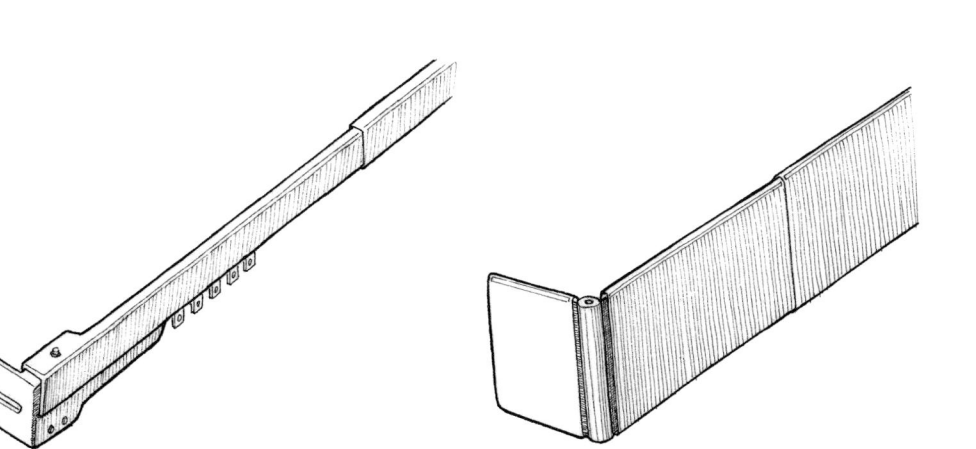

decorative hardware

Decorative curtain rods are made of metal, iron, bronze, enamel, and wood—with varying circumferences. They are often sold in kits that include brackets, finials, and rings. Many have antique or special metallic finishes, with elaborate finials at the ends. These rods are meant to be seen!

Draped swags are stationary. They hang from rods, decorative poles, mounting boards, or swag holders.

You can hang window treatments from pleat hooks, fabric tabs, ribbons, grommets, rings, and clips—depending on the look you're after.

mounting boards

Instead of working with hardware, you can a hang a window treatment by stapling it to a thick piece of wood, which serves as a mounting board. The board can sit inside the window frame or outside, depending on the effect you want. Cover the board with a fabric of your choice for a professional and decorative finish.

1 Cut muslin or decorator fabric to cover the board, allowing a 1" (2.5 cm) overlap along the long edge and a 2" (5.1 cm) overlap at each short end.

2 Center the board on the wrong side of the fabric. Staple one long edge of the fabric to the board. Leave about 6" (15.2 cm) of fabric free at each end.

3 Fold under ¼" (6 mm) of the unstapled long edge. Wrap the fabric around the board and staple in place, leaving 6" (15.2 cm) of fabric free at each end.

4 Fold the unstapled fabric at each end as shown in the drawing. Finger-press to reduce bulk. Staple in place.

inside mount: Cut the board slightly smaller than the width of the window opening so it will fit in place after it is covered with fabric. Attach the board to the top of the window frame with a drill and screws.

outside mount: Cut the mounting board at least 2" (5.1 cm) wider than the window frame. Attach angle irons to the back edge of the board, an equal distance from each edge of the window frame. Hold the mounting board against the wall to determine the best placement.

measuring windows

To determine the finished size of your window treatments, you'll measure the hardware or the mounting board—not the window! These measurements will help you determine how much fabric you'll need.

Work with a retractable metal tape measure. If the area you're measuring is very large, you may also need to enlist the help of a friend.

Hang the hardware or board, depending on your style of window treatment.

If you are making curtains, valances, and draperies with a rod, attach the rod to the wall above and to the sides of the frame.

If you are making roller shades, attach the hardware inside the window frame or directly on the outside corner.

Cut mounting boards so they either fit inside the window frame or hang on the wall, over and beyond the frame. A spring-tension rod always goes inside the frame.

Most window treatments extend to the top of the sill, the bottom of the window apron, or 1/2" (1.3 cm) from the floor or radiator. Valances should extend at least 4" to 6" (10.2 to 15.2 cm) below the top of the window and should be 10" to 16" (25.4 to 40.6 cm) long.

Measuring Width

To determine the finished width of your window treatment, measure the curtain rod, pole, or mounting board, including the return (or projection) on each end.

Measuring Length

To determine the finished length of your window treatment, measure from the top of the hardware to the point where you want the lower edge of the window treatment to fall.

If the window treatment will hang from clips, rings, or tabs, measure from the bottom of the clips, rings, or tabs.

To make a window appear longer, hang the curtain rod or mounting board closer to the ceiling.

fabric requirements

The amount of fabric you'll need depends on several factors: the window treatment style, the style and size of the hardware, the surface pattern of the fabric (you may need more to match a pattern), the hemming method, and the desired fullness.

Fullness

Fullness is the amount of fabric taken up by the construction of the window treatment—usually in gathering or pleating. Fullness may require up to three times the width of the window.

The amount depends on the treatment style, the fabric weight, and your personal preference (fullness affects drape and volume). For some types of pleated window treatments, you actually need to make a paper pattern, arrange the pleat placement, and then measure the width of the pattern (page 91).

Treatment Style & Fabric	Fabric Needed for Fullness
Gathered curtains/sheer and lightweight fabrics	$2\frac{1}{2}$ to 3 times window width
Gathered curtains/medium- to heavy-weight fabrics	2 to $2\frac{1}{2}$ times window width
Gathered curtains/heavy-weight fabrics	2 times window width
Pleated draperies	approximately $2\frac{1}{2}$ times window width, depending on pleat style

Determining Width

When computing the finished width of your fabric, multiply the measurement of your window hardware by the amount of extra fabric needed for fullness.

Cut width = [finished width measurement (including returns and overlap, if applicable)] × [desired fullness] + [side hem allowances (usually 3" (7.6 cm) for each double-fold 1$\frac{1}{2}$" (3.8 cm) hem)]

You'll need exact cut width measurements only for flat window treatments (like shades) and those made with certain heading tapes. For other treatments, you can approximate.

Determining Length

When making window treatments, always use double-fold hems (page 94). Hem allowances vary with the weight of the fabric and style of the treatment.

Treatment Style & Fabric	Hem Allowance
lightweight fabrics	10" (25.4 cm) for a 5" (12.7 cm) double-fold hem
medium to heavy fabrics	8" (20.3 cm) for a 4" (10.2 cm) double-fold hem
short curtains and valances	4" (10.2 cm) for a 2" (5.1 cm) double-fold hem

Cut length = [finished length measurement] + [hem allowances] + [heading] + [rod pocket depth (if applicable)] + [pattern repeat allowance, if applicable (page 91)]

How Much Fabric to Buy

Divide the cut width by the usable fabric width (excluding selvages). Round up to the next whole number to determine how many fabric widths you need. Multiply this number by the cut length to find out how much yardage to buy.

sewing edge-to-edge lining

You don't always need to add a lining, but it will add weight and body to the main fabric and help the window treatment hang better. A lining also keeps the fabric from fading in sunlight, adds opacity, and presents a finished appearance to the outside world.

Edge-to-edge lining is a quick and easy way to line a short curtain or valance. There are no side hems supporting the shape, so this construction is not recommended for full-length curtains. If the curtain or valance will hang from clips, eliminate the rod-pocket opening.

1   Cut the fabric and lining to the same size, piecing if necessary. Determine the fabric amount, following the guidelines on pages 178 to 179—but when computing the cut width, allow only 1/2" (1.3 cm) for each side seam allowance.

2   Hem the lower edges of the curtain and lining with double-fold hems (page 94).

3   Place the curtain and lining right sides together. Pin along the sides and top. Mark the rod-pocket opening with a fabric-marking pen.

4   Sew 1/2" (1.3 cm) seams along the sides and top, breaking the stitching at the marks to leave an opening for the rod pocket. Trim the corners diagonally.

5   Turn the curtain or valance right side out and press.

6   Stitch along the top and bottom of the rod pocket, using a seam guide or a strip of tape on the machine bed to keep the line of stitching even.

7   Insert the curtain rod.

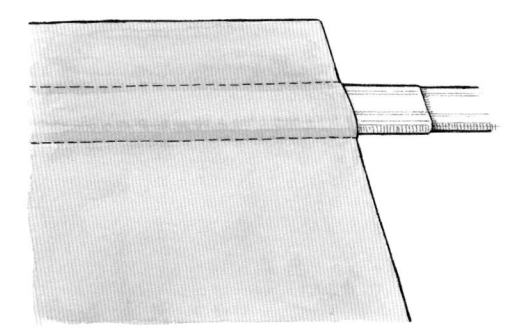

sewing interior lining

Traditionally, lining is cut slightly smaller than the decorator fabric so the lining fabric is not visible at the sides of the curtain. This lining method works well for lightweight curtains that hang from clips or sew-on rings.

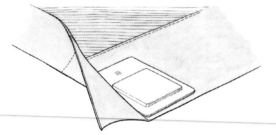

1 Cut the curtain fabric to the desired size.

   Cut length = [finished length] + [4 1/2" (11.4 cm) (2 1/2" [6.4 cm] for the heading and 2" [5.1 cm] for the double-fold hem)].

   Cut width = [finished width] ¥ [desired fullness] + [1" [2.5 cm] (for 1/2" [1.3 cm] seam allowance on each side)]

2 Cut the lining fabric 2" (5.1 cm) shorter and 6" (15.2 cm) narrower than the width of the curtain fabric. Piece curtain and lining panels as necessary (page 137).

3 Hem the lower edges of the curtain and lining panels with 2" (5.1 cm) double-fold hems (page 94). If you are making floor-length curtains, hand-tack a drapery weight in the hem, within each seam allowance of the decorator fabric.

4 Pin the sides of the lining and curtain, right sides together, so that the lining hem is 1 1/2" (3.8 cm) above the hem of the decorator fabric. Stitch the side seams with a 1/2" (1.3 cm) seam allowance. Press the seam allowances toward the decorator fabric.

3

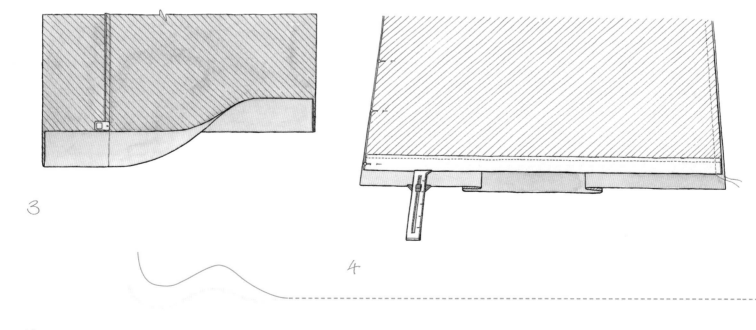

3

4

5   Turn the curtain right side out. Because the lining is narrower than the decorator fabric, the fabric will naturally fold to the wrong side. Center the lining so the overlapping decorator fabric is equal on each side. Press.

6   To form the heading, press ½" (1.3 cm) of the upper edge of the decorator fabric to the wrong side. Then fold over another 2" (5.1 cm), encasing the raw edge of the lining. Edgestitch along the inside fold.

7   Attach clips or sew-on rings at evenly spaced intervals across the width of the heading.

8   Fold the bottom corner of each side hem diagonally to form a 45-degree angle. Hand-stitch closed.

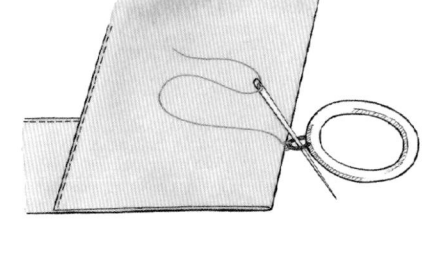

7

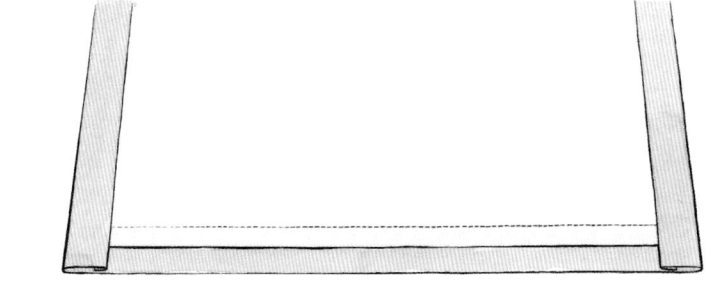

5

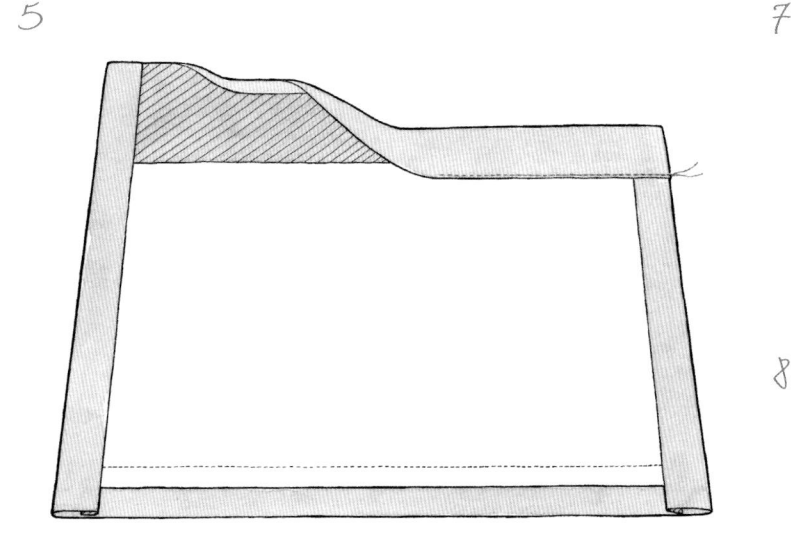

6

8

sewing unlined rod-pocket curtains

A rod pocket is a casing that holds the curtain rod or pole. Traditionally, it is stitched 1" to 4" (2.5 to 10.2 cm) below the upper edge of the curtain. The heading above the pocket forms a ruffle when the curtain is placed on the rod. For curtains used as undertreatment, eliminate the heading and position the pocket at the very top of the curtain.

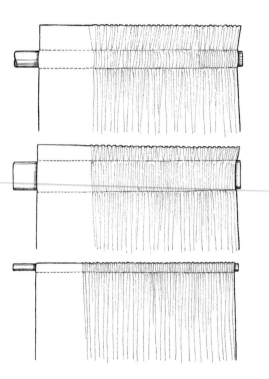

The size of the rod or pole determines the depth of the rod pocket. You can use conventional metal rods (typically 1", 2½", or 4" (2.5, 6.4, or 10.2 cm) wide) or decorative metal rods or wood poles of varying widths.

Measure the circumference of the rod and add ⅝" (1.7 cm) for ease. Divide the number by two to determine the correct depth for the pocket.

1 Cut the amount of curtain fabric you need, following the guidelines on pages 178-179. Add the heading depth and the rod-pocket depth plus ½" (1.3 cm) to determine the amount of turn-under. Piece the curtain panel as necessary.

home décor

2 Press ½" (1.3 cm) to the wrong side along the upper edge. Then press the folded edge to the wrong side for an amount equal to the rod-pocket depth plus the heading depth.

3 Stitch close to the inner fold, backstitching at both ends. Mark the heading depth across the top edge with a fabric-marking pen.

4 Stitch along the marked line to form the rod pocket, backstitching at both ends.

5 Insert the curtain rod into the pocket.

To eliminate the heading, follow the same directions, but make these changes: Don't add the heading allowance in step 1. In step 2, turn the folded edge down only the amount of the rod-pocket depth. Omit step 3. Instead, stitch along the inner fold and, if desired, stitch again close to the upper edge to form a sharp crease.

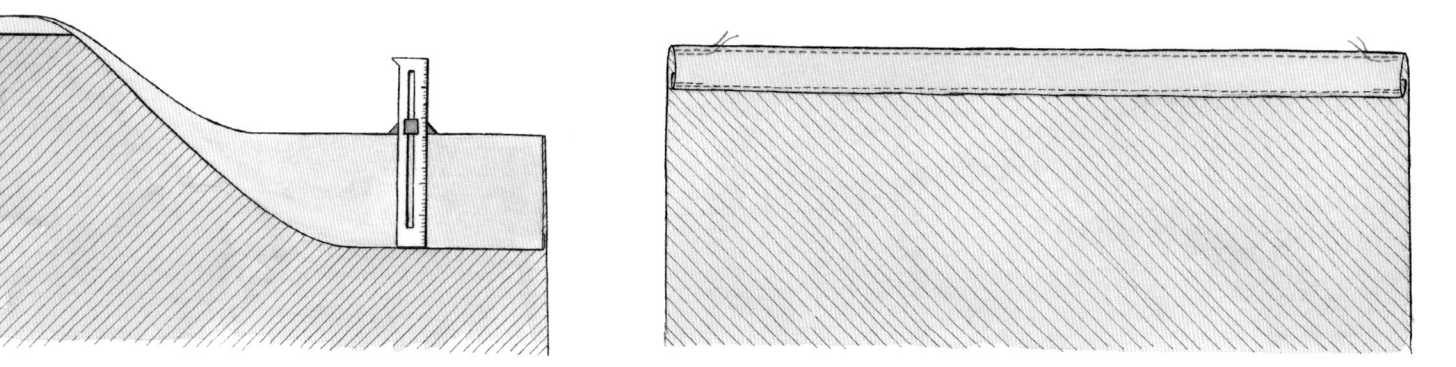

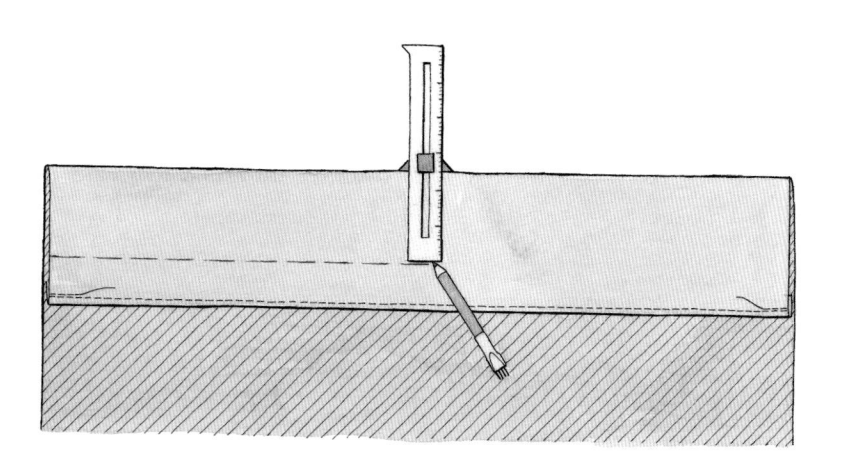

making tabs

Tabs add a nice touch to the upper edge of casual curtains, as attractive alternatives to pleated and gathered edgings. Select a decorative curtain rod or pole to show them off. For the tabs, choose a fabric that matches or contrasts with the curtain fabric—or find a decorative ribbon or sturdy trim. Cut the curtain fabric width adding 1¹/₂ to 2 times fullness (page 178).

Tabs are inserted between the top edge of the curtain and a self-fabric facing. They wrap over the rod, and both ends are caught in the top seam—or one finished end can button to the curtain top for a decorative accent.

To determine tab length, cut a strip of fabric and wrap it around the rod. Mark both ends of the strip at the point where you want the top of the curtain to sit. Measure between the marks and add 1" (2.5 cm)—for a ¹/₂" (1.3 cm) seam allowance at each end—to find the cut length.

Tabs can be any width, depending on the style of the curtain, the fabric weight (wider tabs offer more support), and personal taste. To find the cut width, multiply the finished width by two and add 1" (2.5 cm) for seam allowances.

As a variation, you can also sew strips of fabric or ribbon into the top seam—just as you would the tabs—and tie the loose ends around the curtain rod. There are many other decorative treatments for curtain headings, too—for example, you can simply weave a heavy hemp cording through metal grommets, page 154.

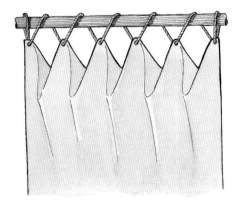  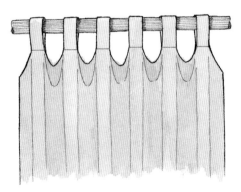

sewing tab curtains

2

1 Cut the amount of curtain fabric you need, following the guidelines on pages 178 to 179. Also cut a facing strip 6" (15.2 cm) long and the same cut width as the curtain. Sew a ¼" (6 mm) double-fold hem in the lower edge of the facing (page 94).

2 Decide how many tabs you need. Plan one at each end of the curtain top, allowing ½" (1.3 cm) seam allowance. Divide the remaining width by the finished width of the tab and the desired space between tabs. Space the tabs 5" to 6" (12.7 to 15.2 cm) apart for short curtains; 8" to 10" (20.3 to 25.4 cm) apart for long curtains. Mark the tab placements on the upper edge of the curtain.

3 You will cut the tabs with their length on the lengthwise grain of the fabric. Cut several fabric strips, each long enough for three or four tabs and wide enough for one.

4 Fold each strip in half, right sides together. Stitch with a ½" (1.3 cm) seam allowance to form a tube. Center the seam and press open. Turn the tube right side out.

5 Cut each long tube into three or four tabs to the length you need.

6 Fold the tabs in half, wrong sides together. Pin them to the right side of the curtain top at the marks, with raw edges even. Pin the facing to the curtain top, right sides together, sandwiching the tabs between the layers. Stitch ½" (1.3 cm) from the top edge.

7 Turn the curtain right side out and press. Hem the sides of the curtain.

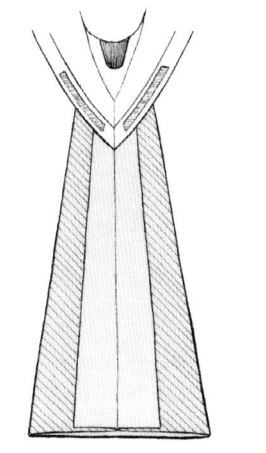

4

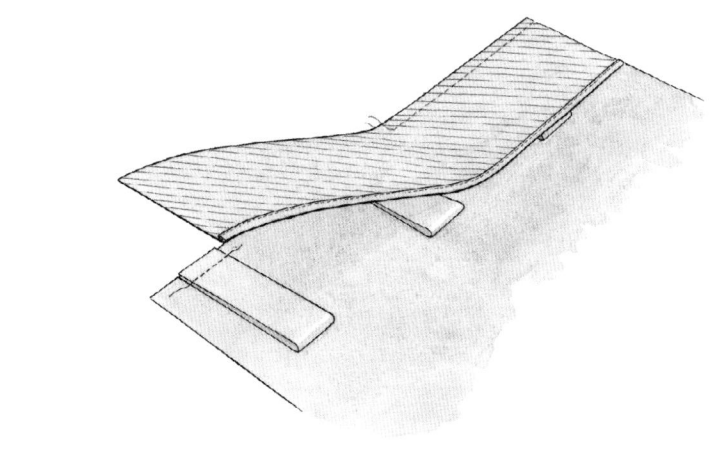

6

heading tapes

Heading tapes add custom detail to plain curtain panels. The tapes have woven-in cords that are pulled to draw the fabric fullness (page 178) into pleats, gathers, or folds. The tapes, which are either sewn or fused, work best on lightweight to medium-weight decorator fabrics.

Most tapes require a flat curtain panel that is 2 1/2 times the finished width for fullness—but to be sure, check the manufacturer s information on the packaging. The tapes are sewn to the wrong side of the upper edge of the curtain panel (pages 188 to 189).

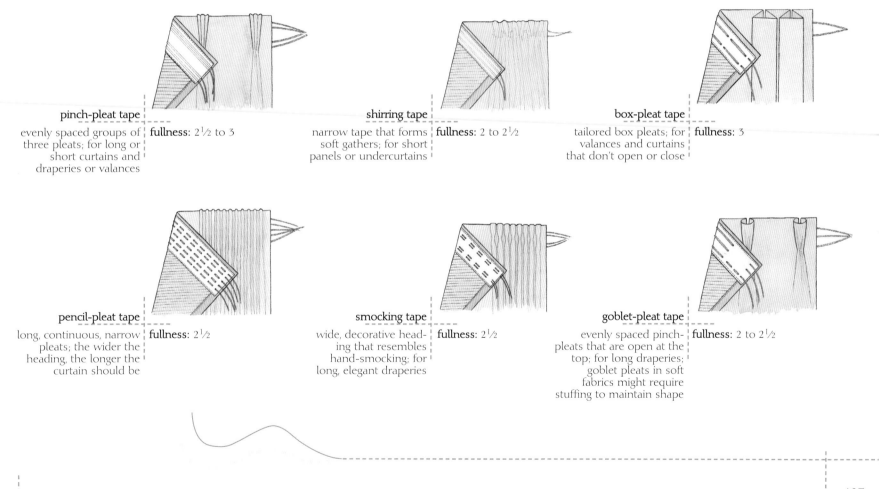

pinch-pleat tape
evenly spaced groups of three pleats; for long or short curtains and draperies or valances
fullness: 2 1/2 to 3

shirring tape
narrow tape that forms soft gathers; for short panels or undercurtains
fullness: 2 to 2 1/2

box-pleat tape
tailored box pleats; for valances and curtains that don't open or close
fullness: 3

pencil-pleat tape
long, continuous, narrow pleats; the wider the heading, the longer the curtain should be
fullness: 2 1/2

smocking tape
wide, decorative heading that resembles hand-smocking; for long, elegant draperies
fullness: 2 1/2

goblet-pleat tape
evenly spaced pinch-pleats that are open at the top; for long draperies; goblet pleats in soft fabrics might require stuffing to maintain shape
fullness: 2 to 2 1/2

attaching heading tapes

When making curtains with heading tapes, you need to plan ahead. Measure the rod to determine the finished width of the panel. If the curtain or drapery will open, divide the finished width by two, allowing for a center overlap and corner returns (the amount the rod projects from the wall), if applicable.

Fabric Requirements

Each style of heading tape requires a specific amount of full-ness in the curtain or drapery (page 178). Most tapes require the cut fabric to be 2½ to 3 times wider than the finished width of the curtain or drapery.

Cut width = [finished width measurement (including returns and overlap, if applicable)] × [fullness required by the tape] + [side hem allowances (usually 3" (7.6 cm) for each double-fold 1½" (3.8 cm) hem)]

On medium- to heavy-weight fabrics, add enough length to finish the top of the panel with a 1" (2.5 cm) fold to provide a flat, stable surface for the heading tape. For lightweight fabrics, cut your fabric to allow 4" (10.2 cm) for a 2" (5.1 cm) double-fold hem for greater stability. (For a clean, crisp edge, edgestitch along the fold. See page 72.)

Cut length = [finished length measurement]+ [lower hem allowance] + [top hem allowance] + [pattern repeat allowance, if applicable]

If your fabric has a pattern repeat, add enough fabric length for one extra, full repeat for matching.

Attaching the Tapes

1 Cut and piece fabric for desired width. Sew double-fold hems at the bottom and sides. The panel should now measure the finished width times the fullness required by the tape.

2 Fold under the upper edge 1" (2.5 cm) and press.

3 Cut the heading tape several inches longer than the panel width. Position the tape, right side up on the wrong side of the panel, ½" (1.3 cm) below the upper edge, covering the raw edge of the fabric.

If you are attaching pinch-pleat or goblet-pleat tape to a curtain with returns, adjust the position of the tape so the first pleat at each end will fall at the corner of the rod.

4 Turn under the ends of the tape so they are even with the edge of the curtain. Pin the tape in place. Pull out the cords at the folds with a pin. Knot the cords together at one end.

5 Stitch across the top and bottom of the tape, taking care not to catch the cords in the stitching. Backstitch at each end. If the tape is wide, stitch across the center of the tape, again being careful not to stitch over cords.

6 Check that the knot is still secure. Gently pull the cords from the other end and slide the fabric along the cords to form pleats or gathers. The panel should now measure the desired finished width.

7 Knot the cords after you have formed the last pleat or gather. Coil and loosely tie the excess cord, so you can release the cord to straighten the panel when you need to launder it. Tuck the cord into the opening between the fabric and the tape.

8 Insert drapery hooks and hang the panel.

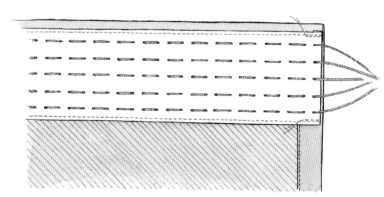

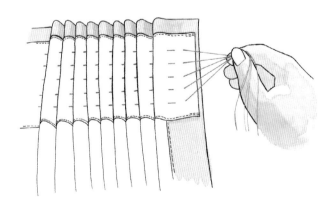

mending & repair

assessing the damage

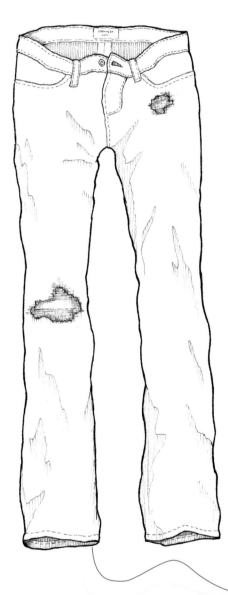

Mending is a simple job. You don't have to be an experienced sewer, but you do have to decide whether the item is actually able to be fixed—and whether your time is worth the effort.

Examine the damaged area. Trim away loose threads to neaten the hole or tear. Try to catch rips and holes before they get too large—the larger the damaged area, the harder it is to fix inconspicuously. Reinforce frayed or thinning fabric before it tears, and take action against stains, spots, and scorch marks as soon as possible.

You can make simple repair jobs (fixing torn hems and ripped seams) while you watch television. Other jobs (replacing a zipper or darning a hole) require a bit more attention. But if the garment in need of repair is your favorite jacket or your most comfortable pants, it just might be worth it.

What's It Worth?

Consider whether the repair will be visible, whether the item will still fit after it's repaired (sometimes you have to sacrifice space in a garment to fix a tear), and whether it might just take less time and effort to replace it. You can easily patch a tear in the knee of a pair of jeans, but making an invisible repair in a fine knit, for example, is a little more challenging.

Expensive clothing, draperies, and cushions are usually made of good quality fabric—which, fortunately, is easier to repair than cheaper fabric. If the item is expensive, one of your favorites, or an heirloom, definitely try to repair it. Even if you are okay with giving the item away—to charity or as a hand-me-down—why not try to fix it first? You have nothing to lose—and the person on the receiving end will appreciate the effort!

checklist of considerations

Simple mending gives almost everything new life. If the damage seems beyond your skill level, take the garment to a tailor. But remember, you'll rarely do more damage if you give the repair a try yourself first.

✓ Is the fabric of good quality?

✓ Is it easy to find a replacement item?

✓ Is the item expensive to replace?

✓ Is the item part of a set or an outfit?

✓ Is the item a favorite, with sentimental value?

✓ Is the fabric easy to work with?

✓ Is the damage in a visible or central area?

✓ How large is the damaged area?

✓ Is the rest of the garment or item still in good shape?

✓ Is the fabric frayed around the damaged area?

✓ Is the fabric stretched out of shape?

✓ Is the area around the tear stretched or distorted?

✓ Will the color and/or design be hard to match?

✓ Will a patch or repair stitching be unsightly?

✓ Can you make a decorative repair?

✓ Are you nervous about taking on this kind of repair?

common repairs

Some mending and repair projects are easy. If a button falls off your jacket, just sew it back on before you leave the house—it's that easy. Other types of repairs, such as mending a torn buttonhole, aren't difficult—they just take a little longer to complete. Here are some of the most common mending projects, listed by degree of difficulty. The biggest factors in complexity are the location of the damage, the type of fabric, and the techniques required to make the repair.

Easiest Repair Projects

Fabrics: fleece, fake fur, moderate to heavyweight knits, patterned and textured fabrics

- Fixing a torn hem
- Shortening any type of garment
- Darning a hole in an unobtrusive location or on sport/casual work clothes
- Darning a hole in knit, fleece, or pile fabrics
- Patching play clothes and casual clothing
- Fixing a ripped seam
- Mending an inseam pocket
- Sewing on a button
- Fixing a partially ripped buttonhole
- Restitching a partially ripped but working zipper
- Replacing elastic in a casing
- Darning a snag or a pulled thread
- Taking in clothing at the seams
- Repairing topstitching
- Restringing a drawstring

More Challenging Projects

Fabrics: broadcloth, denim, machine-made lace, single knits, solid-color fabrics

- Lengthening any type of garment
- Adding a cuff to pants
- Adding a ruffle to the bottom edge of any item
- Darning a hole in an obvious location on everyday clothing
- Darning a hole in flat, woven fabrics
- Re-attaching a torn patch pocket
- Repairing a fabric tear under a button
- Fixing a frayed or substantially ripped buttonhole
- Repairing ripped lining
- Reshaping clothing at the seams
- Fixing a dart or vent that has ripped open
- Replacing stitched-on elastic
- Removing some types of stains

Most Challenging Projects

Fabrics: lace, leather, satin, silk, velvet

- Darning a hole in satin weave and shiny eveningwear fabrics
- Darning invisibly in a conspicuous location
- Fixing a rip in the center (not the seam) of a garment
- Repairing specialty fabrics, such as lace, metallics, sequined fabrics, and leather
- Stabilizing a stretched buttonhole and fixing a completely ripped buttonhole
- Replacing a broken zipper
- Replacing lining
- Darning burn holes
- Letting out clothing
- Removing some types of stains, water marks, or pressing shine

notions

Keep a basic supply of these helpful items on hand and store them in a pretty basket or box. If you have to run to the store every time you need to mend something, the repair probably won't ever get done!

thread: All-purpose thread is all you need for most repairs, including resewing seams, patching, and replacing closures. Buttonhole twist or other heavy-duty thread is handy for attaching buttons on heavy fabrics.

Purchase thread in black, white, and a few other basic colors, such as navy, khaki, and mid-tone gray—these will blend with nearly any fabric color.

fasteners: Look for snaps and hooks and eyes in assorted sizes.

buttons: Keep a supply of white and black flat buttons in a variety of sizes.

seam tape: Basic white and black seam tape is great for quick fixes.

fusible interfacing, web, and stabilizer: Buy 1/4 yard (22.8 cm), for quick patching and stabilizing.

There's no need for a lot of sewing gadgets. A few basics will help you get the job done. Many mending projects are done by hand, so keep a small supply of sewing tools handy.

straight pins, safety pins, and a pin cushion: Keep a supply of dressmaker straight pins and safety pins. To prevent spills and keep them handy, store them in a pin cushion or on a magnetic pin-holder.

hand-sewing needles: Sharps are all-purpose, medium-length needles with sharp points for seaming and general hand sewing.

darning needles: Darning needles are very long with fine points for darning holes by hand.

needle threader: This small wire loop enables you to thread needles easily (see page 66).

thimble: Wear a thimble on the third finger of your sewing hand so you can push the needle through heavy fabrics without hurting your finger.

seam gauge: A seam gauge is great for taking small measurements, especially seam allowances and hems.

measuring tape: A flexible tape measure, 60" (152.4 cm) long, is soft but not stretchy. It is used for measuring the body and curved seams.

beeswax: Run your hand-sewing thread across a piece of beeswax to strengthen it and prevent it from fraying and tangling.

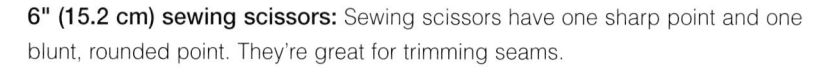

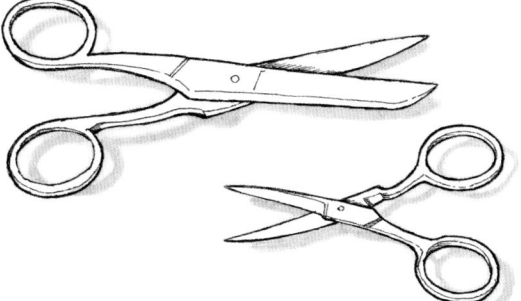

6" (15.2 cm) sewing scissors: Sewing scissors have one sharp point and one blunt, rounded point. They're great for trimming seams.

3" or 4" (7.6 or 10.1 cm) embroidery scissors: These small scissors with two sharp points are ideal for precision cutting and snipping thread ends.

seam ripper: With this precise, invaluable tool, you can remove unwanted stitches without ripping the fabric.

chalk wedge/pencil or fabric-marking pen: These tools will help you accurately copy design lines or mark alteration and new sewing lines.

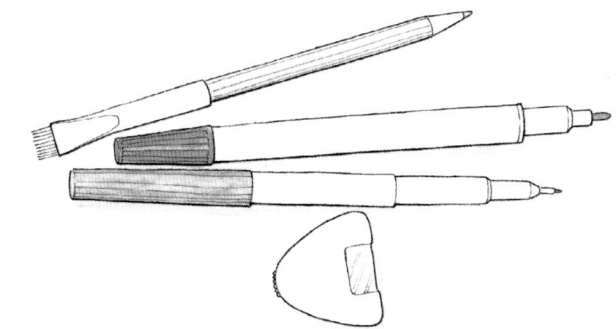

steam iron, ironing board and press cloth (scrap of muslin or plain white cotton): When pressing repair areas, cover the item with a press cloth to protect the fabric from the iron, and the iron from any fusible adhesives that might be present.

liquid fray preventer: This liquid prevents fabric and trim from fraying. It is also used to secure thread ends. It is washable and dry-cleanable and does not discolor or stain most fabrics. (Test it first on an inconspicuous area.)

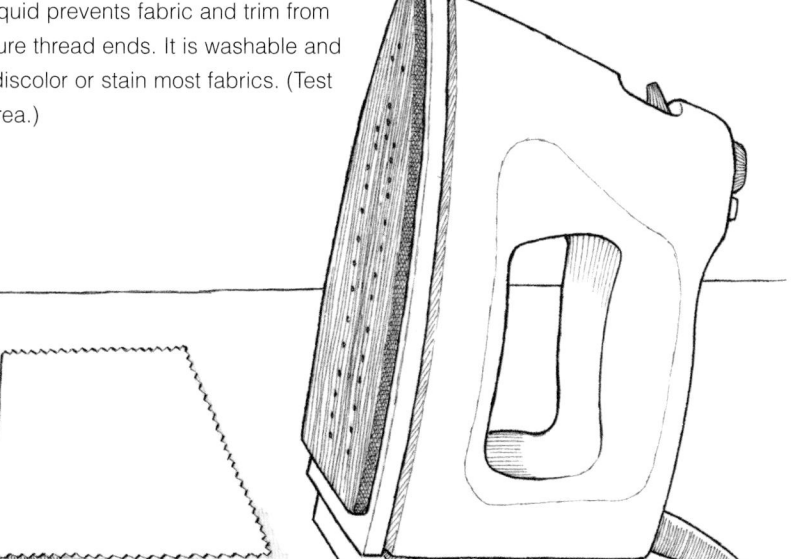

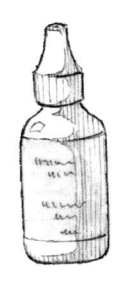

Remove unwanted liquid fray preventer by blotting the area with a cotton ball dipped in rubbing alcohol.

general guidelines

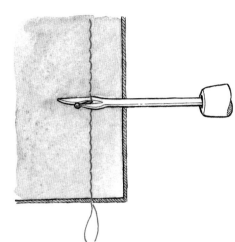

Before you start mending anything, review these simple tips to make your job easier! Damaged areas will always get worse over time, so the sooner you repair them, the simpler the job will be.

- Always work in good light.
- Press the repair area before you begin.
- Mend the item before you wash it, to prevent further fraying or tearing.
- Select a thread that matches the color of the item. If you can't find the exact shade of thread, choose one that is slightly darker than the fabric.

- Take action to avoid having to mend later. Reinforce stressed or worn areas, such as knees and elbows, before the fabric tears. Repair small holes or tears before they get bigger.
- Always remove stitches carefully (with a seam ripper, scissors, or pin) and mark the original stitching line with a fabric-marking pen or chalk.

How to Remove Stitches

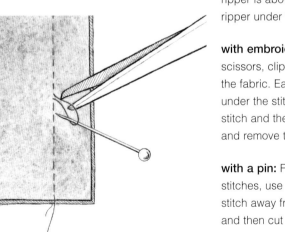

with a seam ripper: Insert the point of the seam ripper under the stitch so the top/ball of the seam ripper is above the stitch. Gently push the seam ripper under the stitch to cut the thread.

with embroidery scissors: With small, pointed scissors, clip the stitching from the right side of the fabric. Ease one of the scissor points under the stitch and cut. Clip every third stitch and then pull the seam apart and remove the loose threads.

with a pin: For very small stitches, use a pin to pull the stitch away from the fabric and then cut it with small, pointed scissors.

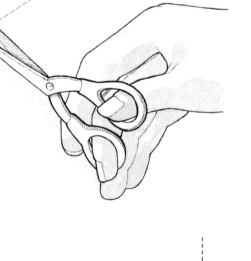

fixing with fusibles

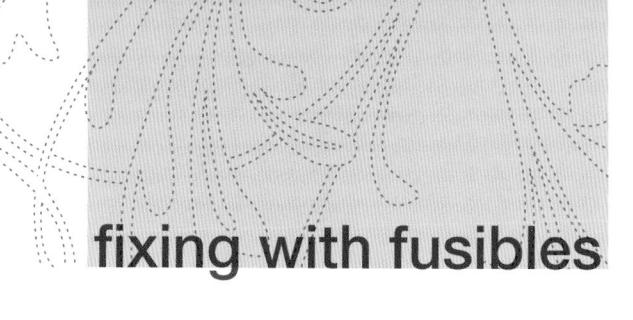

Fusible products offer "no-sew" mending and repair options. Fusibles can help you mend, add stability, attach trim, and support fabrics that are worn thin. Here are a few to keep handy for five-minute fix-ups.

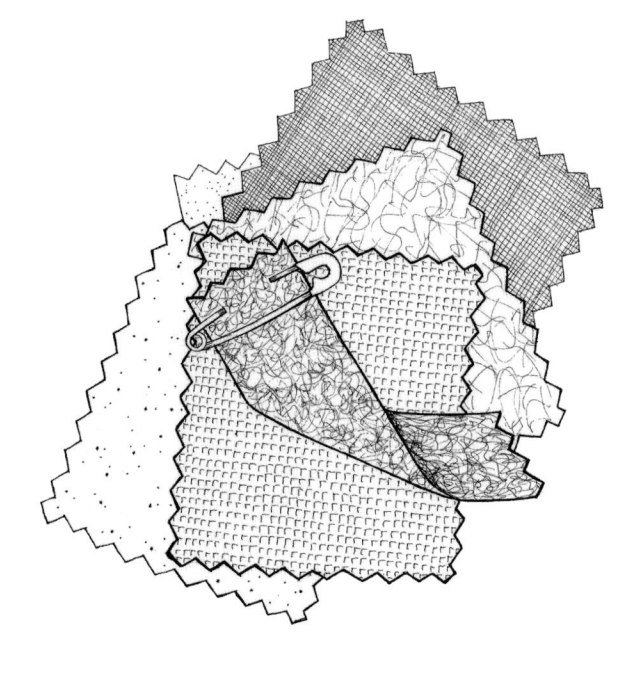

fusible interfacing: Choose this adhesive-backed fabric to add shape and crispness to limp fabric, stability to stretchy fabric, and durability to worn fabrics. Woven, knit, and nonwoven varieties offer many degrees of support and stretch.

Work with iron-on interfacing to hold tears and seams together to make them easier to sew. You can also apply it as an interior patch on fabric that needs support.

fusible web: Sold by the yard or in precut strips, with or without paper backing, this heat-activated product is used to fuse two layers together.

Paper–backed fusible web is fused in two steps. Position it on the first layer and press. Remove the paper backing and fuse the second layer over the first.

Fusible web without paper backing is placed between two pieces of fabric, or between fabric and trim, and fused in one step.

fusible mending tape: Mending tape is heavier than fusible web and works to close a tear. After fusing it in place, stitch over it to reinforce. Fusible mending tape comes in precut strips and patches.

fusible stabilizer: Stabilizer is used to temporarily stiffen a fabric area so that you can stitch on it. After stitching you can tear it away or, in the case of wash-away products, dissolve the stabilizer with a damp cloth. Stabilizer is helpful when you are darning a hole or tear and when you are embroidering by hand or machine.

fusible trim, fusible drapery tapes, fusible rhinestones, and fusible Velcro: These products are designed for convenience. They are like their sew-on cousins, but they have fusible adhesive on the back. Just position them and fuse, following the manufacturer's instructions. Apply them to cover stains or holes or to restyle existing draperies and other home décor.

Fusing Tips

- Follow the manufacturer's instructions and recommendations for heat, pressure, moisture, and drying time.

- Prewash the fabric to remove sizing.

- Prewash the interfacing to eliminate the possibility of shrinkage. Soak it in a basin with hot (not boiling) water for about thirty minutes. Squeeze out excess moisture and hang it to dry.

- Test a small piece of the fusible on the seam or hem allowance or on another inconspicuous area. Make sure the fusible doesn't change the feel of the fabric and that the fused layers don't tear apart.

- Protect the fabric and the sole plate of the iron by placing a press cloth, brown paper, or pressing paper on top of the fabric.

- Place the interfacing (or any fusible with adhesive on one side), adhesive side down, on the wrong side of the fabric. Cover it with a damp press cloth.

  With your iron set to the temperature suggested for the type of fabric you are working with, press (don't move the iron) one section for about fifteen seconds. Lift and repeat until the whole piece is fused in place.

- To maximize the efficiency of the fusible, press on both sides after the initial fusing process.

- You can use fusibles to prevent or minimize raveling and further tearing.

- Fusibles add stiffness and weight, so they are not always suitable for sheer and lightweight fabrics. There are special interfacings specifically made for sheer fabrics.

- Fuse large pieces, like a table runner or a window shade, by covering your kitchen table with a thin blanket and an old sheet to create a large pressing surface.

- Fusibles have different bonding strength. Make sure the weight and strength of the fusible matches the weight of the fabric.

- Avoid using fusible web that is too heavy. The adhesive might seep through the fabric and leave residue on the right side.

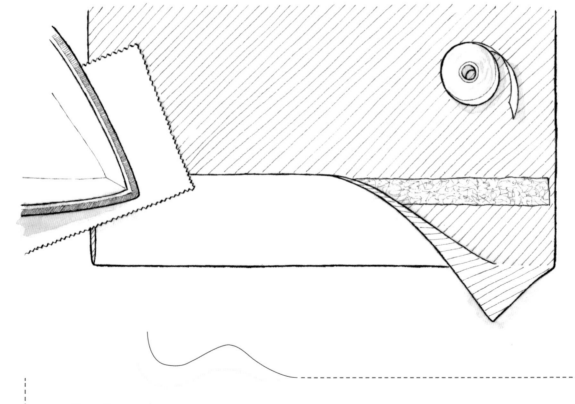

Mark a press cloth with "This side up for fusing" and always use it when working with iron-on adhesive products. You'll avoid getting glue on your iron.

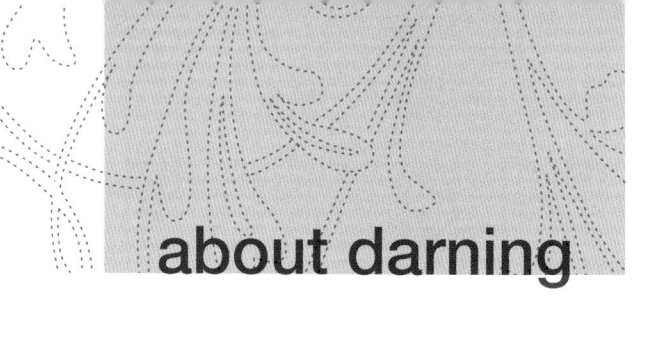

about darning

Darning is the weaving of thread or yarn across a hole in a piece of fabric to fill and conceal the hole. You can also darn across a thin or worn area of fabric to strengthen it, to prevent a hole from forming, and to close a fabric tear.

For support as you darn, place the damaged fabric over a darning egg or mushroom—or other firm, rounded object, such as a smooth rock, light bulb, piece of cardboard, or plastic ball. Stretch the fabric slightly as you stitch.

- Work with darning needles (see page 195), which are longer than other hand-sewing needles and extend across the diameter of a hole more easily.

  For fine fabrics and small holes, work with a smaller darning needle. For knits, wools, and heavier fabrics, choose a longer darning needle with a bigger eye.

- Try to find thread or yarn that matches the color, weight, and texture of the fabric. For lightweight woven fabrics, look for silk, cotton, or polyester/cotton thread.

  Embroidery floss is a good alternative to thread because you can separate the plies to make the darning strand as thick or thin as you want. Wool or crewel yarn is suitable for wool coats, socks, and blankets.

- Pull threads from a cut edge inside the item, such as the seam allowances or hem, if you can't purchase matching thread or yarn.

- Darn solid-color fabric with matching thread or yarn so that the repair is barely visible. A multi-color pattern is a little harder to darn invisibly. You can try to shade the darned area by using two or three different colored threads. For the least obtrusive repair, you may need to simply patch the garment (see page 206).

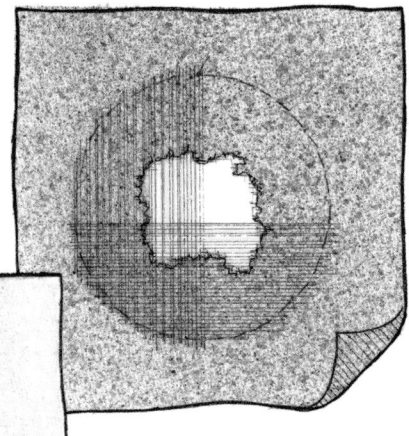

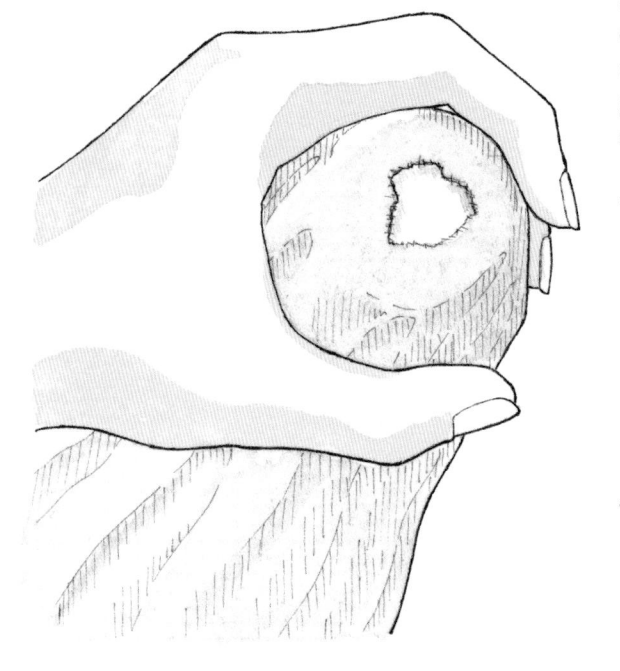

- If a hole is small and unobtrusive, seal it by dabbing it with a liquid fray preventer, such as Fray Check.

- If the hole is large, place a small piece of net or fine muslin in a matching color under the hole on the wrong side and catch it in all the darning stitches. The small piece of fabric provides support for the darning stitches.

- When you work darning stitches, do not pull them tight or you will close the hole and distort the fabric. Keep stitches taut—but not tight—so they span the hole.

- Make sure the darning stitches cover the hole and the surrounding, usually weakened, fabric, too.

- Shape the outer edges of the darned area slightly, so the stitches don't stress the same fabric threads on every stitch. Avoid darning in a perfect square.

- Space the stitches as close together as possible to form a tight weave.

- Before darning a burn hole in fabric, trim away the burned or frayed area first, as shown in drawing below.

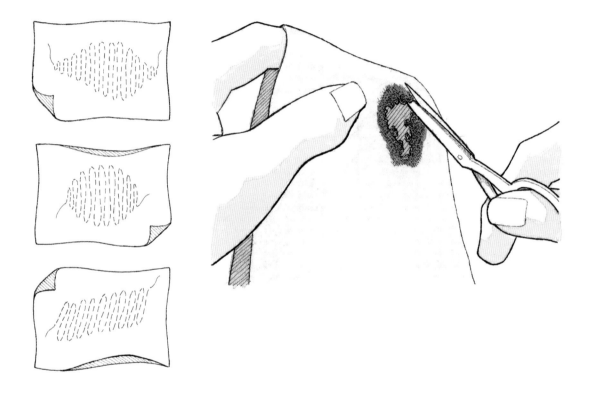

For a casual, "distressed" look, try darning jeans with contrasting color thread.

darning by hand

The best way to hand-darn a hole or tear is by inserting a patch of fabric or fusible interfacing inside the item and darning over the patch. A small hole or tear doesn't require a patch.

Darning a Hole by Hand

1 Thread a needle. Support the weakened fabric near the hole by sewing a line of short running stitches around the perimeter of the hole, about 1/4" (6 mm) from the edge.

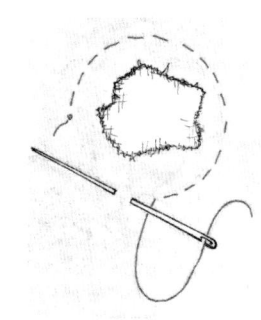

2 Place the hole over a hard surface, such as a darning egg or a smooth rock, to stretch it and support it. Sew closely spaced, long, straight stitches across the hole, starting and ending each stitch at the stitches that encircle the hole.

1

3 With a new thread, weave the threaded needle in and out of, and at right angles to, the first layer of stitches, picking up some garment threads as you go. To finish, pull the thread to the wrong side and run it under previous stitches. Clip the thread.

Darning a Tear by Hand

1 Trim away loose threads. Working on the wrong side, bring the fabric edges together. Sew the sloating stitch (see page 68) to close the tear, beginning and ending 1/2" (1.3 cm) beyond the tear. Backstitch or knot at the end of the tear.

2 If the tear is in a high-stress location, reinforce it by turning the tear upside down and sewing a second row of sloating stitches to form crisscrosses over the first row.

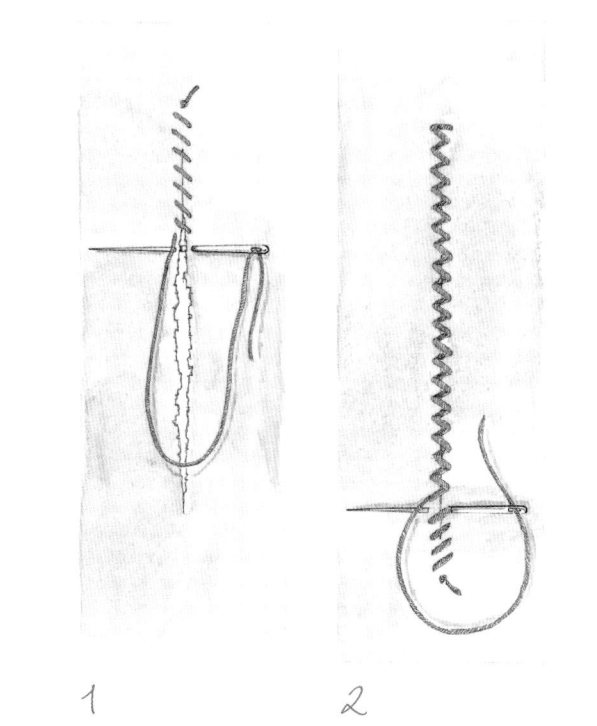

1   *2*

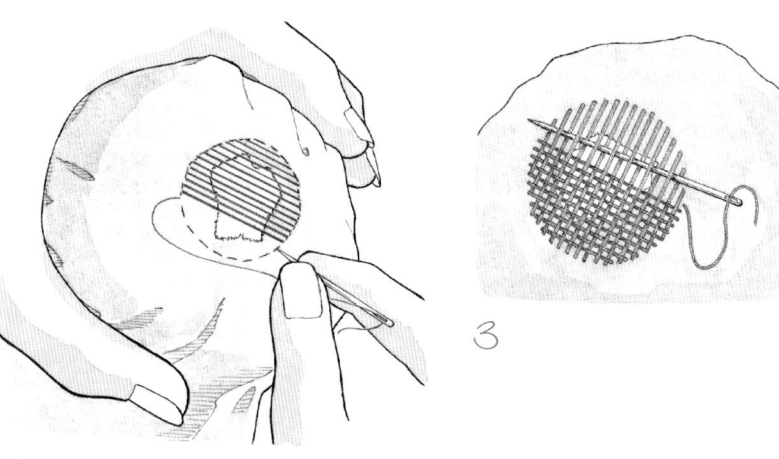

3

2

darning knit fabrics

Darning knits is much the same as darning woven fabrics. You'll get a much better result if you do it by hand rather than by machine. Sweater-type knits are surprisingly forgiving of darning—their lofty texture conceals darning stitches nicely. Whether your sweater has a hole, a moth hole, or a burn, you can salvage it with a minimum of effort. The key to successful darning is to work with yarns that match the garment in weight, texture, and color.

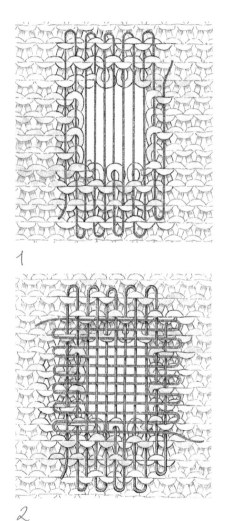

1

2

1   Tuck all loose yarn ends to the wrong side of the garment. Don't clip them, or you'll risk a bigger hole. Starting above and to the side of the tear, weave stitches through the existing stitches and then across the hole. Continue stitching across the entire hole and 1/2" (1.3 cm) beyond it. Don't pull the stitches tight.

2   To finish the repair, weave stitches through the first stitches and perpendicular to them, across the hole and 1/2" (1.3 cm) beyond the edges of the hole. Weave broken yarns into the darning stitches on the wrong side.

darning by machine

Darning by machine requires a few machine adjustments, which enable you to control the movement of the fabric under the needle. Remove the standard presser foot and lower or cover the feed dogs, following the instructions for your machine.

Preparing the Fabric

Mount the damaged fabric in an embroidery hoop: Sandwich the fabric between the hoop's two rings to hold it taut. The hoop will allow you to slide the fabric back and forth under the needle to form the stitches. Darning by machine takes some practice, so practice on scrap fabric first. Machine darning stitches are usually visible from the right side.

Preparing the machine

1 Loosen the upper thread tension slightly (follow the instructions in your owner's manual).

2 Sew without a presser foot or replace the presser foot with a darning foot (see page 12).

3 Lower the feed dogs or attach a darning plate to cover the feed dogs (refer to your owner's manual).

4 Set the machine for a medium-length straight stitch.

Darning a Hole

Center the hole in an embroidery hoop, with the right side up. If the hole is larger than ⅝" (1.5 cm), baste a fabric patch or a piece of stabilizer over the hole on the wrong side of the fabric.

Hand-sew short running stitches around the perimeter of the hole, as shown in the drawing below.

Slip the embroidery hoop under the needle and work rows of straight stitches back and forth over the hole by moving the fabric under the needle. The stitches should be very close together.

Turn the hoop 90 degrees and repeat the sewing to cover the first layer of stitches. Trim away excess fabric or remove the stabilizer after the stitching is complete.

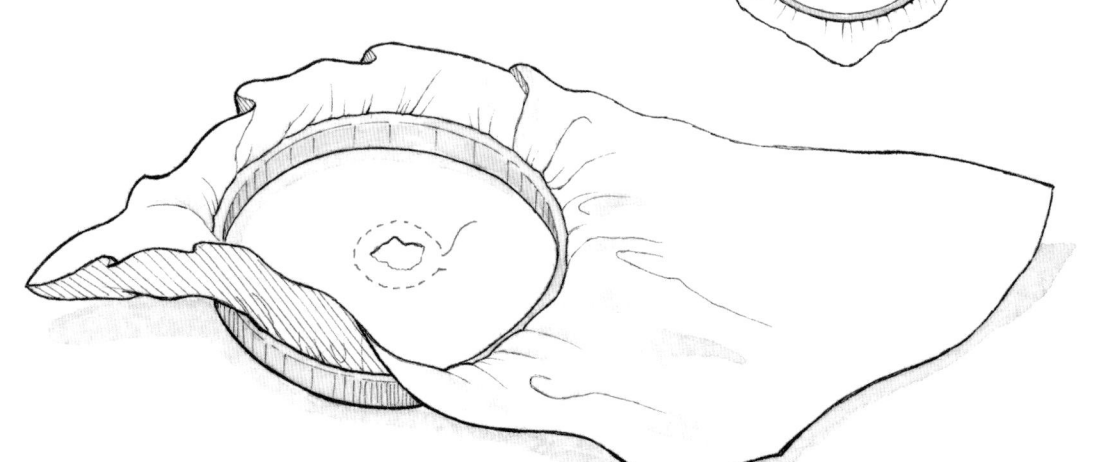

Darning a Small Tear

For tears less than 1" (2.5 cm) long, pin or hold the edges of the tear together and stitch a single row of wide, zigzag stitches directly over the tear.

Darning a Large Tear

Pin, hand-baste, or fuse stabilizer behind the tear. From the right side, zigzag directly over the tear. Then, stitch two or three parallel rows on each side of the first row to cover the weakened area.

Fusing a Tear

If you don't want to see darning stitches in the item or garment, fuse interfacing to the wrong side of the fabric, following the manufacturer's application instructions. Position a press cloth on top of the interfacing to protect the iron.

In some cases the interfacing will hold the tear closed, but not always. A large tear or a tear located in an area that's subject to stress will also need darning by machine or hand over the interfacing. Hand-wash the mended garment to eliminate the wear and tear of machine-washing.

If you don't have an embroidery hoop, place an extra layer or two of stabilizer on the wrong side of the fabric to support the stitching. Trim away excess stabilizer after darning the hole.

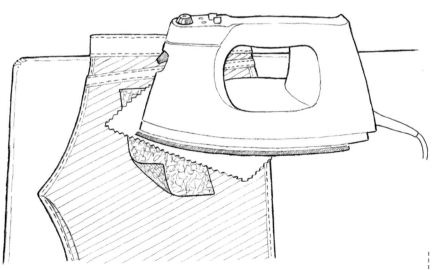

mending & repair

about patches

A patch is a small piece of fabric that covers, replaces, conceals, reinforces, or repairs a torn, worn, or stained area. Select fabric for a patch that's similar in weight and care requirements to the item's fabric. The patch can be sewn or fused in place on the right or wrong side of the fabric.

Decorative Effects

Make your patch a statement by using fabric in a color or pattern that contrasts with the garment fabric. Apply it on the right side of the garment. Use contrast thread for more emphasis.

Unobtrusive Repairs

Choose a matching fabric and apply the patch to the wrong side of the garment. Consider cutting fabric from the garment hem, a facing, the bottom of sleeves, or an interior pocket. Replace whatever you cut from the garment with muslin.

Tips for Patching

• Reinforce high-stress areas, like knees and elbows, with an interior patch before the garment fabric tears or wears through.

• Patch holes and tears as soon as you notice them, before they get larger.

• Consider a decorative patch or appliqué for holes that are large or in a very noticeable location (see page 261).

• Stabilize small holes on the wrong side of the fabric and cover them with beautiful buttons. Choose one button or several to create a "design detail."

• Patch pant legs and sleeves by hand if it's hard to reach the repair site by machine. Or, open the seams of the pant leg or sleeve to access the patch by machine.

fusing an iron-on patch

A store-bought fusible patch is a quick way to mend, especially worn-out knees! Refer to the fusing instructions on the packaging.

- Consider buying iron-on, ready-made patches, especially for denim fabric. You may need to edge-stitch or zigzag them as well as fuse them for long-term durability.

- Before fusing patches in place, trim square corners to round them. The rounded edges help prevent the patch from pulling away from the surface of the garment fabric.

- Work with fusible products to make iron-on patches from your own fabric (see page 198).

- If the hole or tear is large, you might need an inside patch as well, so the fusible product has something to adhere to.

To fuse a store-bought patch, cut it at least 1" (2.5 cm) larger all around than the hole or worn area. Round the corners. Trim away the frayed edges of the damaged area. Position the patch over the hole, with the fusible side down. Insert a piece of paper between the patch and the bottom layer of the garment so the patch doesn't fuse the garment closed.

Adjust the setting of the iron as recommended. Press the patch firmly by lifting and lowering the iron rather than sliding it. When the patch is cool, check that it's securely fused. If not, press it again.

For added strength, zigzag-stitch around the perimeter of the fused patch on the right side of the patch and garment.

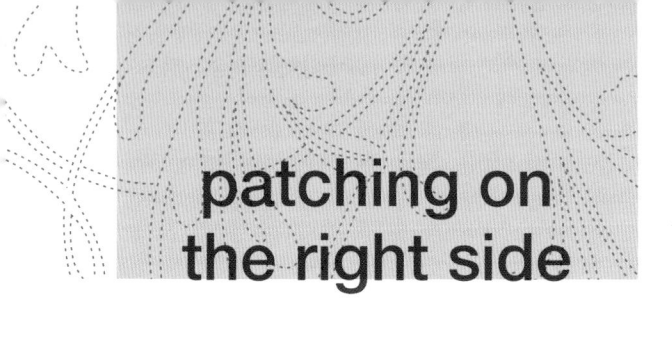

patching on the right side

Patched repairs are certainly more noticeable than darned repairs, but they are also stronger. If you don't mind that the patch is visible—or want to add a decorative touch—just sew it on the right side of jeans, work clothes, children's clothes, sport bags, tents, and workout or sports gear.

Prepare the Patch

1 Cut a patch of fabric 1" (2.5 cm) larger all around than the hole. It can be any shape.

2 If the fabric is light- to medium-weight, press under all the edges 1/2" (1.3 cm).

3 Press the area around the hole or tear and then trim away any loose threads.

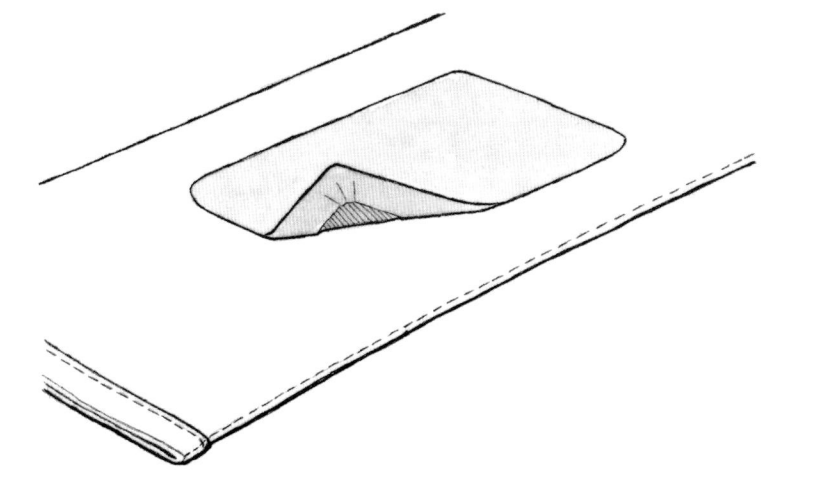

How to Machine-Sew the Patch

1 Center and pin the patch, right side up, on the right side of the garment.

2 Position the garment and patch right side up under the presser foot, with the edge of the patch slightly to the right of the needle.

3 Edge-stitch the patch to the garment (see page 72). Pivot at the corners, if there are any.

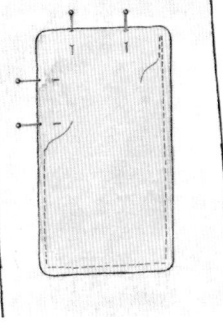
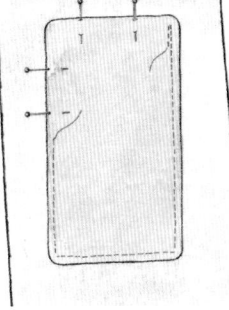

How to Hand-Sew the Patch

1 On the right side of the garment, center and pin the patch over the hole.

2 Backstitch (see page 67) the patch to the garment.

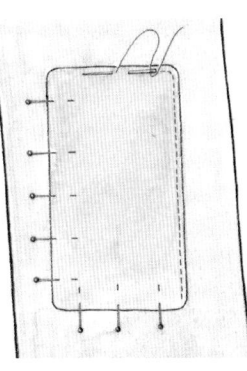

finishing the edges

If you didn't press under the edges of the patch before applying it, you'll want to finish them in one of the following ways to keep them neat through wearing, washing, and drying.

medium- to heavyweight fabric patches: Minimize bulk by attaching the patch without turning under the edges. After edge-stitching the patch to the right side of the garment, set the machine to the widest possible zigzag stitch and a stitch length between 10 and 12 stitches per inch (2.5 cm).

Attach an embroidery presser foot to the sewing machine. With the right side up, position the patch so the cut edge is slightly to the right of the needle. Sew around the patch so that the zigzag stitch spans the cut raw edge of the patch. Pivot at corners, if there are any.

patches of any weight: Edge-stitch the patch in place, leaving the edges raw. Then, outline the raw edges of the patch with decorative fabric paint.

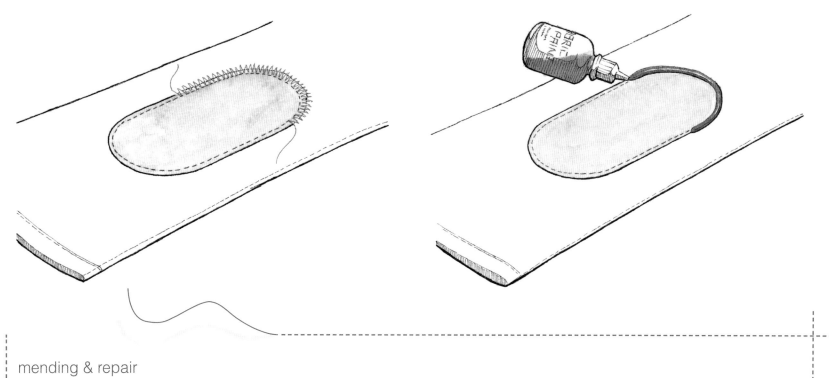

mending & repair

patching on the wrong side

A patch applied to the wrong side is less visible than one applied to the right side. Apply it with a fusible product or sew it. If the fabric ravels a lot, it's best to sew it (see page 211). If you are fusing the patch, you may need to reinforce the edge of the hole with small zigzag stitches or liquid fray preventer to prevent raveling. In either case, use the gentle cycle whenever you launder the mended item.

Fusing a Patch to the Wrong Side

1. Trim the ragged edges from the hole. Cut a piece of matching fabric and a piece of paper-backed fusible web, both 1/2" (1.3 cm) larger than the hole.

2. Center the fabric hole over the paper side of the fusible web. With a pencil, mark the outline of the hole through the fabric onto the paper. Cut out the outlined shape at the center of the fusible web patch to create a ring.

3. Press the fusible web ring to the right side of the fabric patch, following the manufacturer's instructions.

4. Remove the paper backing and position the patch on the wrong side of the garment, so that the right side of the fabric, but not the fusible web ring, is visible through the hole. Fuse the patch in place.

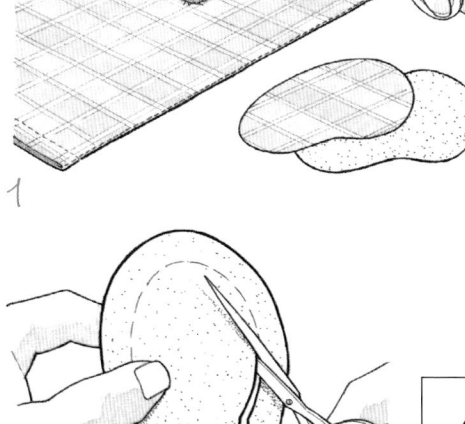

1

2

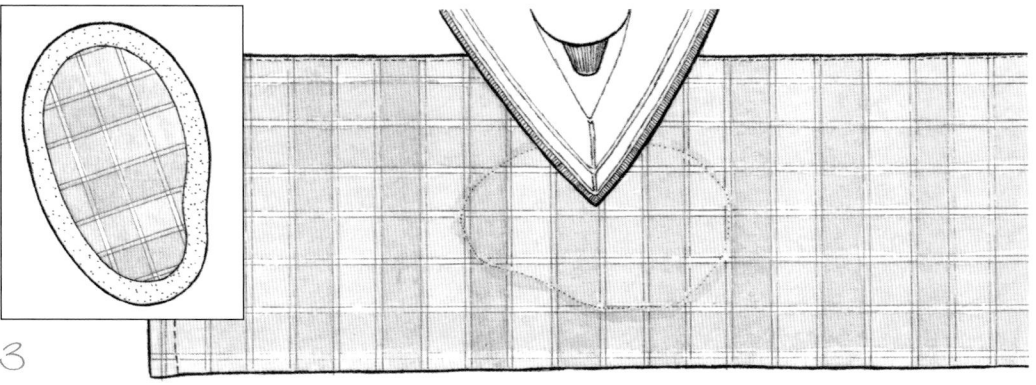

3

4

Sewing a patch to the wrong side

1 Trim the ragged edges from the hole to form a square or rectangle. Snip 1/2" (1.3 cm) diagonally into each corner of the hole. Cut a patch of fabric (matching any stripes, plaids, or pattern) so that it is at least 1" (2.5 cm) longer and wider than the hole.

2 Press the edges of the hole to the wrong side.

3 Cover the hole by pinning the patch inside the garment, right side of patch to wrong side of garment, matching any patterns.

4 Working from the inside of the garment, machine-stitch one side of the patch to the folded-back edge of the hole, sewing along the pressed-in fold. Don't catch the outer layers of the garment in the stitching. Backstitch at the beginning and end of the seam.

5 Repeat step 4 for each side. Trim the patch edges to align with the folded-back edges of the hole. If the fabric ravels, pink or overcast the raw edges of the seams.

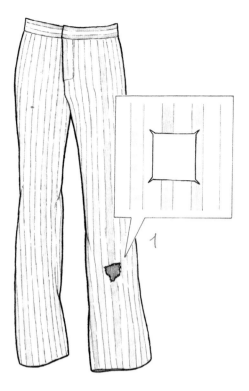

1

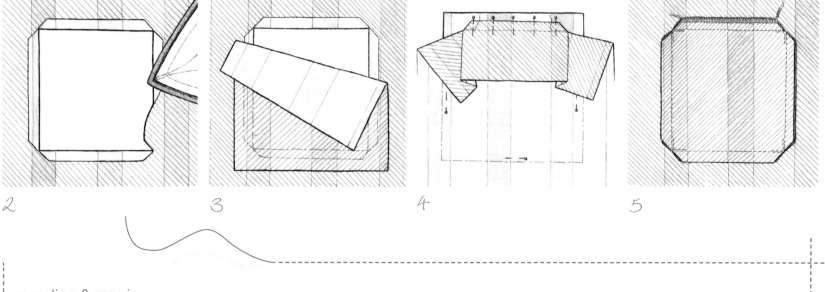

2   3   4   5

thread snags & pulls

Sometimes a snagged thread is as unsightly as a hole or tear. Both knit and woven fabrics, especially those with a loose weave structure, can get caught on jewelry, buttons, or hooks, or any number of other objects you brush against. Don't cut the pulled thread away, or you might end up with a big hole! Instead, try these methods for pushing the snagged thread back into the fabric—or at least to the wrong side where it won't show and can't get snagged again.

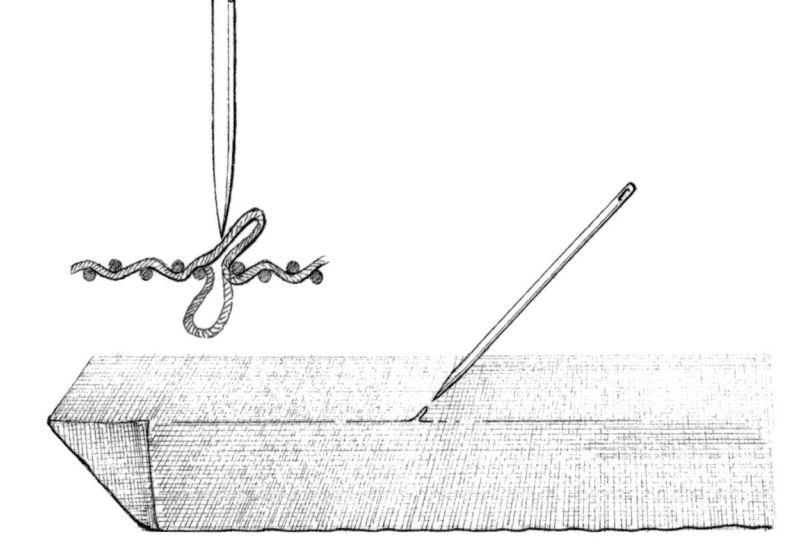

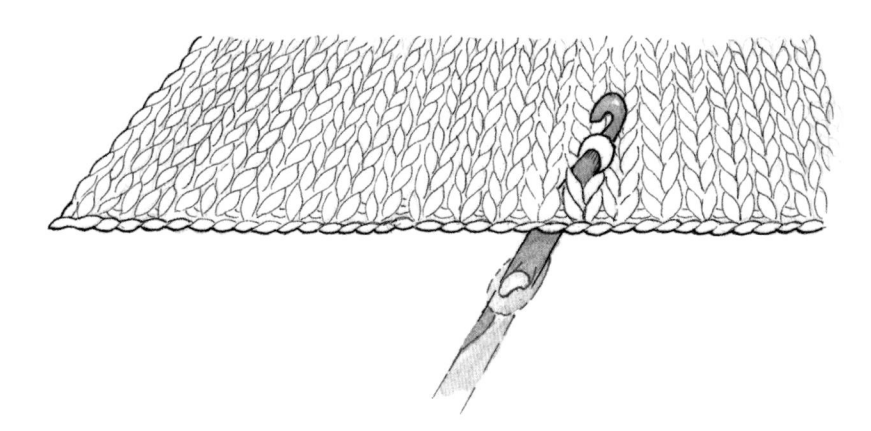

on woven fabrics: Push the thread loop to the wrong side of the garment. Manipulating the thread can be tricky on lightweight and fine fabrics, but if you work under good light it shouldn't be a problem.

Use a needle or very small crochet hook to push the snag through the other threads to the wrong side of the fabric. Hand-sew two or three backstitches over the pulled thread, or dab a liquid fray preventer on the area.

on knit fabrics: Try stretching the fabric gently, just enough so that the snag is pulled back into the fabric.

If this doesn't work, insert a small crochet hook from the wrong side of the fabric next to the snag on the right side. Catch the loop of pulled yarn in the hook and pull it to the wrong side of the fabric. Make a loop with the yarn and pull the end through to form a knot.

repairing straight seams

It's easy to repair seams—because most often they are straight lines of stitching that just need to be reinforced. You can repair seams by hand with a backstitch or machine-stitch them with a straight stitch.

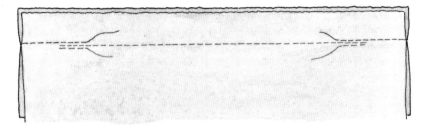

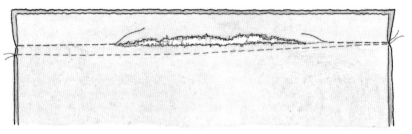

Simple Ripped Seam

Press the seam allowances together. Then cut away the broken threads. Hand- or machine-stitch across the unstitched area, following the original seam line.

Stitch 1" (2.5 cm) beyond the tear at both ends backstitching to secure the thread.

Ripped Seam with Frayed or Torn Fabric

Stabilize the fabric on both sides of the seam before you attempt to fix it. Cut two pieces of medium-weight fusible interfacing that are long enough to cover the tear and about 1" (2.5 cm) wide.

Fuse one piece to the wrong side of the fabric on each side of the seam, pulling together the torn edges of the tear to bond them closed with the fusible. Restitch the seam as you would for a simple ripped seam.

Ripped Seam in a Loose-Fitting Item

If there is enough extra room in the item or garment, sew a slightly wider seam allowance.

Begin the new line of stitching well above the end of the tear and parallel to the original line of stitching, increasing the amount of fabric in the seam allowance. The tear in the fabric will be concealed and enough out of the way so it won't cause further damage.

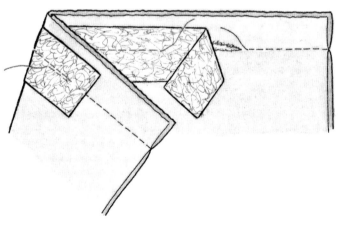

mending & repair

reinforcing stressed seams

When a seam rips in a high-stress location—such as an underarm, pocket, dart, or vent—it is important to reinforce the fabric, so the seam doesn't rip again.

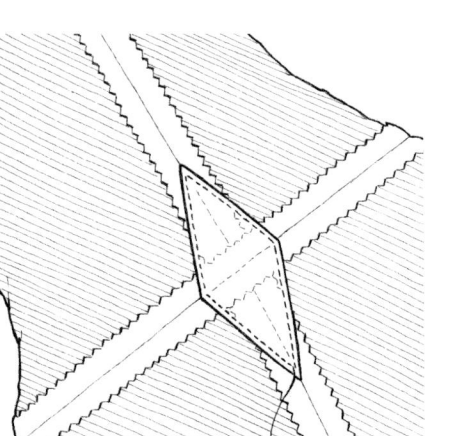

Underarm Seams

Underarms often rip because they are so well used. Resew the seam patch, then patch.

Cut a lightweight muslin patch in the shape of a diamond, about 4" (10.2 cm) long and 1¹/₂" (4 cm) at its widest point. Press ¹/₄" (6 mm) of the edges to the wrong side of the fabric. Center and pin the patch on top of the underarm seam. Stitch along the patch edges and over the seam line, through all layers.

Darts

To repair a dart, turn the garment inside out and pin along the fold of the dart. Redraw the stitching line with a fabric-marking pen. Straight-stitch by machine or backstitch by hand along the marked line, tapering gently toward the point. Tie the thread ends into a knot at the point.

Vents and Slits

If only the vent seam is ripped, turn the garment inside out and stitch over the previous seam line, as you would for a simple straight seam (see page 213).

Unfortunately, when a vent or slit rips open, the fabric frequently rips, too. Reinforce the fabric with a patch before repairing the seam. Remove the stitches that hold the vent facings in place, and press the facings and seam allowances together.

Patch the torn fabric by applying fusible interfacing on the wrong side. Resew the seam. Press the vent facings back into position, then hand-sew them to secure.

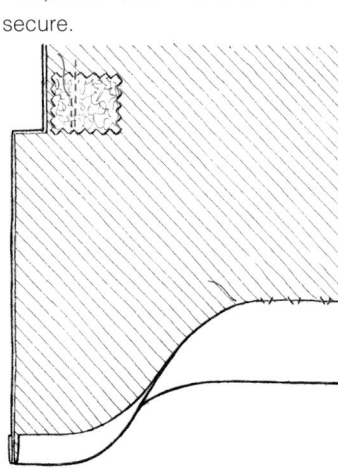

mending patch pockets

The edge stitching that holds a pocket in place sometimes breaks—most often, at the top corners—because of the stress the wearer causes by inserting hands, keys, and other heavy or bulky objects. You can reattach a patch pocket with a hand-worked backstitching, but a machine-stitched repair will be stronger.

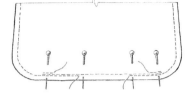

When the stitching on a patch pocket breaks, remove all the strands of broken thread. Pin the pocket to the fabric and restitch on the previous stitching line, starting and finishing 1" (2.5 cm) beyond the intact stitches. Backstitch at the beginning and end of your stitching line.

When the top corner of a patch pocket comes unstitched, you need to add a reinforcing fabric patch on the inside of the garment. Cut a small square of muslin and fusible web. Fuse the fabric patch to the wrong side of the garment, over the weakened or torn area.

Then, restitch the top corners with one of several reinforcing stitch options. You can either:

- Stitch a narrow zigzag stitch for about 5/8" (1.5 cm), just inside the edge stitching.
- Sew a small triangle of straight stitches. To make sure they are all the same size, measure and mark 3/4" (2 cm) from the corner across the top and side edges. Join the markings with a diagonal stitching line.
- Backstitch 5/8" (1.5 cm) directly over the edge- or topstitching.

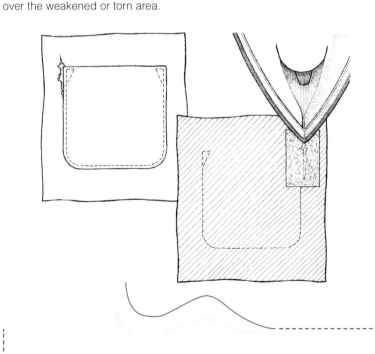

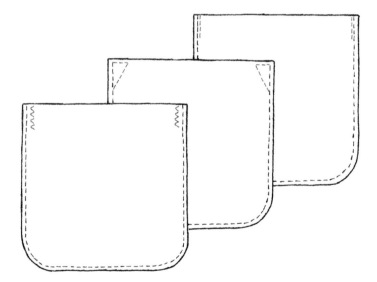

repairing in-seam pockets

In-seam pockets can tear either in the bag of the pocket or at the garment seam. Both types of tears are easy to fix.

in-seam pocket bags: Pocket bags are subject to a lot of wear and tear. If you fix the broken stitching as soon as it rips, you won't lose anything out of your pocket.

Machine- or hand-stitch directly over the torn stitching line, beginning and ending 1" (2.5 cm) beyond the rip. Be sure to backstitch at the beginning and end of the new stitching.

in-seam pockets at the garment seam: The bottom of the pocket opening is subject to a lot of friction. If the garment seam starts to open, turn the garment inside out and press the side seam allowances together, with the pocket extending away from the seam.

Re-stitch over the seam line, starting and ending 1" (2.5 cm) beyond the torn area, and backstitching at both ends. If the fabric has ripped, fuse a patch over the broken stitching to strengthen the area, then restitch the seam. Backstitch at the beginning and end of the new stitching.

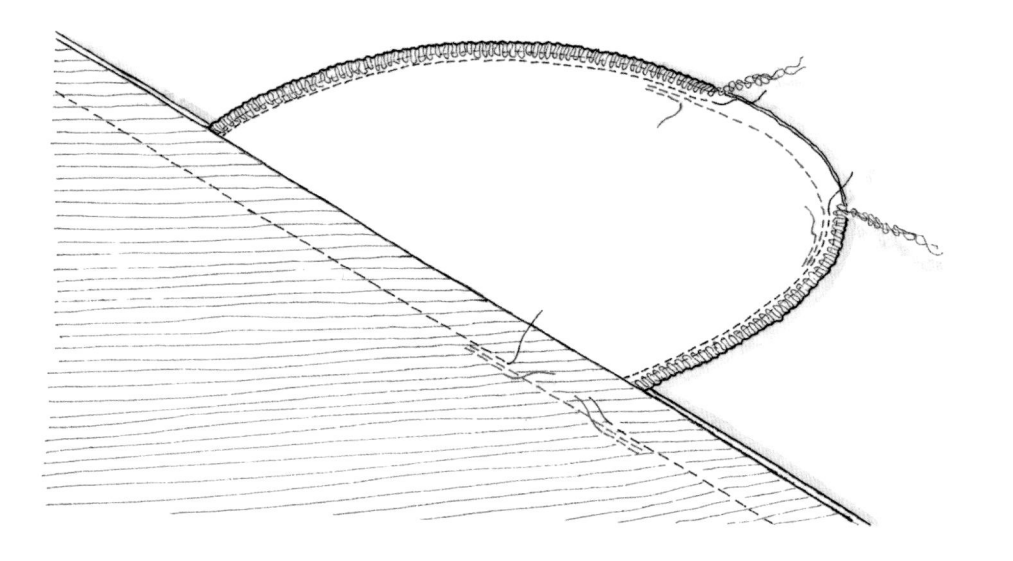

If a pocket bag is badly tattered, cut it away and sew the pocket closed.

reattaching decorative trim

Decorative trim is designed to be seen, so when it frays, tears, or comes undone, it's usually pretty noticeable—and unattractive. Fix the trim right away with a few stitches or fabric glue, and it will be as good as new. Notice how the trim was originally attached and follow the same method for the repair.

frayed ends: Ribbon, cording, and other flat trims tend to fray if the ends are not caught in a seam. Zigzag-stitch over the ends with matching thread, to prevent more raveling and to keep the ends flat and less noticeable. You can also dab liquid fray preventer, fabric glue, or even clear nail polish on the ends.

loose trim: Secure a loose section of trim or appliqué with basting tape, fabric glue, or a fusible web (see page 198). If the trim was sewn in place, stitch back over the missing stitches. If it was glued in place, apply pressure and heat, if necessary, to make sure the adhesive sets.

lost trim: Rhinestones, sequins, and beads often fall off the fabric surface. It's fairly easy to find matches in fabric and craft stores. Sew or glue the replacements in place (see pages 262 and 263).

If you can't find acceptable replacement pieces, you might want to consider replacing all of the rhinestones, sequins, or beads so they match—a big job! You can also remove a piece from a less obvious area of the item and reposition it where you need it.

repairing edge finishes

Edge finishes and embellishments are often subject to a lot of wear—even when the rest of the item is still in good shape. Repairing the edges of a garment, accessory, or soft furnishing will extend their life.

piping or welting comes unstitched: Piping or welting is inserted into a seam. Sometimes the seam opens, letting the trim hang loose. To put the item back together, turn it inside out. Pin the seam closed, along the previous stitching, sandwiching the piping in place as it originally was.

Attach a zipper foot to your machine. Begin and end stitching 1/2" (1.3 cm) beyond the tear, and stitch the seam closed.

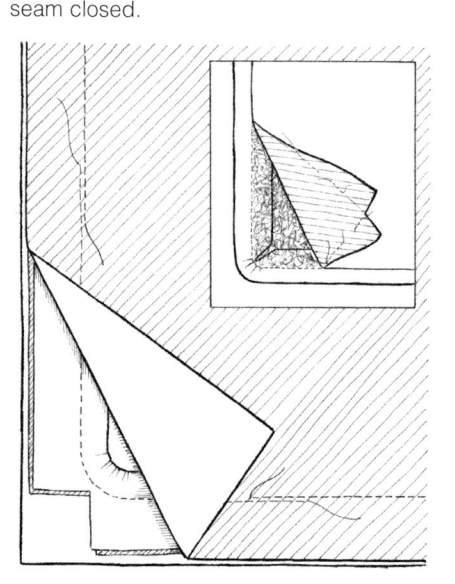

binding tears away from the fabric edge: Sometimes the fabric edge pulls out of its binding; this is common with the satin binding on blankets. With a seam ripper, remove the stitches that hold the binding in place 2" (5 cm) beyond the rip in both directions.

If the fabric edge is frayed, fuse a narrow strip of fusible interfacing to it to create a more stable edge. Trim the interfacing so it fits in the binding.

Fold the binding over the edge and pin. Edge-stitch the binding, starting and ending 1" (2.5 cm) beyond the opening.

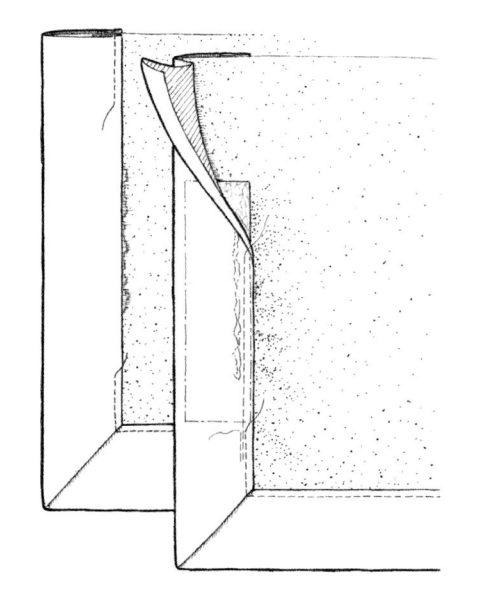

damaged trim: A snag, rip, or hole in a decorative trim is hard to repair without removing the entire length of trim. Instead, consider adding a second trim to cover the damaged area.

Lay a length of ribbon over damaged trim and stitch along both edges to secure it.

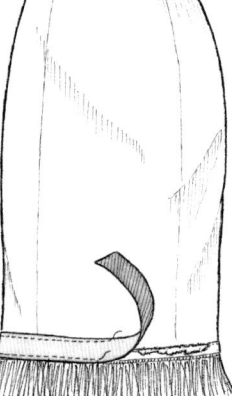

Make sure the care requirements of trim and fabric are the same. You might need to prewash the trim so it doesn't shrink in the wash.

about closures

When a plain white button falls off your favorite shirt, it doesn't mean you have to put a plain white button back on. Just because the snaps keep popping open on your son's pants, you don't have to toss them into the rag bag. And if the zipper feels lumpy on your duvet cover, you don't have to toss off the bedcovers.

There are many kinds of closures—buttons, snaps, hooks and eyes, zippers, hook-and-loop tape, and drawstrings, to name a few. Closures help you open and close your clothing, bags, and other fabric items. When they work, you hardly notice them. When they break or fall off, you notice!

It's easy to replace exactly what was there—but it's also easy to change the fastener to something more interesting, decorative, or effective if you prefer.

There are two types of situations that require closures, and each requires different types. Once you know that, you can get as creative as you want when it's time to replace or mend.

overlapping edges: Choose buttons, snaps, hooks and eyes, or hook-and-loop tape (also known by its trade name, Velcro).

abutting edges: Opt for zippers, decorative and functional hooks and eyes, and drawstrings.

- Buttons are like miniature works of art. You only need to be sure that the new button fits through the original buttonhole (if you're using the buttonholes), and that the weight of the button is compatible with the weight of the fabric.

- Rough and textured buttons are easier to grasp if you have special needs or arthritic fingers.

- Replace snaps and hooks and eyes with small squares or circles of hook-and-loop tape, which is easier to manipulate.

- If you don't like the bulk and the ripping sound of hook-and-loop tape, sew on snaps or hooks and eyes instead.

- Replace a zipper closing with multiple tie closures, evenly spaced across the opening.

- Sew-on snaps are not strong enough to hold overlapping edges in high-stress areas. Substitute hook-and-loop tape or gripper snaps.

- Position the loop-shaped eye of a hook and eye set so that it extends beyond the fabric edge—for a neat, secure, but unobtrusive finish at the top of a zipper or in lingerie and bridal wear.

choosing replacement buttons

If a button falls off, just sew it back on the same spot (see page 109). If you lose a button, you have a few options. Start by identifying the style you need: sew-through (flat, with two or four holes), or shank (raised up on a neck or small loop).

If you decide to simply buy a replacement button, take the garment with you to the store to shop for a match. As long as you buy the same size and style, it will fit through the buttonhole. If you can't find the same button, consider replacing all the buttons so they match.

- Check inside the garment along the side seams for an extra button supplied by the manufacturer.

- Remove a button from the lower edge of the garment, especially if it's a shirt that you tuck in. Replace the lower button with any button of similar size. You can also "borrow" buttons from inside waistbands and substitute same-size buttons there.

- Replace the top button on a garment with a unique, antique, or jeweled button, and use the top button to replace the one you've lost.

- Remove a button from a shirt cuff and roll the cuffs instead of buttoning them.

- To camouflage the mismatched button, change a couple of the other buttons, too, to create a decorative "mix and match" style of closure.

- Cover all the buttons with decorative button covers (sold in craft, fabric, and specialty stores and catalogues) to hide the fact that your replacement button isn't a match.

- Buy a fabric-covered button kit and make matching fabric-covered buttons with small pieces of fabric cut from the hem or facing of the garment. Instructions are included in the kit.

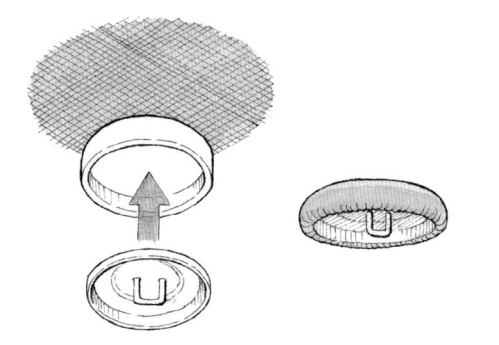

Keep a button box or jar filled with assorted buttons. Remove any wonderful buttons — and plain white shirt buttons, too — from clothes and other items that you're discarding.

multiple buttons & fabric mends

Whether you're faced with a lot of buttons to sew on, or a nasty fabric tear under a button, there's an easy way to approach the task.

Attaching Buttons by Machine

When you need to attach several sew-through buttons, you might want to use your sewing machine. Attach a button-sewing presser foot (check your manual).

1   Set the machine for a zigzag stitch, with the stitch length at zero.

2   Place the button under the button presser foot, with one hole under the needle. If you need to create a thread shank (a shank makes it easier to button garments made from heavy fabrics), lay a toothpick on top of the button.

3   Adjust the stitch width so the needle goes in and out of the two holes with each stitch. Take several stitches.

4   If the button has four holes, stitch the first two holes. Raise the needle and presser foot and slide the button so the needle goes through the remaining holes. Pull the top thread to the wrong side and knot.

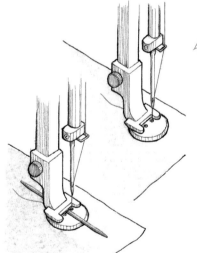

Repairing Torn Fabric

Sometimes, the fabric under a button weakens or tears. You'll need to reinforce the fabric before resewing the button.

1   Cut off any loose threads around the hole.

2   Cut a small patch of fabric, backed with fusible web, or fusible mending tape into a circle or oval that is a little larger than the hole.

3   If there is a facing in the item, insert the patch between the facing and the outer fabric. If there is no facing, place the patch on the wrong side of the fabric. To fuse the patch, follow the manufacturer's instructions.

4   Stitch over and across the patch. The stitches should extend slightly beyond the edge of the patch and be invisible on the right side of the fabric. Sew the button, stitching through the patch and creating a thread shank (see page 109).

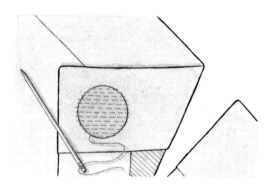

fixing frayed buttonholes

Repair a buttonhole as soon as you notice that it's fraying. You want to fix it before more of the stitches tear or the fabric stretches.

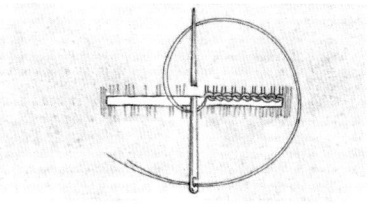

1

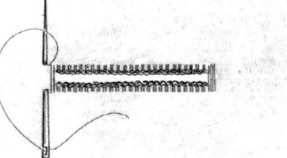

2

Working by Hand

Thread the needle with a double length of thread that matches the existing thread. Trim away any loose threads to neaten the buttonhole area.

1   Insert the needle to the right of the torn stitches on the wrong side of the fabric. Take two or three backstitches. Pull the needle up through the opening and take enough buttonhole stitches (see page 68) to cover the frayed and torn area.

   If the entire buttonhole is weak, stitch over the existing stitches all the way around the buttonhole. Pull the thread firmly, but not too tightly, so that the loops fall exactly on the edge of the buttonhole.

2   Restitch the bar tacks if necessary.

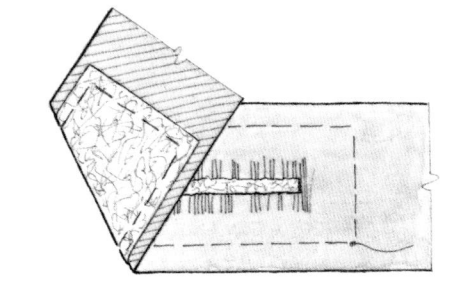

1

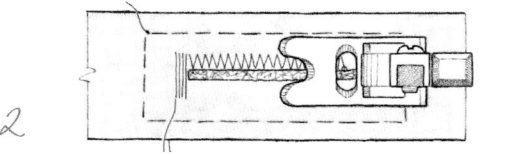

2

Working by Machine

Before repairing a buttonhole by machine, make a practice row of narrow and short zigzag stitches on scrap fabric. Make sure the stitches resemble the original buttonhole stitches.

1   Carefully remove the frayed stitches. Baste or fuse a small piece of stabilizer or interfacing around the back of the buttonhole to support the area. Make sure the two buttonhole edges are close together, but not touching.

2   On the right side of the fabric, zigzag-stitch over the frayed area, starting and continuing slightly beyond the frayed area.

If the buttonhole is just starting to fray, dab it with Fray Check to keep it from getting any worse.

making a new buttonhole

If a buttonhole is frayed beyond repair, you can easily stitch a new one with the sewing machine. Either use the built-in buttonhole function, if your machine has one, or follow these easy steps to make a bar-tack buttonhole.

Preparing the Buttonhole

1   Working with a seam ripper, remove any remaining buttonhole stitches from the wrong side of the fabric. Pull out the remaining thread bits with tweezers. Mark the ends (just outside the bar tacks) of the old buttonhole with a fabric-marking pen.

2   Fuse a piece of interfacing or baste tear-away stabilizer to the wrong side of the fabric under the old buttonhole, to hold the opening closed.

Making a Bar-Tack Buttonhole

1   Attach a zigzag or buttonhole presser foot to your machine. Lower the foot over the center marking. Set the machine for a very short stitch length and stitch three or four wide zigzag stitches across the end to form the first bar tack.

2   Reduce the stitch width. Zigzag-stitch down one side of the buttonhole opening to the other marked end.

3   Reset for the wider zigzag stitch setting and sew the remaining bar tack.

4   Adjust the machine setting for a narrow zigzag stitch. Turn the fabric around. Stitch the opposite side, back to the first bar tack. Make one or two small stitches to secure threads.

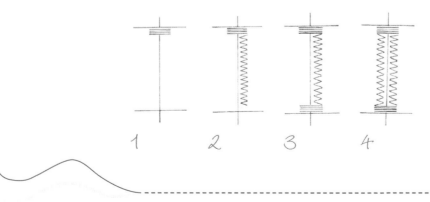

Cutting Open the Buttonhole

Be careful not to cut through the bar tacks. Insert straight pins just inside the bar tack at each end of the buttonhole. With sharp scissors or a seam ripper, carefully cut along the center of the buttonhole between the rows of zigzag stitches.

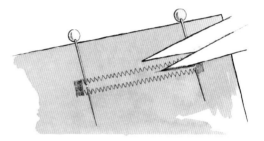

quick fixes for buttonholes

Buttonholes that are subject to a lot of stress—for example, at a waist-band or bust line—can easily tear, along with the fabric around them. Luckily, button-holes with tears, stretched fabric, and loose stitching can be repaired with a quick fix.

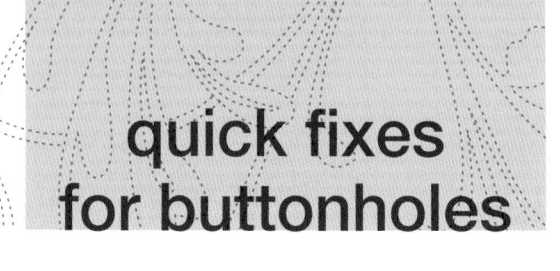

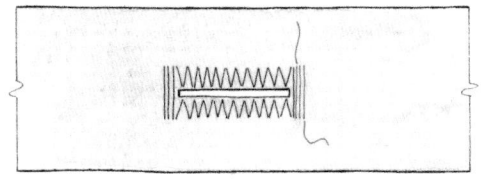

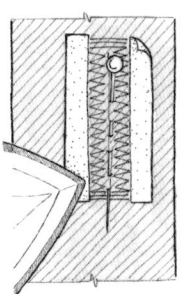

torn fabric: If the fabric tears at one or both ends of the buttonhole, mend it by fusing a fabric patch to the wrong side to hold the torn edges together. Fuse a patch of similar color and weight as the fabric.

Darn over the tear (see page 204). Restitch the torn buttonhole stitches, following the instructions on page 222.

torn bar tack: To strengthen a bar tack, sew several wide, closely spaced zigzag stitches over the ripped stitches.

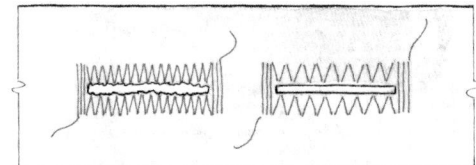

rippled buttonholes: If the buttonhole stitching is too dense in a knit or stretch fabric, the buttonhole will ripple. Stabilize the area with a scrap of fusible interfacing and pull out the old buttonhole with a seam ripper. Restitch a new buttonhole using a longer zigzag stitch.

stretched-out buttonholes: Pin the buttonhole closed. Stabilize the area by fusing two narrow strips of interfacing as close as possible to each side of the buttonhole on the wrong side of the fabric.

gaping buttonholes: On the wrong side of the fabric, run a heavy thread under one row of stitches, around one end, and back up under the opposite row. Pull the thread slightly to straighten the buttonhole. Knot the ends and hide the knot under the stitches.

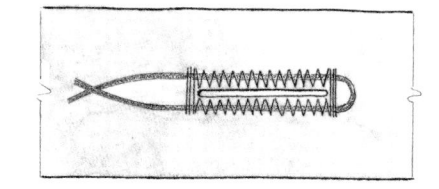

Shorten a buttonhole that keeps popping open by sewing several wide zigzag stitches inside one or both bar tacks.

creative buttonhole repairs

Want a more creative fix for torn or frayed buttonholes? You have several choices. Color-blocked patches, ribbon trim, fabric bands, and even purchased appliqués are great ways to cover damaged or torn buttonholes. The challenge is to make the repair look like part of the design.

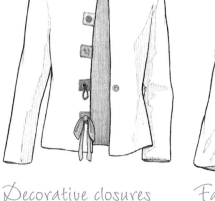

Fabric ties

Before applying a new closure, remove the buttons. Pin any facing off to the side so you don't catch it in the repair. Fuse a small piece of interfacing to the wrong side of the fabric to permanently close the buttonholes or hand-stitch them closed.

fabric ties: Sew your own ties from fabric or decorative trim or cording. Cut two lengths, making sure they are long enough to tie in a knot or bow. Trim later. Topstitch one tie so it covers the buttonhole. Topstitch the other to the right of the original button location. Knot the ties to close.

flat trim: Fuse or baste a length of flat ribbon or trim along both edges of the opening, covering the but-

tonholes and button locations. Fold the ends of the trim under to conceal them. Edge-stitch by machine to secure the trim in place.

fabric patches and decorative closures: Cut fabric or leather patches to cover the buttonholes. If the patch fabric ravels, fold the edges to the wrong side. Fuse and then topstitch the patches in place. Sew decorative buttons, toggles, or bows over the patches. Sew metal snaps or hooks and eyes on the inside to keep the garment closed.

fabric flower or appliqué: When you have sewn or fused the buttonhole closed, pin a large fabric flower over it, or hand-sew an appliqué in place to cover it. Sew a metal hook and eye on the inside of the opening to securely close the garment.

Flat trim   Decorative closures   Fabric flower

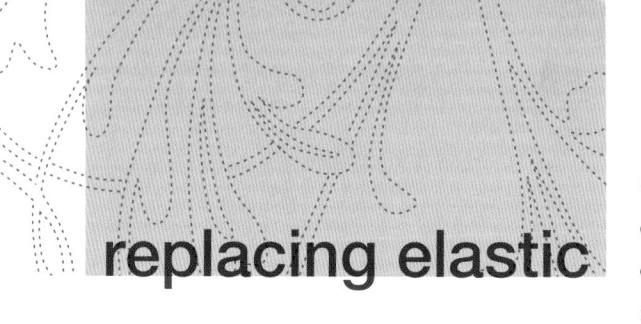

replacing elastic

Elastic is a narrow, flexible, stretchable strip that is either enclosed in a casing or stitched directly onto a garment. Time and many trips through a hot clothes dryer can damage elastic, causing it to stretch and lose recovery (the ability to spring back to size). To replace elastic, measure the width of the existing elastic and replace it with a strip of the same type and size. If you plan to sew the elastic to the garment, cut it slightly shorter because it will stretch while you are stitching.

Applied Elastic

1   With a seam ripper (see page 197), remove the stitches that hold the existing elastic. If you are replacing elastic on a sleeve or pant hem, convert your sewing machine to a free arm to make it easier to sew (check your machine manual). Or, open the seam far enough so you can flatten the area to make it easier to sew.

Divide the area where you will apply the elastic into four equal sections. Mark with pins. Divide and pin-mark the elastic into equal fourths, too. Leave the width of the seam allowance free at both ends of the elastic and the garment section.

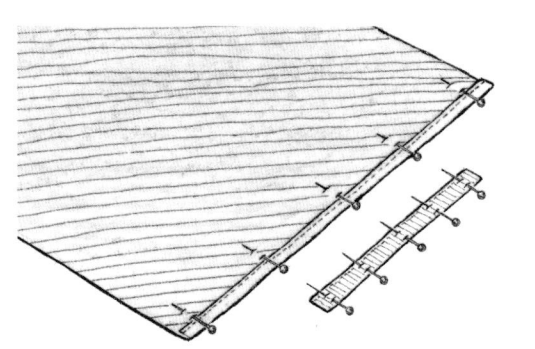

2   Pin the elastic to the wrong side of the garment, matching the quarter markings on the elastic and the fabric. Leave the seam allowances free at each end. Add pins as needed to stretch the elastic across the entire length of fabric. The fabric will gather.

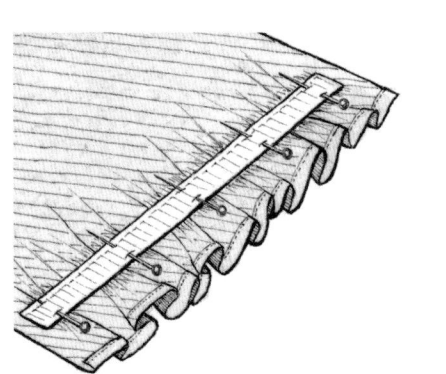

3   Zigzag-stitch the elastic to the fabric, stretching it between the pins. Hold the fabric taut with one hand behind the presser foot and the other hand in front of the foot. Let the feed dogs move the fabric.

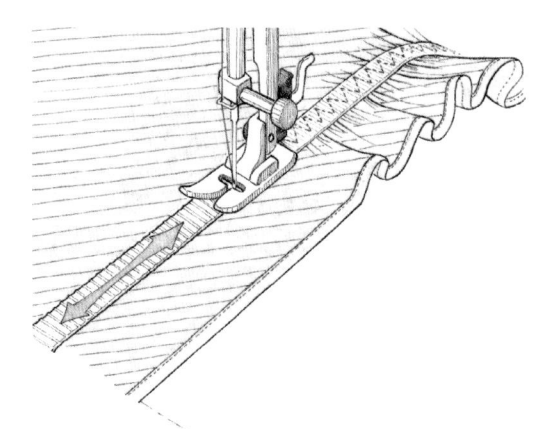

Elastic in a Casing

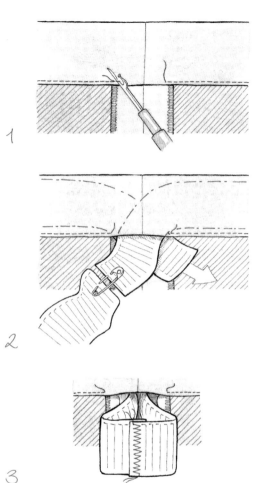

1 Remove about 1" (2.5 cm) of the casing stitches with a seam ripper (see page 197). Work in an unobtrusive area, such as the side seam, and along the lower edge of the casing.

2 Pull a tiny bit of elastic out of the opening and cut it. With a safety pin, join one of the cut ends to one end of the new elastic. Round off the corners of the new elastic so it moves through the casing more easily.

Pull the unpinned end of the old elastic out of the casing, drawing the new elastic into the casing. Leave the last 2" (5 cm) of the new elastic exposed at each end.

3 Unpin and remove the old elastic from the end of the casing. Make sure the new elastic lies flat inside the casing. Overlap and join the ends of the new elastic by hand or zigzag stitch by machine.

4 Stretch the elastic to pull the ends into the casing and distribute any gathers in the fabric. Edge-stitch or hand-stitch the opening closed, being careful not to catch the elastic in the stitches.

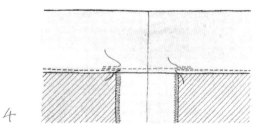

To determine how much elastic you need, wrap the new elastic around your body (at waist, wrist, or ankle) and add 1" (2.5 cm) for finishing the ends.

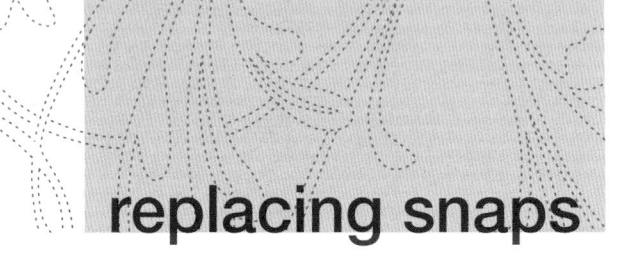

replacing snaps

A snap that keeps popping open doesn't do much good. It just needs to be replaced. Traditional ball-and-socket snaps are great for overlapping edges that aren't subject to a lot of strain. You'll find snap tape on babies' clothing and some home décor items.

If one side of a gripper snap falls off or is torn off, you'll have to replace both elements to ensure the right fit. Cut around the snap pieces, then patch the holes (see page 206). Following the instructions in the snap and applicator package, apply new ball and socket pieces over the patches.

Ball-and-Socket Snaps

1 Attach the ball section to the wrong side of the overlap, close to the edge. Take three or four straight stitches through each hole. Take care that your stitches don't go through to the right side of the garment. Secure with two or three backstitches and a knot near the snap.

2 Position the socket so it aligns with the ball section and sew it to the fabric as in step 1. Your stitches can go through the fabric because they'll be hidden inside the garment.

Snap Tape

If a single snap on a strip of snap tape stops working, the other snaps will probably keep the garment or item closed. If they don't, however, remove both pieces of snap tape by picking out the stitching that holds it in place.

Pin the two halves of a new tape in place. Double-check that the ball and socket elements align properly. Working with a zipper foot, edge-stitch by machine through all layers of the tape and fabric.

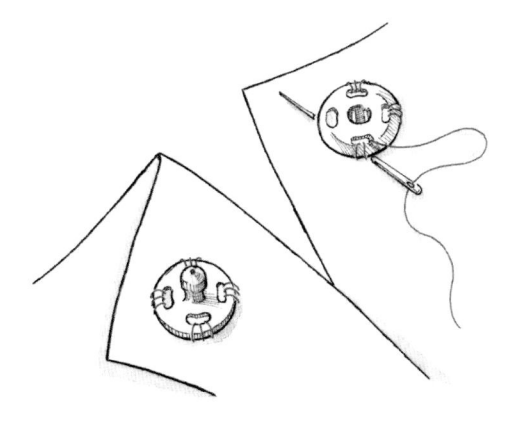

replacing hook fasteners

Hooks and eyes and hook-and-loop tape are simple and unobtrusive fasteners. They keep your garments securely closed without adding bulk. When they fall off, you soon realize how important they are. Note and mark the location of the original fasteners before replacing them.

Hooks and Eyes

Hooks and eyes are usually found at the top of a zipper and on fur garments. This two-part fastener comes in several shapes and sizes and is easy to replace.

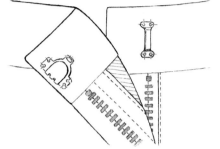

1. Sew the hook section on the underside of the overlap about 1/8" (3 mm) from the edge. Take four or five small, straight stitches around each hole, picking up only one or two threads of fabric so the stitches don't show on the right side.

2. Stitch two or three stitches across and under the hook to keep it flat. Secure the stitching with several small backstitches and a knot buried under the thread.

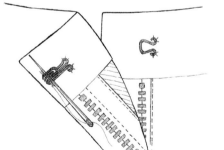

3. Position the eye in place, either so the fabric overlaps or so the edges meet (for example, at the top of a centered zipper), and stitch around the holes as in step 1.

4. If the eye extends beyond the fabric edge, take two small stitches on each side to better secure it. Take several backstitches on the wrong side and knot the thread.

Hook-and-Loop Tape

Hook-and-loop tape, commonly called Velcro, is a popular tape fastener because it's easy for children and people with weak fingers to manipulate. It's also easy to topstitch in place.

If the stitching breaks, just restitch around the edges. If you need to replace the tape, remove the two halves with a seam ripper and replace with new pieces. You can sew them on by hand, but its easier—and more durable—to machine-sew them.

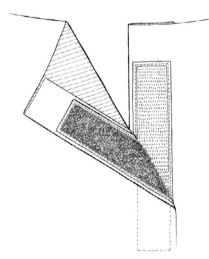

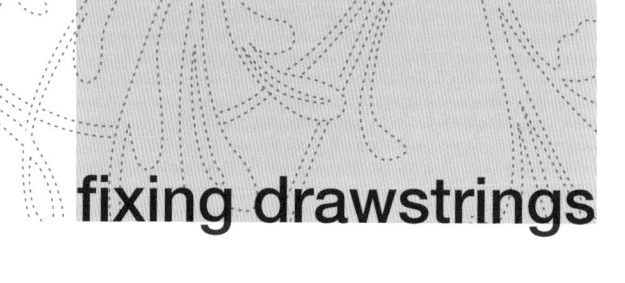

fixing drawstrings

Don't despair if the drawstring in your favorite pants pulls out—it's easy to replace it and to make sure that it doesn't slip out again.

Reinserting a Drawstring

If one end of the drawstring has disappeared into the casing, pull out the entire string. Attach a safety pin to one end and insert it into the casing.

Push and pull the safety pin through the casing and out the opposite opening. Be careful not to pull the unpinned end of the drawstring all the way into the casing. Pull on both ends to even their lengths.

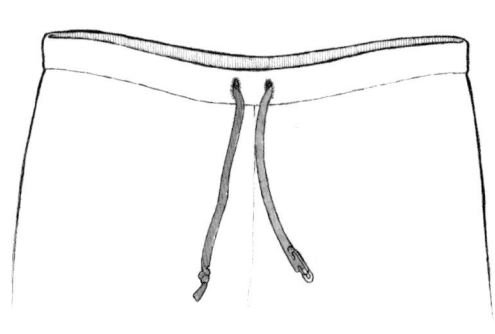

Keeping the Ends in Sight

To avoid losing the ends in the casing, make small overhand knots at each end. Or, at each end, sew a button, tassel, or charm that is too large to fit through the casing. You can also simply tie the ends together when you launder the item.

Securing the String

You can stitch the drawstring in place to secure it. Center the string inside the casing, so equal amounts extend from each opening. At the center of the casing, topstitch across the width of the casing and drawstring to secure the string in place.

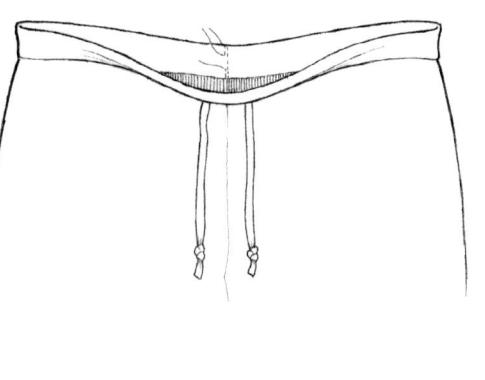

If the fabric around the casing opening is torn, remove the drawstring and darn the area as well as you can without sewing the casing closed.

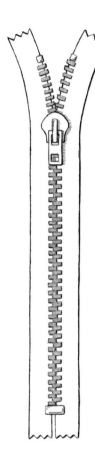

zipper care

Zippers are hard-working closures. They're strong, convenient to use, and can be decorative or practically invisible. These simple tips will keep your zippers in good working order and will ensure that they have a long life.

- Keep the zipper closed when you clean or store the item.

- When opening or closing the zipper, move fabric overlaps, seam allowances, and linings away from the teeth of the zipper so the fabric doesn't get caught. Trim any loose threads in the seams.

- If fabric or threads are caught in the zipper teeth, pull the slider down to dislodge them. Never try to force the slider up.

- Brush or hose off zippers in outdoor gear, if they have collected grit, salt, or sand.

- Press the zipper area with a cool to medium-hot iron. Don't lay the iron directly over the zipper coil or teeth.

- Fix broken topstitching immediately to prevent the entire zipper installation from weakening. Attach a zipper foot and machine-stitch directly over the stitching line to connect and reinforce the still-secure stitches.

Replacing a Zipper

Most zippers are so durable they outlive the rest of the item, but they sometimes break. Try a quick fix first (see pages 232 to 233), but if the zipper breaks a second time, you should replace it (see page 234). If the teeth or coil is damaged and the damage is not near the bottom of the zipper, the zipper probably needs to be replaced.

It isn't hard to replace a zipper, but it can be time-consuming—and in many cases it's best to work on a sewing machine. Before you take on the task yourself, call a tailor and see how much it will cost for a professional repair. Compare the expense of the repair with the cost of your free time, then decide whether the item is worth the money or the time!

repairing a zipper

It's much easier to repair a zipper than it is to replace it. Here's a list of common problems and some tips on how to fix them.

sticky zipper: Rub a candle, beeswax, or bar of soap along the teeth and then zip and unzip it a few times.

threads caught in zipper: Cut the threads with a seam ripper or sharp scissors at the point where they enter the slider. Pull out the cut threads.

fabric caught in zipper: Don't try to force the zipper open or closed. Gently pull the inside fabric (usually a lining) away from the zipper teeth or coil. Don't pull on the zipper itself.

If you can't release the fabric, carefully pry the slider or teeth off the fabric with needle-nose pliers. (The zipper might break, but it's easier to fix a zipper than to repair torn lining or fabric.)

missing teeth: If the missing tooth is near the top of the zipper, you need to replace the zipper. If a tooth is missing near the bottom of a closed-bottom zipper, move the slider above the gap.

Create a new zipper stop by stitching several straight stitches back and forth across the teeth just above the gap—or make a machine bar tack with zigzag stitches.

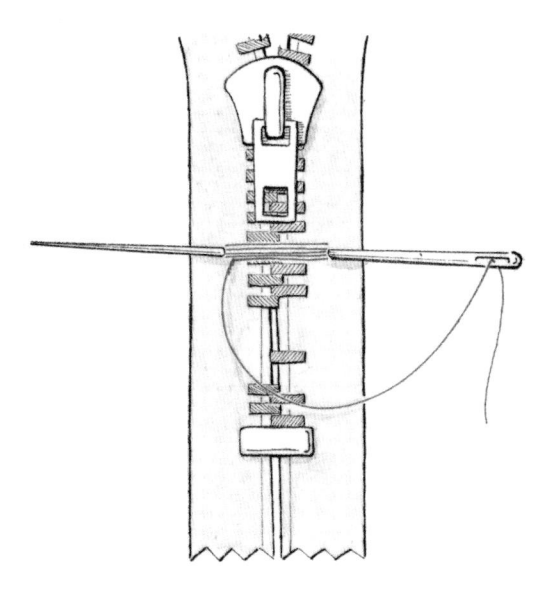

If the zipper pull is broken, you can add a decorative zipper pull that clips onto the slider. You may want to use one even if the zipper pull isn't broken!

fixing a zipper slider

The slider is the part of the zipper that opens and closes the zipper teeth or coil. Often, fixing or replacing the slider will solve your zipper problem. A pair of pliers might be all you need to return a broken zipper to good working order. Here's a list of symptoms and solutions:

slider separates from teeth or coil in the middle of the zipper: First, pry off the bottom metal stop with needle-nose pliers (or cut away the bottom 1/2" [1.3 cm] of the zipper, if that's easier). Move the slider all the way to the bottom of the zipper and off the zipper tape.

Realign the teeth and insert them back through the slider, so the zipper closes smoothly. Raise the slider. If the teeth aren't aligned and the zipper doesn't lie flat, pull the slider down and try again. Repeat until the zipper lies flat.

Close the zipper and hand-sew several straight stitches across the bottom of the zipper to create a new zipper stop. Alternatively, attach a new metal stop, as you would for a broken slider, as described below.

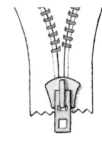

broken slider: Buy a new slider or a zipper repair kit. The kit includes a new slider and metal stops. Pry off the bottom stop with needle-nose pliers. Zip the old slider off the bottom of the zipper. Place the two zipper ends into the front two openings of the new slider. Hold the teeth together and move the slider up and down, aligning the teeth—this might take a few tries. Attach a new bottom stop by locking the ends of the metal stops around and under the zipper teeth. Or, sew the zipper closed across the bottom with several straight stitches or a zigzag bar tack (see page 232).

zipper separates in the middle or doesn't stay closed at the top: The slider is too loose. With pliers, gently squeeze the right and wrong sides of one half of the slider together then squeeze the other half of the slider together. Apply even pressure. If this technique doesn't work, replace the slider.

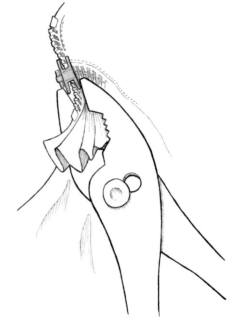

about replacing zippers

If you can't repair the zipper, you need to replace it. Prepare the new zipper by pressing the tape with a cool iron. Attach a zipper foot to your machine and adjust the needle or presser foot position so the needle is between the foot and the zipper teeth or coil.

Replacement guidelines

- Try to buy a zipper that is the same length and color as the broken zipper. If you can't find the same length, use one that is slightly shorter—or buy a longer zipper and shorten it.

- Mark the original zipper's stitching lines with a marking pen or tailor's chalk before removing it.

- Work with a seam ripper to remove the old zipper (see page 197). If the zipper is caught in a waistband or facing, unstitch the top edge about 1" (2.5 cm) on each side of the teeth or coil to release the zipper tape.

- Extend narrow seam allowances by stitching seam binding to the raw edges. The extensions will make it easier to install the new zipper.

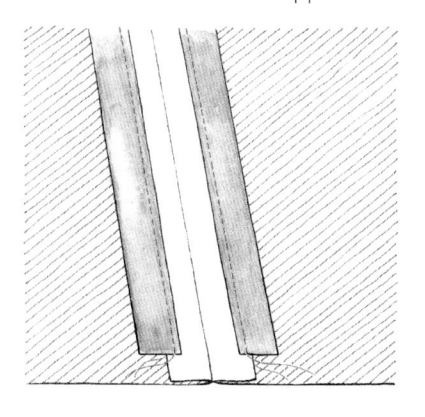

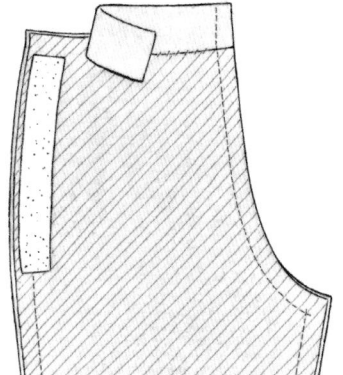
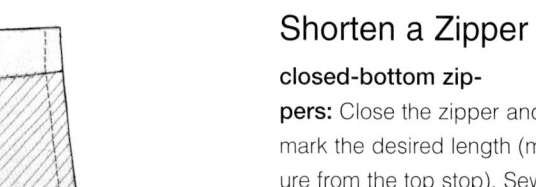

- Stabilize stretched or easily distorted fabric in the zipper area by fusing a narrow strip of interfacing to the wrong side of each seam allowance.

- Convert your machine to a free arm (check your owner's manual) to work more easily on a garment. If the zipper is in a tight or hard-to-reach spot, you might need to replace it by hand.

Shorten a Zipper

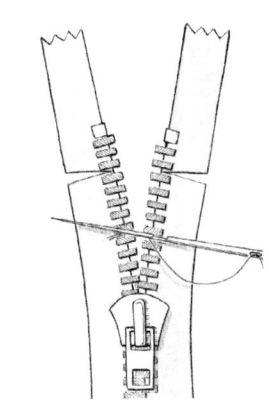

closed-bottom zippers: Close the zipper and mark the desired length (measure from the top stop). Sew a bar tack by machine or by hand (with several straight stitches). Stitch over the coil or teeth at the mark to make a new bottom stop. Trim the zipper 1/2" (1.3 cm) below the stitches.

separating zippers: Close the zipper. Measure from the bottom and mark the desired length on each side of the coil. Open the zipper and sew zigzag bar tacks at the marks on each side of the coil to form new top stops. Trim the excess zipper tape and remove the exposed coil with small, sharp scissors.

replacing a centered zipper

A centered zipper has two parallel rows of stitching that are each the same distance from the zipper opening in the garment. This zipper treatment is usually found in the center front or back of a dress or skirt and also in some pillow and cushion covers.

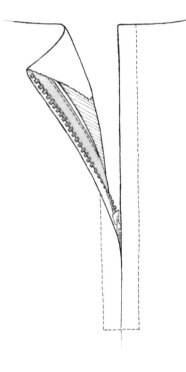

Working by Machine

Machine stitching is the best way to secure zippers that endure a lot of wear.

1 Mark the original stitching with a marking pen or tailor's chalk, using a ruler as a guide.

2 If the zipper is enclosed at the top by a facing, collar, or waistband, open the stitching at the ends of the enclosure with a seam ripper. Unstitch just enough to free the top of the zipper tape as shown in the drawing. Remove the stitches in the rest of the zipper.

3 Baste the zipper opening closed (see page 70). Press open the seam allowances.

4 With the zipper face down, center the teeth or coil over the basted seam line and position the top stop in the same location as the old top stop. Temporarily attach the zipper to the seam allowances, using a glue stick, basting tape, or basting stitches as shown in the drawing below.

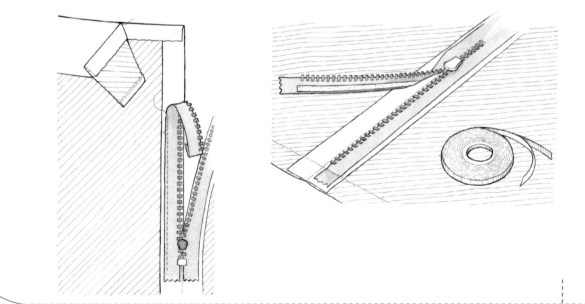

5   Attach the zipper foot so it is on the right side of the needle. Sew directly on the marked sewing lines, starting at the bottom of the zipper. Stitch across the bottom, beginning at the seam. Pivot at the corner and stitch up the side, as shown in the drawing below.

6   Adjust the zipper foot so it is on the left side of the needle. Again, stitch across the bottom of the zipper, beginning at the seam and pivoting at the corner. Stitch up the remaining side.

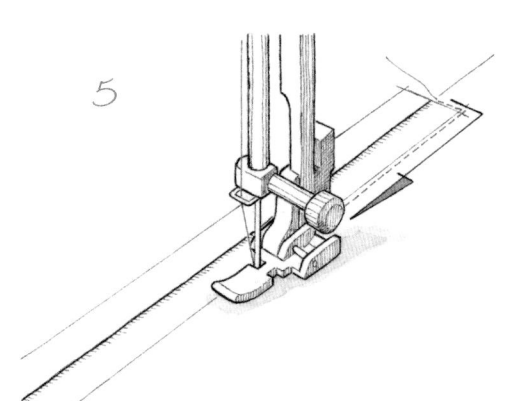

7   Remove basting and markings. Press with a press cloth.

8   Stitch the facing, collar, or waistband closed, catching the top of the zipper tape in the seam, as shown in the drawing below.

Working by Hand

Long centered zippers—especially in finished garments like dresses—are hard to reach with a sewing machine. When replacing this inaccessible type of zipper, it's best to work by hand to keep the zipper and fabric from rippling.

3   Follow steps 1 through 3 for replacing the zipper by machine.

4   Starting at the bottom of the zipper, hand-sew across the bottom and up one side of the zipper. With a backstitch or a pick stitch (see page 68), stitch directly over the stitch markings as shown at right.

3   Repeat step 2 on the opposite side of the zipper. Follow steps 7 and 8 of machine application (above left).

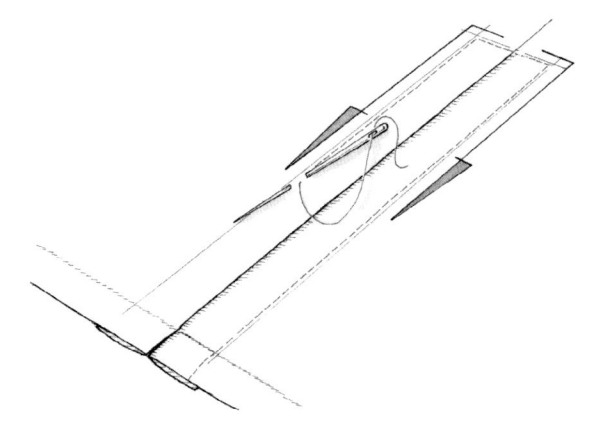

replacing a lapped zipper

Lapped zipper applications conceal the zipper. You often find them in side seams or at the center backs of dresses, skirts, and pants. They're ideal when the color of the zipper tape, teeth, and garment fabric don't match. One row of stitching is visible on the right side of the zipper opening. The second row is stitched so close to the zipper teeth that the fabric overlap covers the zipper and the stitching. Most lapped applications use coil zippers, which are more flexible and less decorative than other zippers.

Replacing by Machine

1. Mark the previous stitching lines with a marking pen or tailor's chalk, using a ruler as a guide.

2. If the zipper is enclosed at the top with a facing, collar, or waistband, open the stitching at the ends of the enclosure just enough to free the top of the zipper tape (see the drawing on page 235). Remove the stitches in the rest of the zipper.

3. Open the replacement zipper. Position the finished, hidden edge of the garment opening on the zipper tape, close to the teeth and with right sides up as shown in the drawing at right. Temporarily hold the zipper in place with basting tape, glue stitch, or hand-basting stitches.

4. Attach a zipper foot and edge-stitch along the zipper opening, as shown in the drawing.

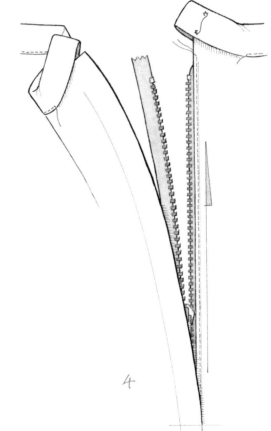

4

5   Close the zipper and pin the remaining finished garment edge in place, covering the zipper and the first row of stitching. Hand-baste through all layers as shown in the drawing below.

6   Move the zipper foot to the right of the needle. Starting at the seam line at the bottom of the zipper, topstitch across the bottom and up the outside edge of the zipper along the previous stitching marks.

Replacing by Hand

1   Follow steps 1 through 3 for replacing the zipper by machine.

2   Sew short backstitches (see page 67) to attach the first half of the zipper, as in step 4.

3   With a backstitch or a pick stitch (see page 68), sew the second half of the zipper as in step 6. These stitches will be visible on the right side of the item, so keep them neat and even. Press with a press cloth.

4   Restitch the facing, collar, or waistband, catching the top of the zipper tape in the seam.

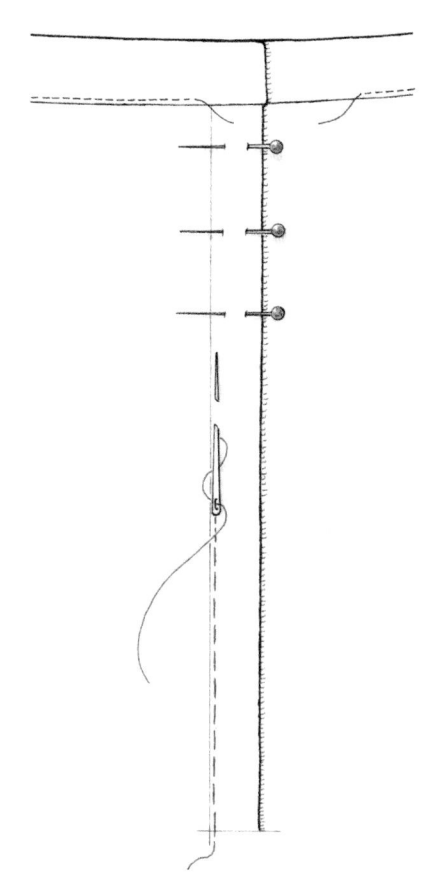

7   Remove the basting and marks. Press with a press cloth.

8   Stitch the facing, collar, or waistband closed, catching the top of the zipper tape in the seam.

Position 1/2" (1.3 mm)-wide household tape at the seam line to act as a topstitching guide.

replacing a fly-front zipper

A fly-front zipper application—the style found in blue jeans—is strong and sturdy. A fly zipper has a single or double row of topstitching that curves as it nears the bottom of the zipper. This type of zipper is found only in the center front of pants or a skirt. These instructions are for a woman's garment, which laps on the left side; reverse the instructions below if your zipper laps on the right side of the zipper.

1 To avoid having to match any decorative top-stitching, remove only the stitches that hold the zipper in place (as shown in the drawing below). Cut the zipper tape at the waistband and at the lower edge to release it. With a fabric-marking pen, mark the areas where you removed stitches. If the new zipper is longer than the old one, shorten it (see page 234).

2 Fold the top edge of the side of the zipper tape to the wrong side. Slide the zipper tape into the opening you created when you removed the broken zipper. Pin the tape so the finished edge of the zipper opening is close to the teeth or coil. Hand- or machine-baste the zipper in place as shown in the drawing below.

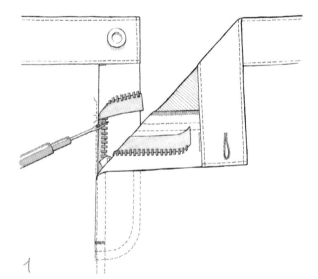

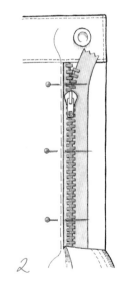

3 With the zipper foot to the left of the needle, stitch along the edge of the fabric, sewing as far down the zipper as possible. Stitch through all the layers (including the folded top of the zipper tape).

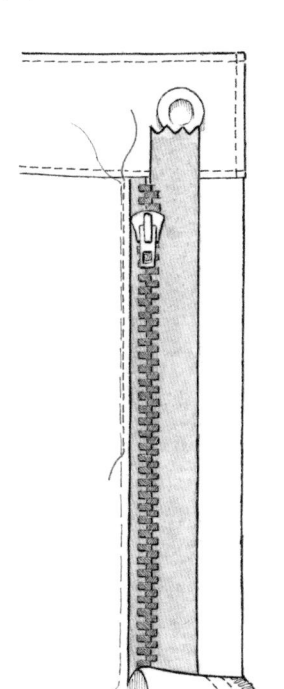

4 Close the garment and zipper. Fold the remaining top edge of the zipper tape to the front. Pin the free zipper tape in position, following the markings. Pin or hand-baste the zipper in place. Open the zipper.

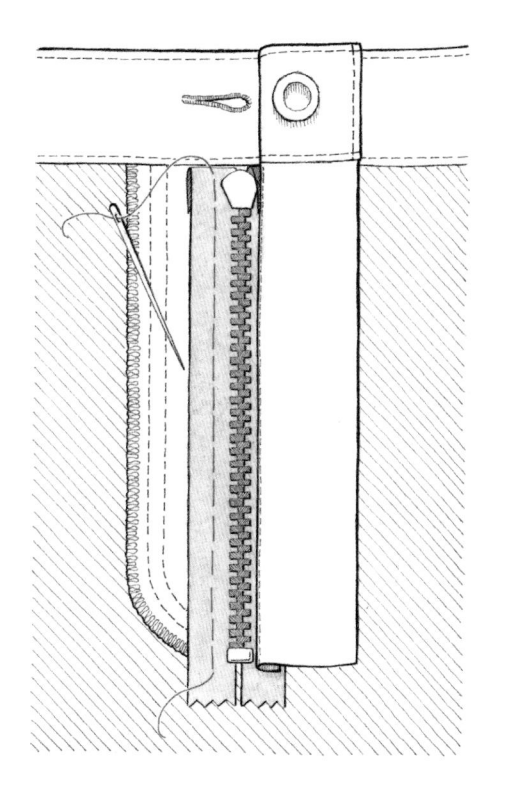

5 From the inside, backstitch the zipper tape to the fabric, sewing through only the inner layers of the fly overlap, as shown in the drawing. No stitches should show on the outside of the garment. Secure by making extra stitches at the bottom of the zipper tape. For added strength, hand-sew a few short, straight stitches across the bottom of the fly-front opening.

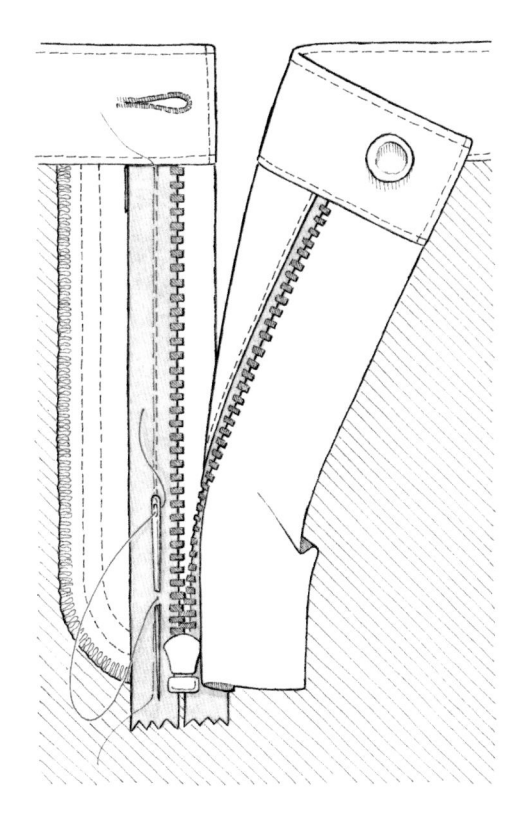

replacing a separating zipper

A separating zipper opens completely. This style is typically found in coats, jackets, outdoor gear, and sleeping bags. The zipper teeth may be concealed or exposed. You can replace a separating zipper by hand, but machine stitching is stronger. Mark the original stitching with a marking pen or tailor's chalk, using a ruler as a guide.

1. If the zipper is finished with a facing or collar, open the stitching just enough to free the top and bottom of the zipper tape. Then remove the stitching from the rest of the zipper.

2. If the new zipper is longer than the old one, shorten it (see page 234). Unzip the new zipper and work with one side at a time.

3. Pin the right side of the new zipper tape to the wrong side of the garment opening, with the teeth aligned along the garment edge as shown in the drawing below. Fold the top of the zipper tape under. Baste in place. If there is a facing, pin the facing in place along the zipper tape, then baste. If there is a lining, pin it out of the way.

4. Attach the zipper foot and topstitch from the right side through all layers, along the original stitching line.

5. Zip the two zipper pieces together. Pin and baste the loose half of the zipper to the other side of the garment as in step 3. Unzip the zipper and attach the remaining zipper half, repeating step 4.

6. If the garment has a lining, hand-sew it in place. With a hand-worked slipstitch, re-attach the collar or facing.

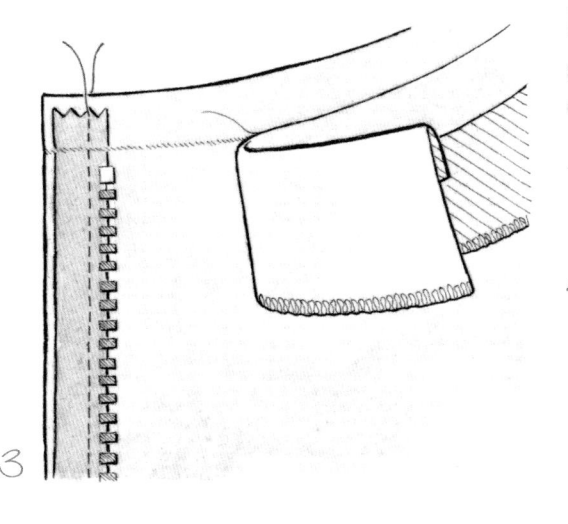

3

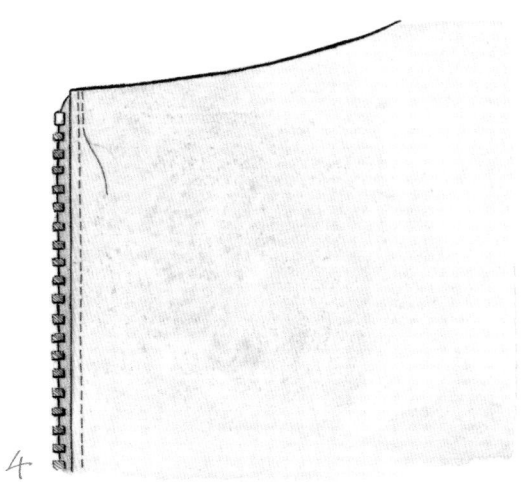

4

Replacing an Exposed Separating Zipper

Sometimes, the colorful, plastic zippers found in active sportswear and children's clothing are installed with the teeth exposed for a casual, sportier look.

1 Follow steps 1 and 2 for replacing a separating zipper.

2 Lay one side of the zipper face down on the right side of the fabric, with the teeth 3/4" (1.9 cm) away from the garment edge. At this point, the zipper teeth should be facing away from the opening of the garment. Pin the zipper in place. Attach the zipper foot. Stitch close to the zipper teeth as shown at lower left.

3 Fold the zipper tape to the inside of the garment, if it won't be caught in a facing or collar. Finger-press and then edge-stitch along the folded garment edge through all the layers as shown at lower right.

4 Zip the two zipper pieces together. Pin the loose half of the zipper to the other side as in step 2, aligning the upper and lower garment edges. Unzip the zipper and sew the remaining zipper half to the garment, repeating steps 2 and 3.

5 Follow step 6 for replacing a separating zipper.

repairing lining

A lining adds longevity to an item, but, unfortunately, it often wears out before the fashion fabric does. It's easy to patch a small damaged or worn area, but if the lining is visible, it's best to replace the entire piece or panel. In tailored garments—jackets and coats, for example—it's sometimes easier to just cut away the damaged lining and live without it.

Patch garment linings with fabric that matches the existing lining in color, weight, and fiber content. Patch home-décor items with muslin or cotton sateen. Preshrink the lining fabric.

patching lining: To patch a small or inconspicuous area, cut a patch that is slightly larger all around than the worn area. Press 1/4" (6 mm) of the patch under on all sides. Pin the patch in place. Edge-stitch the patch by machine or slip stitch it by hand.

mending lining: To mend a torn lining, pin the edges of the tear with right sides together and stitch it closed. Machine-stitch from the wrong side if you can. If you can't, hand-stitch from the right side.

removing lining: If the lining is badly torn, replace or remove it. The simplest way to remove lining is to cut it as close as possible to the seams—although you'll leave a few threads. If the inside of the item is visible, you might prefer to open the seams to remove the lining.

Working with a seam ripper, open the seams that secure the lining. Remove the entire lining, then resew the seams. It's often easier to sew these seams by hand because they can be difficult to reach by machine.

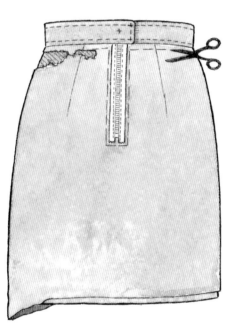

guidelines for adjusting fit

If you're one of the few people who can buy clothing right off the rack, congratulations! The rest of us usually need to make some small (or large) fitting adjustments. If you've got a couple of impulse purchases still hanging in the back of your closet or you just can't seem to fit into some of those old favorites—a quick tuck or a loosened seam might be just what your wardrobe needs!

Fitting Tips

- Launder the item first. If it's new, it might shrink in the wash. If not, you want to remove any dirt so you don't press it into the fabric as you are making the alteration.
- Try on the garment while wearing the proper undergarments and accessories.
- Bear in mind that it's easier to make something smaller than larger.
- Pin the alterations from the right side of the garment. Double-check to make sure that you like how the alteration looks before you begin sewing.
- Mark the pin locations on the inside of the garment and baste along the markings.
- Try on the garment again after basting to make sure the alteration is still correct.
- Save the altering of tailored garments, eveningwear, and specialty fabrics for the tailor. Narrowing pant legs, shortening spaghetti straps, and letting out a seam are quick fixes that can even be done by hand.
- Press often as you sew for a crisp, precise result.
- Make some notes about the garment, so you can match the thread, stitch length, and construction methods.
- Work with a seam ripper to take out any seams that need adjustment (see page 197).
- Press out all crease lines.
- Plan to conceal any crease lines that can't be eliminated by pressing.
- Press with a damp press cloth to close visible holes left after ripping out a seam.

It's hard to see the back of a garment when you're wearing it, so enlist the help of a friend to pin and mark adjustments — and possibly offer an opinion on the fit.

when it's too tight

When a garment is too tight, the first and easiest option is to let out a side seam or another vertical seam. The standard seam allowance is 5/8" (1.5 cm), but in manufactured garments the allowance is often trimmed. Usually you can gain 1/2" (1.3 cm) at each seam, which might be just enough to make the garment fit more comfortably.

adjusting at the seams:
Measure from the original seam line to the edge of the fabric to see how much extra fabric you gain.

You'll need a minimum of 1/4" (6 mm) for a new seam allowance. If there's 1/2" (1.3 cm) or more beyond that, you'll be able to increase the garment by at least 1/2" (1.3 cm) per seam.

Side seams, sleeves, and armholes are the easiest seams to let out. Pull out the seam with the seam ripper. Press both sides and restitch close to, but not on, the raw edge.

widening seam allowances:
If the seam allowances are too narrow to allow much extra width, sew a strip of twill tape or seam tape to the edges. Press. Resew the seam very close to the tape extensions, without catching them in the seam.

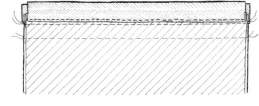

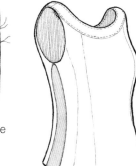

adding a gusset: A gusset is a piece of fabric of any shape that is inserted into a seam to allow greater ease of movement. A gusset is usually added at side seams and is made of matching fabric (if possible), but you can also use contrast fabric or trim.

To make a gusset, rip out the seams that are too tight. Try on the garment and measure the gap in the open seams. Cut a gusset large enough to fill the gap. Pin the gusset at the seams.

Try on the garment again and adjust the gusset to ensure a comfortable fit. Sew the new seams.

closing side-seam pockets:
If pockets on the side seams gape open, turn the garment inside out and sew the pockets closed. Cut away the pocket bags inside the garment and zigzag the edges.

when it's too loose

Changing an entire garment to a smaller size is a job best left to a tailor. Otherwise, to fix a loose fit, you can just take in any one of a number of seams. The biggest challenge you face when taking in seams is preserving the silhouette and drape of the garment.

Taking in Straight Seams

Pin the alteration and try on the garment. Baste the new seams and try on the garment again. When you are satisfied with the fit, stitch the seams with a standard stitch length. Trim the excess fabric. Press and zigzag the edges. Whenever possible, distribute the adjustment by altering two or more seams a little, rather than one seam a lot.

Taking in a Pant Waistband at Center Back

1   Try on the pants and have a friend pin the excess fabric at the center back seam.

2   With a fabric-marking pen or tailor's chalk, mark the pin locations to create a new stitching line inside the pants.

   Remove the belt loop and waistband facing and open the center back seam with a seam ripper. If there is no seam, cut the existing waistband at center back.

3   Stitch the new center back seam, extending it through the waistband facing. Trim the excess fabric, if desired. Press the seam allowances open and resew the facing. Reattach the belt loop.

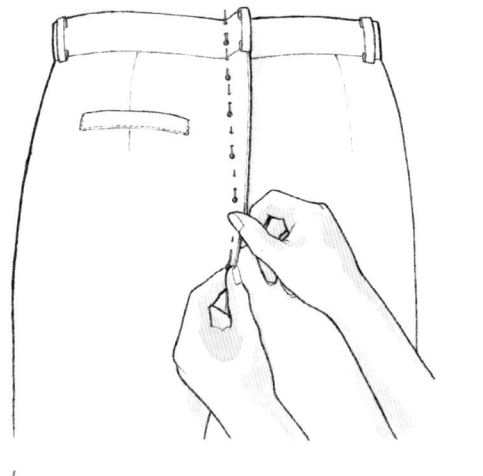

1

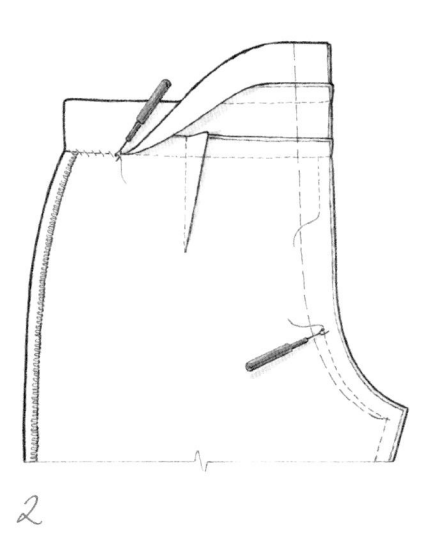

2

3

when it's too wide

Silhouettes change with fashion, for both clothing and home décor. An easy way to update the look of trousers, skirts—and even curtains and drapes—is to remove some of the fabric's fullness, or volume.

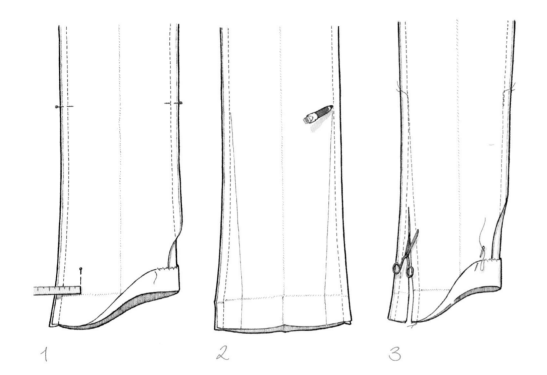

1

2

3

Narrowing Pant Legs

1 Try on the pants and pin them to see how much fullness you want to remove. Measure the total amount. Rip out the hem with a seam ripper (see page 197). Press.

On the hem crease line, measure and mark half the total desired amount from each seam. Make equal adjustments to the outer and inner seam so that the pants hang straight.

2 With tailor's chalk or a fabric-marking pen, mark the new seam lines, starting at or just above the knee and continuing to the hem.

3 Stitch the new seams. Adjust the depth of the hem allowance to accommodate the new pant-leg width. Trim the seam allowance and zigzag the new edges. Rehem the pants (see pages 251 and 252).

Turn a blousy shirt into a more tailored style by sewing a series of vertical darts or tucks around the torso.

stretched & frayed necklines

Necklines and collars receive a lot of wear and tear—and they often look worn before the rest of the garment does. To add years to the life of a good-quality sweater or shirt, just fix the collar or neckline.

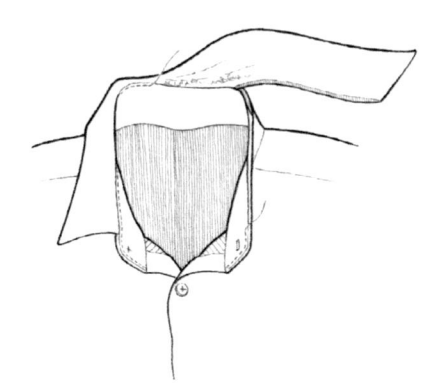

ribbing on sweaters: Thread a long needle with elastic thread and knot the end. Working from the wrong side of the sweater, sew small running stitches from one rib to the next all around the neckline (this works for cuffs and hems, too). Make sure the stitches aren't visible on the right side.

Repeat with two or three additional rows of running stitches, spaced about 1/2" (1.3 cm) apart. Steam the elastic thread to shrink it slightly.

off-the-shoulder necklines: To form a casing, hand-sew ribbon or seam tape on the wrong side of the garment just below the finished neck edge. Insert narrow elastic through the casing with a safety pin.

Adjust the elastic so it doesn't gather the neck edge but instead holds the edge of the garment close to the body. Hand-sew the elastic ends together and tuck them inside the casing.

shirt collars: When the roll line of a collar becomes worn, turn the collar to reveal the fresh underside. With a seam ripper (page 197), remove the collar from its stand.

Turn the collar over, insert the raw edges into the collar stand, and edge-stitch them in place. (You can make the same repair with shirt cuffs, too.)

You can convert a traditional shirt collar to a band collar. Just unstitch the collar stand to release the collar, then edge-stitch the stand to close it.

fixing a torn hem

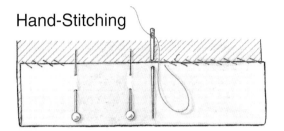

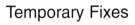

One of the most common repair jobs is fixing a torn or loose hem. It's also one of the easiest. If you don't want or need to change the length of the item, simply restitch the loose section, exactly as it was originally stitched.

Hand-Stitching

For the most invisible repair, restitch hems by hand. Press the hem and pin it back in place. Use any hand-hemming stitch shown on page 251 that resembles the original stitching and doesn't show on the right side of the fabric.

Temporary Fixes

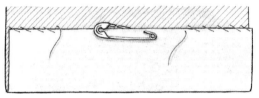

For a quick, emergency fix, hold a torn hem in place with double-sided tape or duct tape. The repair will last at least a few hours. Or safety-pin the hem at the side seams and intermittently across the ripped area—but try not to pin through to the right side so you keep the repair invisible.

If you're in a real bind, you can also staple the hem allowance to the side seams of the garment. Join the hem allowance only to the seam allowances inside to avoid damaging the outer fabric of the garment.

Fusing

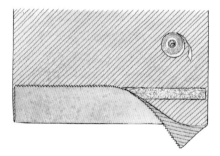

Keep fusible web or fusible hemming tape on hand for quick, no-sew hem repairs. Fusibles are best suited to light- to medium-weight woven fabrics and straight hems.

Insert a ¹/₂" (1.3 cm)-wide strip of fusible web between the hem allowance and the garment along the hemline and press to secure (see page 198).

Machine-Stitching

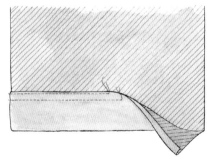

If the original hem of the garment was machine-sewn, repair it by machine, duplicating the original stitching as closely as possible. Topstitch knits by machine with a stretch stitch. If there are two rows of topstitching, you can work with a twin needle (see page 195) to create perfectly parallel stitching.

repairing hems by hand

To sew hems by hand, thread the needle with a single strand of matching color thread and knot one end (see page 69). Begin sewing about ¹/₂" (1.3 cm) before the beginning of the torn stitches. Don't pull the stitches too tightly. To secure the new stitching, take a small backstitch in the hem allowance every 4" to 6" (10 to 15 cm).

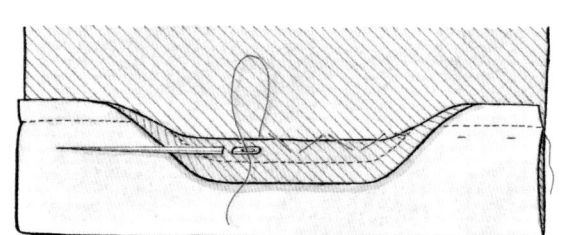

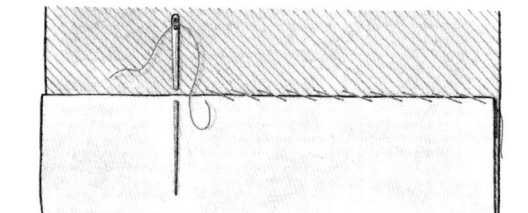

blindstitch: Fold back the top edge of the hem. Take a tiny stitch in and out of the garment fabric, catching only one or two threads on the surface. Take the next stitch ¹/₄" (6 mm) away within the allowance. Repeat, keeping stitches small and ¹/₄" (6 mm) apart. The stitches will be hidden between the layers of fabric.

hemming stitch: Take a tiny stitch in and out of the garment, catching only one or two threads of the garment. Then bring the needle through the edge of the hem. Repeat, evenly spacing and slanting the stitches.

slip stitch: Insert the needle inside the fabric fold of the hem allowance and bring it out through the folded edge about ¹/₄" (6 mm) away. Insert the needle in and out of the garment fabric, catching only one or two threads of the fabric. Repeat, alternating from the hem allowance edge to the garment with each stitch.

Press only the bottom edge of the hem so the thickness of the fabric layers at the top of the hem won't leave an imprint on the front of the garment.

repairing hems by machine

Some hems are perfectly suited to a quick mend by machine. It's always easiest to copy the hemming method that was originally done, especially if only part of the hem has ripped out.

machine topstitch: You'll often find a machine-topstitched hem on casual clothing, curtains, draperies, and outdoor gear. Fold and pin the torn hem in place.

Topstitch on the right side so that the stitches are the same width from the edge as the existing hem stitches. Start and stop stitching 1/2" (1.3 cm) before and beyond the ripped section.

If the item has a double row of topstitching, stitch the first row of topstitching the same width from the edge as the intact stitches. Then use the toe of the presser foot as a guide for the second row, as shown in the drawing. Stitch slowly to keep the two rows parallel.

machine-stitched narrow hem: Narrow hems are usually found on sheer, silky, and bias-cut garments. Most narrow hems are folded twice, to enclose the raw edge, and then stitched.

Before stitching, you need to repress the hem as it was originally pressed, to make sure it's even and that the raw edge is caught in the hem. Machine-stitch close to the inside fold.

If the fabric is torn near the hem, you might need to trim off the entire bottom of the garment, just above the tear, and re-sew the hem. For a new narrow hem, press under 1/2" (1.3 cm) and then 1/2" (1.3 cm) again. Machine-stitch close to the inside fold.

machine blindstitch: Install the blindstitch presser foot. Refer to your manual for instructions for your machine. Place the hem allowance face down on the machine bed and fold back the rest of the fabric. Allow about 1/4" (6 mm) of the hem edge to extend under the presser foot, aligning the soft fold against the guide in the foot.

Stitch along the hem, close to the fold, catching only one or two threads of the garment with each left-hand stitch. Open the hem and press it flat.

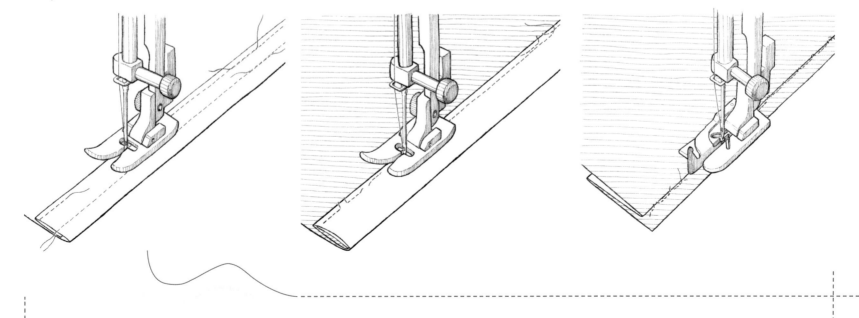

making a simple hem

You can shorten any type of garment. You might want to hide a frayed edge or update the look of a favorite skirt or coat. Items with straight hems are the easiest to shorten, but you can rehem pleated, tapered, flared, and cuffed garments, with just a couple of extra steps. With these same, simple techniques, you can make a change that is barely perceptible or one that will alter the entire look.

Marking for a Hem

Begin by removing the stitching in the original hem. Put on the garment, while wearing the appropriate undergarments and footwear. Enlist the help of a friend to mark the hem with chalk or pins so that it is an even height from the floor all the way around the bottom of the garment.

Stand in place and ask your helper to move around you, measuring with a yard-stick while marking. Pin up the hem along the marked line and double-check to be sure you like the new length.

Mark a new hem on a curtain or other home accessory by placing the item in position and pin-marking its desired length with a yardstick. Measure from the floor to make sure the hem is even.

Adding a Hem Allowance

When you are satisfied with the new hemline, mark a cutting line, allowing extra for the desired hem allowance below the new hemline. The standard hem allowance for a straight garment is up to 3" (7.5 cm) wide. For a flared garment, it is 1/2" to 2" (1.3 to 5 cm) wide. (Allowances for hand-sewn hems are usually wider than allowances for machine-sewn hems.)

The hems on curtains, draperies, table, and bed linens vary—from a 6" (15 cm) double-fold hem to a 1/2" (1.3 cm) double-fold hem. After adding the hem allowance cut the excess fabric from the item, leaving 1/4" to 1/2" (6 mm to 1.3 cm) for a clean-finished edge.

If you don't have a sewing buddy who can mark your hem, you can purchase a floor-standing chalk hem marker. This handy device marks the hemline an even height from the floor.

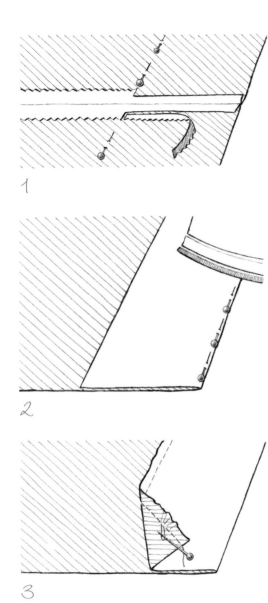

Preparing to Hem

For the neatest, smoothest hem, follow these prep steps, then sew. It's worth the time to press, clean-finish, and ease the hem allowance before stitching the hem—a puckered, bulky hemline can ruin an otherwise gorgeous garment.

1   Trim the garment's seam allowances in the area below the marked hemline to reduce bulk.

2   Fold up the hem along the pin-marked line and press.

3   If the garment is wider at the raw edge than at the hem fold line, stitch ¼" (6 mm) from the raw edge with a long machine stitch. Pull up the bobbin thread every few inches to gather the fullness very slightly.

Stitch a new hem by hand or machine, as described on pages 250 to 251.

Finishing the Cut Edge

• Clean-finishing the cut edge of the hem allowance prevents fraying and raveling, so your new hem lasts longer and looks neater from the inside. There are many ways to clean-finish the cut fabric edge before hemming.

• Turn under ¼" (6 mm) of the hem to the wrong side. Press and machine-stitch close to the fold.

• Machine-zigzag along the raw edge.

• Edge-stitch a length of seam binding or hem tape to the right side of the garment's edge, overlapping short ends.

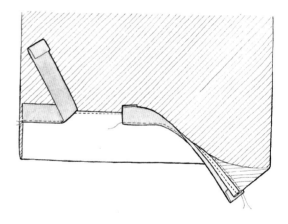

shortening with fabric tucks

Fabric tucks are a creative and effective way to shorten an item without cutting fabric or removing the existing hem. This quick fix is especially useful when shortening clothes for children—tucks are quickly and easily reversible as children grow taller.

Hidden Tucks

To shorten cuffed pants or shirts—without removing the cuff—simply sew a tuck at the cuff's seam line.

to shorten pants, fold and pin the pant legs with an even tuck of fabric on the inside of the pant leg, hidden behind the cuff. Try on the pants. If they're okay, sew the tucks in place, making sure the seam is below the upper edge of the cuff. Press the tuck toward the hem.

to shorten a cuffed shirtsleeve, fold the extra length at the cuff seam, so that the fold of fabric extends behind the cuff, inside the garment. Stitch the tuck, close to or directly over the cuff seam.

If the tuck is bulky, cut away the excess fabric close to the stitching, then zigzag-stitch the cut edges.

Decorative Tucks

Shorten garments or curtains with horizontal tucks positioned near the hem edge. Make one or more tucks to remove the desired amount of length.

Working with a fabric-marking pen on the wrong side of the fabric, mark two parallel tuck fold lines for each tuck, separated by twice the desired finished depth of the tuck. Pin the tucks along these lines, then sew them in place with a machine straight stitch. Press the tuck folds toward the hem.

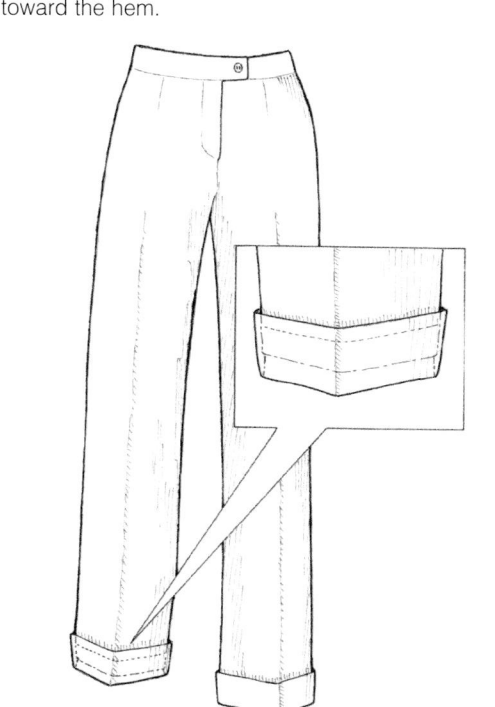

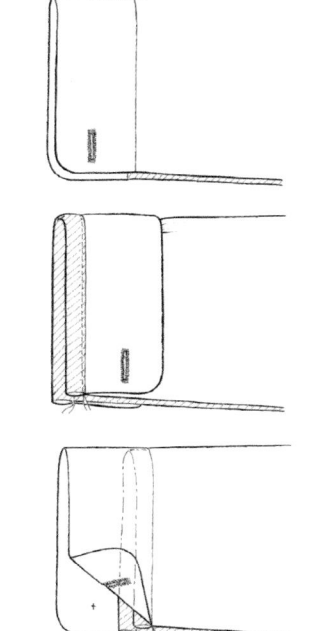

hemming decorative edges

Fancy border prints or embroidered hemlines call for special hemming treatment. You can't just fold up the bottom. Instead, subtract length farther up the seam.

shortening above the embellished section: Decide how much shorter you want the item to be. Mark one cutting line 1/2" (1.3 cm) above the top edge of the border. Mark a second line the amount you want to shorten the item (and subtract 1/2" [1.3 cm] for the seam allowance). Cut along the marked lines, as shown in the drawing.

With right sides together and cut edges aligned, place the border section on the new hemline. Join the two pieces with a 1/2" (1.3 cm) seam allowance. Press the seam allowances toward the hem and zigzag the edges.

shortening at the waist: Decide how much shorter you want the item to be and determine how many inches you need to remove. Measure down the garment from the waist and mark the amount to be shortened (and subtract 1/2" [1.3 cm] for the seam allowance).

Remove the waistband (and zipper if there is one) with a seam ripper. Cut the fabric at the marked line. Replace the zipper, resew the darts, and reattach the waistband at the new top edge of the garment.

If you shorten a darted garment at the waist, you don't have to copy the original darts. Put on the garment and pin in custom-fitted darts. Stitch them in place, and resew the waistband.

shortening tapered or flared garments

Have you ever tried to shorten a flared skirt and found you have cut away all the styling? Or have you ever tried to shorten a tapered pair of pants and found the hem allowance too tight to work with? Sometimes shortening a garment changes its fit, silhouette, and drape. Here's how to handle a variety of shaped hems.

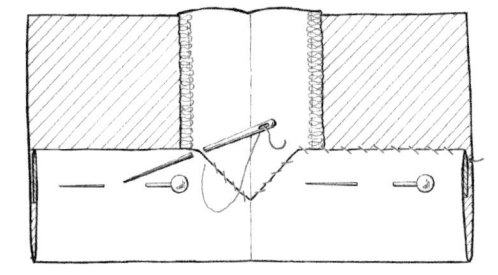

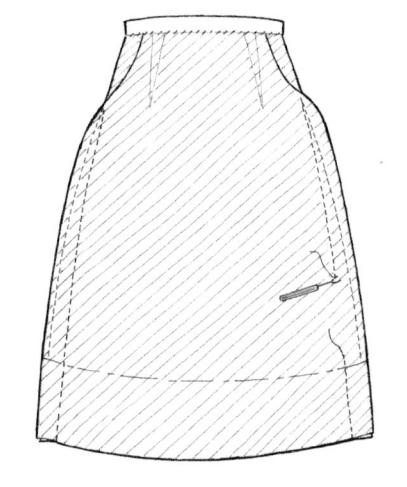

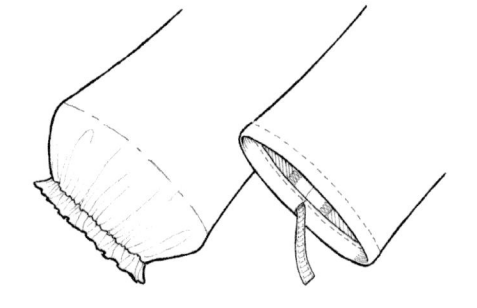

shortening narrow, tapered skirt or pants: Measure, mark, and prepare the hem, as described on pages 252 to 253. Open the side seams of the hem allowance with a seam ripper, so you can spread the allowance to fit. When sewing the hem, secure the opened hem allowance to the side seam allowances.

shortening flared pants, skirts, or dresses: You'll change the shape of a flared garment if you shorten it more than 2" (5 cm). Let out the side seams below the hipline to put flare back into the hem area. Work with a seam ripper to open the side seams from the hipline to the hemline.

Draw a new stitching line from the hipline, gradually narrowing the seam allowances to almost nothing at the hemline. Stitch the new side seams and then stitch the flared hem, easing as described in step 3 on page 253.

shortening pant legs or sleeves with elastic casing: Open the casing and remove the elastic. Mark the desired new hem length, adding an allowance for the new casing (make the casing the width of the elastic plus 1/4" [6 mm]).

Cut off the excess fabric and fold the casing to the wrong side. Sew the casing in place, stitching close to the cut edge and leaving an opening for inserting the elastic. Insert the elastic from the old casing into the new one (see page 227), then sew the opening closed.

Or you can cut off the elastic casing entirely and simply machine-stitch a narrow hem, but keep in mind that the pants or sleeves will then be much wider at the hem.

lengthening at the hem

Lengthening is a bit more challenging than shortening, but definitely doable. The first and easiest option is to simply remove the stitching, let down the hem allowance, and press it flat. If there isn't enough fabric in the hem allowance, to lengthen as much as you want there are several options.

narrow hemming: If there is enough fabric in the hem allowance to lengthen the item as much as you'd like to, resew the hem with a narrow double-folded hem (see page 251).

If the garment has a cuff, you can narrow the cuff or use the cuff allowance to add length.

topstitching decorative trim: Attach trim to the lower edge of the unfolded or stitched hem with basting tape, glue, or running stitches (see page 67). Topstitch it in place (see page 72) with one or more rows of stitches—you can use straight or decorative stitches. Make sure the care requirements of the trim match that of the item itself.

attaching bias binding: You can add length with extra-wide bias binding. Cut the binding so the length equals the hem circumference plus 1" (2.5 cm). Sew the short ends of the binding with right sides together.

Pin one edge of the bias binding to the hem edge with right sides together and raw edges aligned.

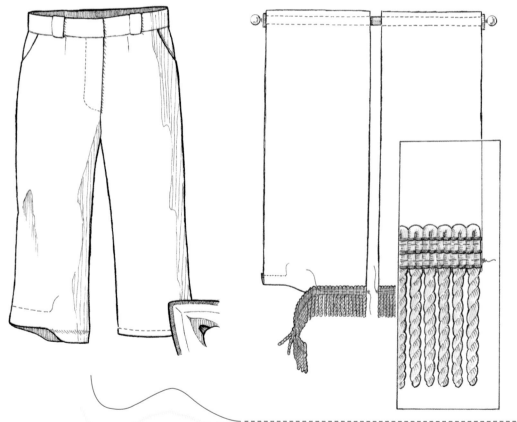

Press the seam allowances toward the binding. Fold the free edge of the tape under to enclose the raw edge and just cover the stitching. Machine- or hand-stitch in place.

lengthening with a facing or ruffle

It's easy to add length by attaching extra fabric at the hem. Open the existing hem, press the crease flat, then add a facing or ruffle. A facing will be invisible, while a ruffle changes the look of an item.

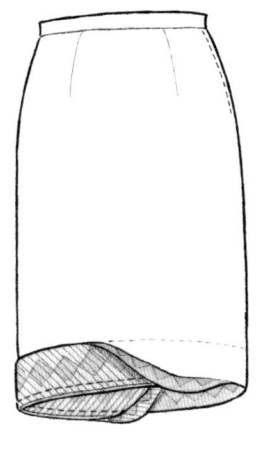

making a faced hem: Cut a hem facing from lining fabric or seam tape. The facing length should equal the hem circumference plus 1" (2.5 cm). The width should be about 2" (5 cm) or the finished width of the seam tape.

For circular hems (as on skirts), sew the short edges of the facing with right sides together, using ½" (1.3 cm) seam allowances.

With right sides together, sew the facing to the lower edge of the item. Clean-finish the unstitched facing edge if necessary. Turn the facing to the inside, rolling the seam so it doesn't show on the right side. Press it in place.

Hand- or machine-hem the upper edge of the facing to the fabric (see pages 250 to 251). From the outside, the facing should be invisible.

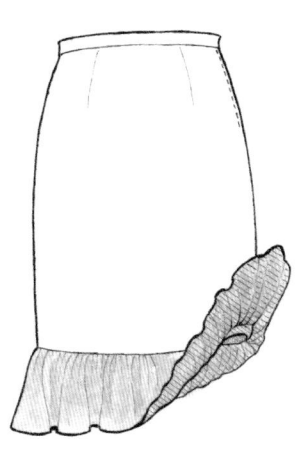

adding a ruffle: Cut a ruffle from fabric or trim equal to 2½ times the circumference of the edge it will be sewn to. Make the ruffle as wide as you want plus ½" (1.3 cm) for the seam allowance and 1" (2.5 cm) for the hem allowance. For circular hems, join the short ends with right sides together to form a ring. Hem the lower edge with a narrow hem (see page 251). Sew two parallel rows of basting stitches along the upper edges of the ruffle. Then, pull the threads gently to gather the ruffle.

With right sides together and raw edges aligned, pin the ruffle to the bottom of the item. Stitch in place as shown. Press the seam allowances away from the ruffle, and remove the gathering threads.

If the hemline crease is difficult to press flat, try these tricks: Rub it with a clothes or lint brush. Treat it with a stain remover and clean the item. Spray it with spray starch or equal parts of white vinegar and water.

lengthening with a cuff

Cuffs are a great way to add length to clothes. You can vary the style for a sporty, casual, or tailored effect.

adding a ribbed cuff: Ready-made ribbing makes a perfect cuff for pants or sleeves. It comes with the hem edge already finished. Remove the stitching from the existing hem and press out any creases.

Measure your wrist or ankle and cut a piece of ribbed knit to fit, adding 1/2" (1.3 cm) for the seam allowance. Sew the ends together to form a ring. With right sides together, sew the unfinished edge of the rib knit to the hem edge of the item. Fold the cuff down and to the outside.

adding a woven cuff: A woven cuff is the right sort of addition to dressy or business pants or trousers. The biggest challenge is finding suitable fabric. Make sure the cuff fabric matches the garment in color, surface texture, fiber content (if possible), and weight.

1   Decide how wide you want the cuff to be. Double this measurement and add 1" (2.5 cm) for hem and seam allowances. Measure the circumference of the garment at the lower edge and add 1" (2.5 cm). Cut two pieces of fabric to these measurements.

2   With right sides together, sew the short ends to form a ring. Fold 1/2" (1.3 cm) to the wrong side of one of the cuff edges and stitch.

3   Sew the cuff and lower garment edge with right sides together, raw edges even, and with 1/2" (1.3 cm) seam allowance.

4   Fold the cuff to the inside just below the seam. Hand- or machine-stitch the finished hem edge to the garment. The stitches won't show once the cuff is formed.

5   Turn the cuff to the right side, pin and press. Tack the cuff in place at the side seams.

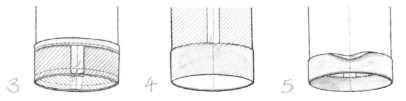

camouflaging flaws

Instead of simply mending a flaw, you might want to camouflage it in a decorative and creative way. Some fabrics are difficult to mend inconspicuously and sometimes the damage is difficult to reach by hand or machine—so a creative solution may be your only solution. Here are a few shortcuts that also add a touch of style.

- To hide a wine spot or thread snag on a cocktail dress or gown, fuse individual rhinestones in strategic places.

- Hand-sew a feather boa along the neckline of a dress to hide make-up stains or broken stitching.

- Shorten a floor-length dress to eliminate a ruined hem (see page 249). Add lace trim if you want to keep the length but hide the problem.

- Sew beads or sequins over a small, darned hole to hide the repair stitches (see page 262).

- Patch casual or children's wear with ravel-free felt and fleece appliqués in matching or contrasting colors (see page 261).

- Sew ribbon trim on old table linens to cover stains and add a splash of detail or color.

- Camouflage a mended area with fabric paint. Consider painting other areas to balance the embellishment.

- Make a ruffle or appliqué patch from a worn pillowcase. Add it to a new pillowcase that coordinates with your bedding set.

- Cut lace appliqués from scraps of lace fabric to cover anything; a neckline, a center front, a repaired zipper, the lapel of a jacket.

- Apply machine or hand embroidery stitches to cover repaired tears, snags, or stains (see page 264).

- Cover stains on upholstery by making armrest or headrest covers in beautiful, complimentary fabrics.

- If cushion covers are worn, consider remaking them by turning the original fabrics inside out (assuming the right and wrong sides are identical).

- Turn floor-length curtains into café curtains to eliminate sun-faded or frayed edges.

- Add a patch pocket in a fabulous fabric (see page 266).

adding an appliqué

A purchased or custom-made appliqué is one of the easiest ways to cover damaged fabric. Appliqués are really just decorative patches that add an additional design detail, while also hiding a flaw or repair.

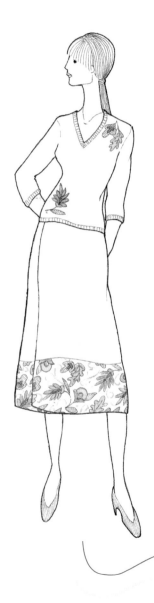

ready-made appliqués: Appliqués come in all sizes, shapes, and designs. Some have a fusible resin on the wrong side to make them easy to position in place. Always follow the manufacturer's instructions.

If the appliqué is not fusible, dab a spot of fabric glue on the back to hold it in position while you stitch it down.

If the edge of the appliqué is finished with a satin stitch, sew it to the fabric with a straight stitch just inside the satin stitch. If not, zigzag around all the edges with a short zigzag stitch to create your own satin-stitch edging.

fabric appliqués: Make your own appliqués from leftover fabrics. If the fabric has an allover design, you can select an individual motif for your design and cut it out, allowing an extra ½" (1.3 cm) all around. Press under ½" (1.3 cm) around the appliqué, and pin or baste the appliqué in place.

Or you can make your appliqué fusible by cutting a square of fabric that is large enough to cover the damaged area.

Fuse paper-backed fusible web to the wrong side and cut the fabric and fusible web to the desired size and shape of your appliqué patch, without turn-under allowances. Remove the paper backing and fuse the appliqué with the right side up over the damaged area (see page 198).

To secure the appliqué, stitch a piece of tear-away stabilizer to the wrong side of the fabric, under the appliqué location. Set your sewing machine for a short, narrow zigzag stitch and stitch around the outside edges. Remove the tear-away stabilizer.

For a playful variation, apply fabric paint to outline and finish the edges of the appliqué patch.

adding beads, sequins & stones

Beads, sequins, jewel stones, and rhinestones are beautiful repair tools. Mend holes or tears with a fusible product to add strength (see page 198). Then sew, fuse, or clamp the embellishments over the repair. Make sure the care requirements of the embellishments match those of the item.

Work with a beading needle or a needle that is slender enough to fit through the holes in your beads or sequins. Work with a single or double strand of invisible thread (look for monofilament nylon thread in the sewing store), or thread that matches the color of the embellishments.

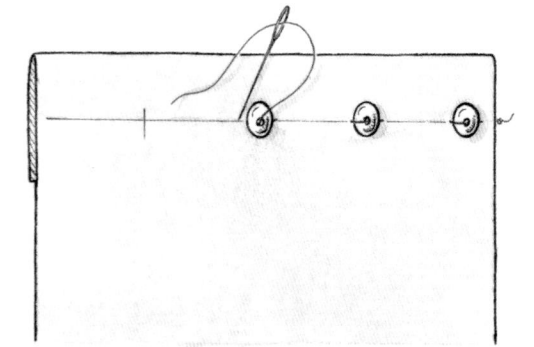

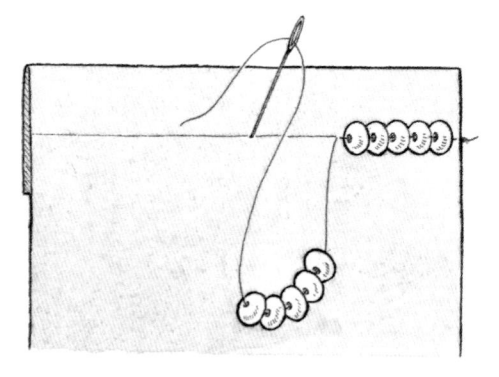

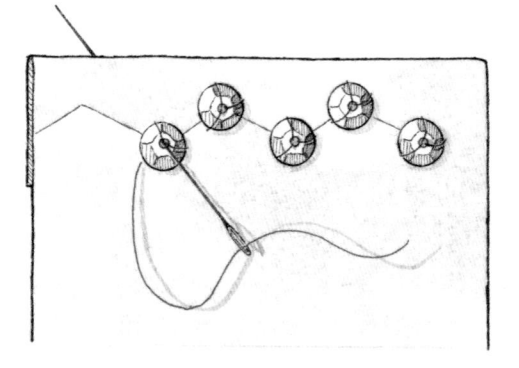

scattered beads: Knot the thread and bring it up from the wrong side at the desired location. String a bead on the needle and slide it down to the surface of the fabric. Insert the needle back through the fabric, next to the bead. Either knot the thread or sew on another bead. Repeat until you have sewn as many beads as you want.

rows of beads: Draw a line with a fabric-marking pen to mark the position of the row of beads. Knot the thread and bring the needle through the end of the line and to the right side of the fabric. Slide several beads onto the thread and insert the needle back through the fabric so the beads lie flat along the marked line.

Bring the needle to the right side of the fabric again and repeat until all the beads are attached. Knot the thread or backstitch on the wrong side every few inches and at the end of the row.

sequins: Bring the threaded needle from the wrong side of the fabric through the hole in the sequin. Carry the thread over the sequin and back through the fabric right next to the edge of the sequin.

Repeat so there are two or more straight stitches from the center to the edge of the sequin, holding it in place. Repeat with additional sequins or knot the thread on the wrong side.

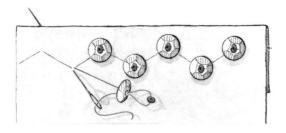

sequins with seed beads: Bring the threaded needle from the wrong side of the fabric through the hole in the sequin and then through a seed bead. Insert the needle back through the sequin hole to the wrong side of the fabric, positioning the seed bead at the center. Knot the thread end or continue sewing more sequins and beads.

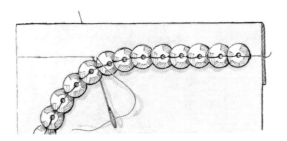

pre-strung sequins: Draw a line with a fabric-marking pen to mark the desired position of the string of sequins. Lay the string of sequins in place along the line. Bring the threaded needle to the right side of the fabric close to one end of the string.

Make diagonal stitches, every three to four sequins, so that the thread travels under the sequins and wraps around the thread that holds the sequins together. Knot the thread to finish.

crystals and jewel stones: If the jewel stones have holes in them, sew them on by hand, as you would sew beads (see page 262). If they do not have holes, choose stones with a flat underside. Dab the underside with non-water-soluble craft glue. Press the stones in place and let set for several minutes, or as directed by the glue manufacturer.

rhinestones: There are many types of rhinestones, so check the package for the best application method. Some types can be hand-sewn in place, others are glued. The newest type has a heat-activated backing that allows them to be ironed on or applied with a heated wandlike tool.

If the rhinestone has a pronged back, you can buy a special tool to bend the prongs to attach the rhinestone to the fabric.

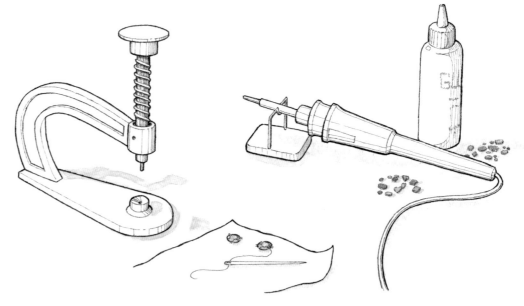

decorative stitching

Embroidery floss, wooly nylons, metallic yarns, and rayon threads are wonderful—and the colors and textures are as inspiring as a brand-new box of crayons! Hand embroidery and decorative machine embroidery made with these materials can hide stains, tears, crease lines, and worn areas of fabric. Mend, darn, or patch the damaged area first.

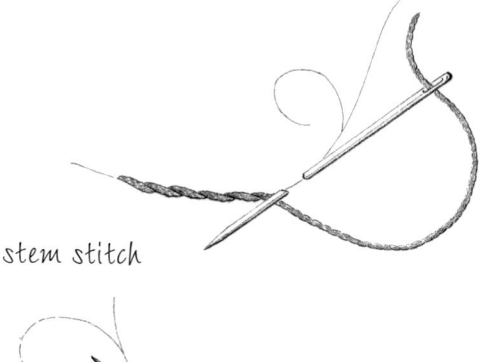

stem stitch

chain stitch

French knot

hand embroidery: This ancient and lovely form of embellishment can be as simple or as complex as you please. Embroider a single motif, a cluster of motifs, or a linear arrangement.

Plan your design on paper first and then draw it on the fabric with a fabric-marking pen. Stitch tear-away stabilizer to the wrong side of the fabric, under the embroidery area, so the fabric doesn't stretch while you're stitching.

Mount the fabric in an embroidery hoop, centering the motif. Work with a short thread, about 12" (30.5 cm) long, so the thread doesn't fray. Three of the most popular and versatile hand-embroidery stitches are the stem stitch, chain stitch, and French knot.

machine embroidery: Any type of sewing machine can produce decorative stitching. Even the basic zigzag, sewn with decorative thread, makes a great border, edging, or surface detail. Most machines also have a selection of built-in stitches that resemble hand embroidery.

The style of machine embroidery called motif machine embroidery requires an embroidery module and a hoop system. (Refer to your machine owner's manual for more complete instructions.)

Four of the most popular machine-embroidery stitches—the cross stitch, fagoting stitch, satin stitch, and scallop stitch—can be used alone or together for a variety of decorative and camouflage effects. When machine-embroidering, always apply stabilizer to the wrong side of the fabric, to support the embroidery area.

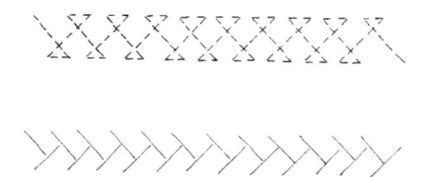

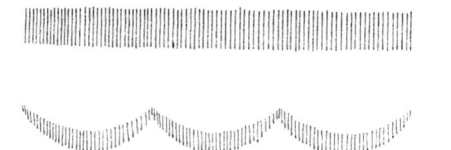

Iron-on embroidery design transfers offer a wide variety of ready-made designs.

decorative trim

Many beautiful trims are sold in fabric stores, and they are perfect for covering damaged fabric. Choose a trim that blends with the fabric of your garment or household item—or, for a more dramatic effect, choose one that contrasts.

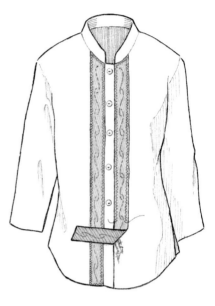

ribbon: Ribbon and other flat trims provide a quick and easy way to mend tears or holes. Baste or fuse the damage closed. Draw a placement line with a fabric-marking pen. Fuse or sew the trim directly to the damage.

bias binding: Bindings of any width enable you to easily conceal a torn fabric edge or dirty cuff edge or hem. Blanket binding, bias tape, and fold-over braid can all be machine-topstitched over any edge as shown in the drawing at the bottom left.

insertion trim: This special trim is stitched along both edges, perfect for replacing damaged fabric that is difficult to darn and too visible to patch. Position and baste the trim to form a panel over the damaged area.

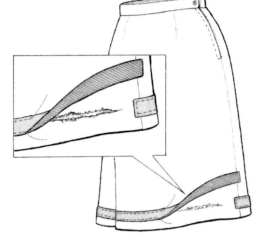

Machine-stitch both edges of the insertion trim to the fabric with a narrow zigzag stitch. Cut the fabric away behind the insertion trim, close to the stitching. Apply liquid fray preventer to the cut fabric edges.

lace fabrics and trims: You can cut lace motifs and medallions from lace fabric and hand-stitch them (or zigzag-stitch by machine) in place to cover a tear or stain. Machine-topstitch lace trims along a fabric edge or hem edge to cover ravelling or abraded edges.

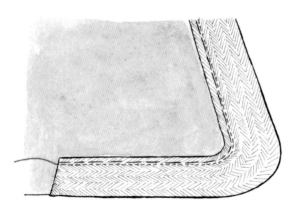

adding a patch pocket

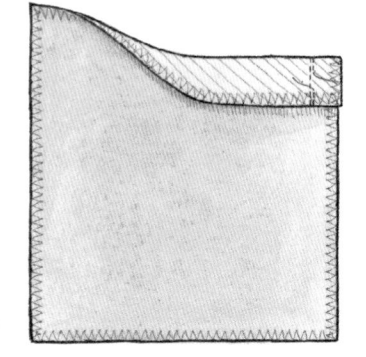

3

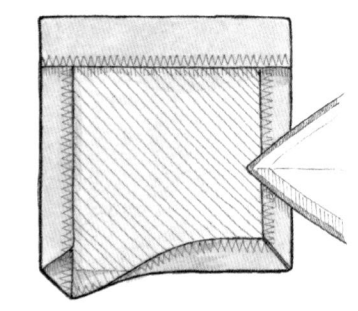

4

5

Cut from matching or contrasting fabric, patch pockets are great for casual wear, children's clothing, and home décor items—such as pillows, towels, tents, and tote bags. A pocket will not just cover a flaw, but add style and function to the damaged item. Make a simple, unlined patch pocket or line the pocket edge to edge with lining or self-fabric.

1   Make a paper pattern to determine the pocket size. Add 1" (2.5 cm) at the top for a fold-over facing, plus $5/8$" (1.5 cm) on the remaining sides. Follow the paper pattern when cutting the fabric.

2   Zigzag-stitch around the edges of the pocket.

3   Fold the 1" (2.5 cm) facing to the right side. Allowing a $5/8$" (1.5 cm) seam allowance, stitch the facing in place along the pocket sides. Trim the upper corners diagonally.

   Turn the facing back to the pocket's wrong side. Press.

4   Press under the $5/8$" (1.5 cm) allowances on the remaining sides. Miter the corners.

5   Topstitch the pocket facing in place as shown at left.

6   Position the pocket on top of the damaged area and edge-stitch it in place. Backstitch or sew a small reinforcing triangle at each top corner for extra strength.

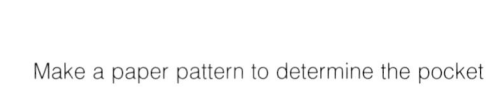

adding a pocket flap

A pocket flap usually covers the tailored pockets of suit coats and jackets. If you need to conceal a hole or stain, however, you can make a false pocket flap. A pocket flap looks best when it's lined with lining or fashion fabric. Mend any tears before covering them with flaps.

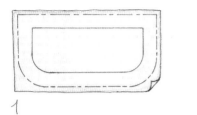

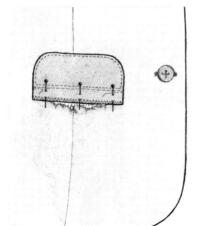

1 Determine the flap size and shape by cutting a piece of paper and placing it over the damaged fabric. Add 5/8" (1.5 cm) all around for seam allowance.

Follow the paper pattern to cut two pieces of fabric for each flap, one of fashion fabric and the other of lining.

2 Sew the pieces with right sides together, leaving the top edge open and backstitching at the upper corners. Trim the seam allowances and clip corners as needed. Turn the flap right side out and press.

3 Edge-stitch around the sides and bottom of the flap if desired to match the detailing of the garment. Zigzag-stitch the top edges together.

4 Press the top 1/2" (1.3 cm) of the flap under. Position the flap over the damaged area. Pin only the folded upper edge to the garment. Open the flap. Stitch 1/2" (1.3 cm) from the top edge, along the pressed fold line.

5 Fold the flap back over the stitching. Machine-topstitch along the upper fold to hold the flap in place.

mending & repair

refolding pleats

There are so many ways to hide fabric flaws, you might never have to throw anything away! If you can't mend or clean something so that the repair is entirely invisible, you can sometimes conceal the telltale signs by refolding the pleats in the opposite direction. Mend holes or tears first, so they don't get larger.

box pleats: To conceal a hole, tear, or stain, simply convert a box pleat to an inverted pleat—or vice versa. Remove the stitching that holds the pleat in place. Refold the pleat in reverse to hide the fabric flaw. Press to set the new folds and restitch, as shown in the drawing below. If the garment has more than one pleat, reverse the other pleats, too.

knife pleats: Knife pleats are a series of pleats that are all folded in the same direction. You find them most often on skirts. To hide damage on the garment, remove the waistband and refold the pleats in the opposite direction as shown in the drawing below at right. Press the new pleats to set them. Then replace the waistband.

mini makeovers

With creative mending, repairing, and decorating, just think about how you can transform once-loved but out-of-date clothes. Instead of staring at a closet full of clothes that don't inspire you, you can step out in style! Here are a few suggestions to get you started.

- Dye the garment. This solution works best for light-colored fabrics.
- Fix a dirty hemline by covering it with trim, shortening the item, or using your overlock machine to create a lettuce edge finish.
- Add or remove trim, whichever suits your taste.
- Narrow the garment's silhouette by tapering the skirt, legs, or sleeves.
- Add volume and flow to skirts by inserting fabric panels in seams.
- Open a seam up from the hem to create a slit or vent in skirts or pants.
- Add a layer of organza under the skirt or as an overskirt.
- Remove sleeves from tops or dresses and add trim around the armholes—or create straps with purchased trim. Convert a jacket into a vest.
- Lower the neckline.
- Reshape the neckline.
- Fuse iron-on rhinestones for extra sparkle.
- Shorten the garment dramatically. Turn a dress into a tunic, or a jacket into a cropped bolero.
- Update closures with decorative buttons, hooks, zipper pulls, etc.
- Cut off pants at hip level and add fabric bands or ruffles to make a skirt.

If you love wearing one-of-a-kind garments, shop at thrift stores for inexpensive garments, then restyle them to create your own look.

mending lace

Lace appears fragile and delicate, but it's simple to mend. The repair stitches disappear into the intricate pattern of the lace.

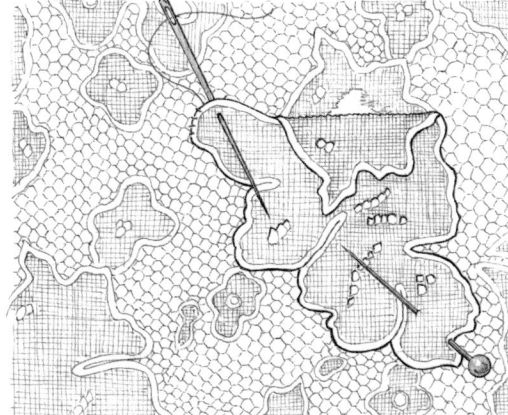

mending a hole: To repair a section of lace, cut a similar or similar size motif from a lace that is the same color, texture, and density. Center the motif over the hole and slipstitch around the edges. Work with a single strand of matching thread—silk thread is best, if you have it. You can also repair holes by machine with small zigzag stitches.

mending a tear: Bring together the edges of the tear, overlapping them slightly. Hand-baste them together. Machine-zigzag over the edges with thread of matching color.

shortening lace: If the lace has a finished or shaped edging that you don't want to fold under, mark a straight line across the top of the edging. Cut along the line. Shorten the item (see page 255) to the desired length.

Zigzag-stitch or hand-sew the section you removed onto the shortened lower edge with matching thread. You can also shorten the item from the waist (see page 255). If the original hem was folded and stitched, shorten it using the same method.

lengthening lace: The easiest way to lengthen lace is by topstitching another piece of similar lace as an edging to the lower edge of the original fabric. Machine-stitch with a zigzag stitch and a matching color thread.

If the lace is very fine, attach a straight-stitch presser foot and small-hole throat plate to the machine to prevent the fabric from being pulled into the feed dogs.

mending leather & suede

It's a challenge to make inconspicuous repairs in leather and suede. These techniques work well, however, for both real and synthetic leather and suede. Synthetic leather and suede are nonwoven so they don't fray. Do not use fusibles on these fabrics.

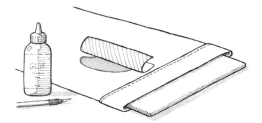

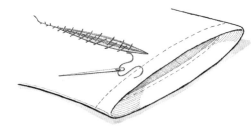

patching a hole: Neaten the edges of the hole with a razor blade, cutting carefully on a cutting mat. Place a piece of paper under the hole and trace the opening to create a paper template. Cut a patch of matching leather to the same size as the template. Insert the leather patch into the hole.

Cut a piece of fabric backing from medium-weight, firm cotton or linen or from lightweight canvas. The piece should be about 1" (2.5 cm) larger all around than the patch.

With the wrong side up, apply leather adhesive or strong fabric glue to the wrong side of the fabric backing. Center it over the wrong side of the patch and finger-press it in place. Put a heavy weight on the patch and let the adhesive set for at least an hour.

mending a tear: Abut the edges of the tear so their surfaces are flush. If the tear is in a location that is subject to strain, hand-sew the wrong side closed with a widely spaced slanting stitch. Work with a heavy needle and polyester thread.

If necessary, apply adhesive to a cotton or canvas backing and apply the backing to the wrong side of the leather, covering the tear, as described earlier.

repairing a snag: If you catch your favorite leather jacket on a sharp object and it tears slightly, don't worry. Repair the surface tear by carefully applying a small dab of clear nail polish under the snag. Firmly but gently press the mended area

shortening leather: Cut the leather to the length desired, adding 1/2" (1.3 cm) for hem allowance. Fold the allowance to the wrong side, then topstitch or glue it in place. To set the new hemline, pound the folded hem edge with a rubber mallet or cloth-covered hammer.

lengthening leather: You can't let down a hem in leather. The easiest option for lengthening is to add a decorative trim to the lower edge of the garment.

Stitch with a longer-than-usual stitch (5–8 stitches per inch [2.5 cm]). Remember, needle holes are permanent in leather.

mending pile fabrics

Pile fabrics are also referred to as fabrics "with nap"—a fabric whose surface fibers have an obvious direction. Pile fabrics include favorites such as terrycloth, velvet, corduroy, sweatshirt fleece, wool flannel, suede cloth, and fake fur.

- Set the sewing machine for about 5 to 8 stitches per inch (2.5 cm).

- Stitch a straight seam on most napped fabrics. For fabrics with a stretch knit backing, use a narrow zigzag stitch.

- Press the fabric on the wrong side, with the pile face down on a terrycloth towel or on a piece of self-fabric with the pile side up.

- Reduce bulk by trimming pile from the seam allowance.

- Zigzag all the raw edges of medium- to heavyweight fabrics.

- Clean-finish the seam allowances of lightweight fabrics with a zigzag stitch or fold the edge to the wrong side and stitch it in place.

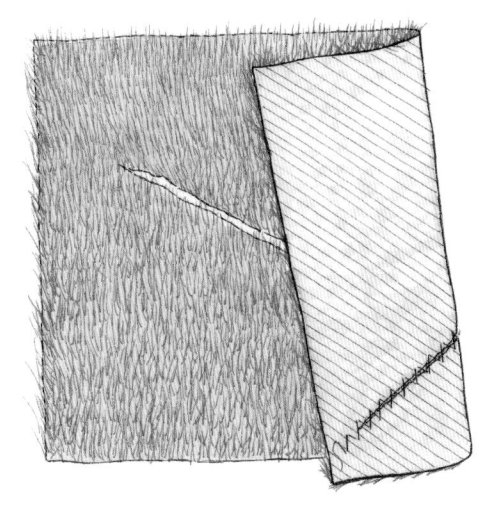

Saving Crushed Velvet

If a velvet fabric has been crushed, you can turn the crush marks into a design feature by adding embossed motifs around and over them. Place the velvet face down over a rubber stamp. Spray the wrong side with water. With a dry iron, press over the stamp for 20 to 30 seconds (or until the water is dry). Lift the iron straight up and peel the fabric off the stamp.

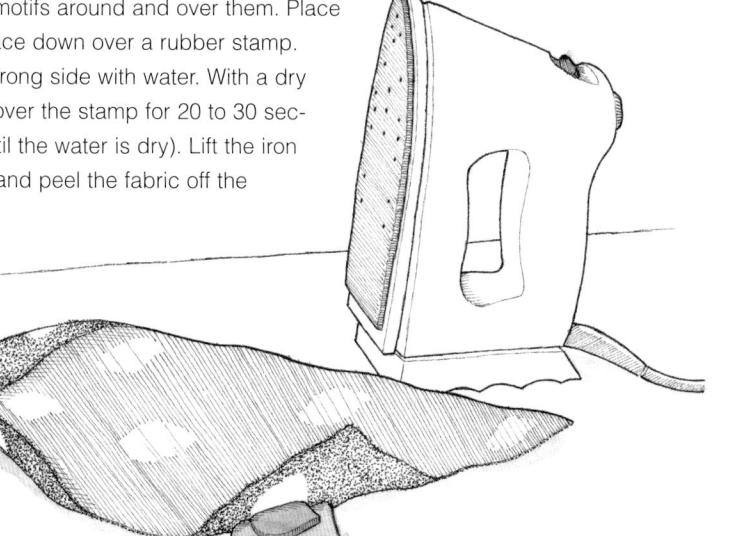

Any patches you apply to a pile fabric need to have fibers that run in the same direction as the original fabric. Work all the mending on the wrong side, as shown, and brush the pile to cover the mending. If you need to patch fake fur, try the same patching technique that you would use for leather (page 271).

mending stretch knits

Machine-knit fabrics are easy to sew, but not as easy to mend. Lightweight, smooth-surfaced knits, like jersey or interlock, are often difficult to darn or patch invisibly. Consider these techniques—or a decorative repair for your more casual garments and items.

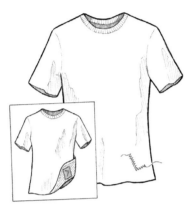

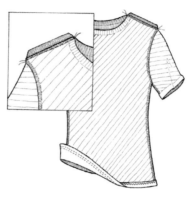

mending a hole or tear: Fuse a patch of interfacing with moderate stretch to the wrong side over the hole or tear. On the right side, machine-zigzag over the tear to reinforce the fusible patch.

reshaping: Often, a trip through the washer and dryer brings a stretched-out knit back to shape. You can also lay the garment on an ironing board and steam-press it into the desired shape by holding the steam iron above it slightly to dampen the fibers.

stabilizing seams: Some seams—usually shoulder, neckline, and waist seams—need to be stabilized so they don't stretch. To do so, sew a piece of twill tape or ribbon to the seam allowance.

shortening: Hem knits with a twin needle or a straight stretch stitch as shown at center, above. Match the number of rows of stitching to those used elsewhere on the garment.

repairing ribbed trim: Many knit shirts have a band of ribbed trim at the neckline, hem, armholes, or sleeve hems. Neckline seams are narrow and often come unstitched.

Turn the garment inside out and pin the edges of the opening together. Machine-zigzag the two edges together, close to the raw edges.

washing & drying

When it comes to mending and repairing, you can fix a lot of problems before they even begin with regular laundering and cleaning of your clothing, upholstery, and carpet.

If you'd like to water-proof a garment, check at your local fabric or outdoor gear store for a wash-in or spray-on product, such as Nikwax.

Machine-washing

- Read all care labels, pretreat stains (see page 279) and repair tears or loose trim.
- Zip zippers, empty pockets, unroll cuffs, and turn colored items inside out.
- Wash brightly colored, new items alone for the first time to make sure the dye doesn't run.
- Sort clothing and other items into separate wash loads by color, fabric weight (heavy jeans should be separated from delicate items), lint production, and whether they are heavily soiled.
- Set the washing machine to the regular cycle for sturdy fabrics and very dirty clothing, to the permanent press cycle for most laundry loads, and to the delicate cycle for lightweight and delicate items.
- Wash most laundry in warm water. Hot water is suitable for white clothing or very dirty, colorfast clothes. Bright colors and delicate fabrics are best suited to cold-water wash.
- Select a washing time of 6 to 8 minutes for an adequate washing time.
- Add the recommended amount of detergent to the washing machine. Extra detergent is actually harmful to many fabrics.
- Start the water; add detergent; add the clothes. Fill the washing machine 3/4 full so the clothes have room to move around.

Machine-drying

- Remove delicate items while they are still damp and hang them or lay them flat to dry.
- Opt for the air-fluff cycle, which circulates unheated air to plump pillows and refresh clothes that have been packed away.
- Do not machine-dry clothes or home décor items that may shrink.
- Keep dryer loads small. Clothes dry faster if they can circulate.
- Don't dry heavy clothes with delicate ones, or the delicate items will overheat.
- Do not put wool or silk garments into the dryer.
- Remove the lint from the dryer every time you use it. A lint-filled filter is a fire hazard and uses more energy than a clean filter.
- Wash the filter with soap and water periodically.
- Don't machine-dry stained items. The heat will permanently set the stain. Instead, hang the item to dry, then retreat the stain.

Hand-Washing and Hang Drying

- Hand-wash delicate items, specialty fabrics, wool sweaters, stained items, items with specialty trims, and any item you aren't sure of the best way to clean.

- Pretreat stains.

- Fill a basin or sink with cool water and mild detergent. Put the clothing in the basin and let it set for a few minutes. Gently work the suds through the fibers. Do not rub the fabric layers together. Rinse with cool water several times. Do not wring out the water. Gently squeeze the item or roll it in a clean towel.

- Lay knits or other stretchy items flat on an absorbent towel to dry. Hang wovens and nonstretch items on a hanger in the bathroom or laundry room to dry. Straighten and close garments so they maintain their shape as they dry.

Dry Cleaning

- Dry cleaning relies on special solvents and a minimal amount of water.

- Some items can be hand-washed even when the care label indicates to dry-clean. If in doubt, take the item to the dry cleaner.

- Items that should be dry-cleaned include: delicate fabrics like silk, chiffon, fur, and some wools, items that shrink easily, and tailored items.

- Empty pockets and remove specialty buttons or trims.

- Point out any stains to the dry cleaner.

If a velveteen or corduroy fabric becomes flat or matted, put it in the dryer with a damp towel to "raise" the nap.

fixing ironing accidents

It doesn't matter how careful you are, everyone has ironing accidents. Often the damage is reversible—especially if you get to it right away.

for crushed pile: Pile fabrics can become crushed in a crowded closet or along crease lines if they're stored folded. Machine-wash and machine-dry the damaged item right away.

Throw a damp towel in the dryer with it, and the moisture will help revive the pile.

You can also hang the item in a steamy bathroom while the shower is running. Brush the area with a stiff-bristled clothes brush to lift the pile.

for a scorch mark: Place the damaged fabric on a dry towel. Blot it with diluted hydrogen peroxide and let it set. Rinse with clear water. Move the treated area to a dry area of the towel.

If the scorch mark is still visible, apply diluted detergent and water. Alternate the cleaning solutions, dabbing them gently on the burn marks.

for pressing marks: steam the area really well. Gently rub the pressing marks with a soft cloth or your fingers. If the fabric is machine washable, spray it with water from a spray bottle and rub gently.

for iron drips or water spots: place an absorbent cloth over the water spot, and as long as the item is machine washable, spray it with a fine mist of water from a spray bottle. Press, the extra moisture should disperse the water ring.

Don't press over a stained area, or you will permanently set the stain.

storing garments

Whether you are storing garments for a season or for a longer time, make sure they are clean and stain-free before you put them away. It's okay to wash and dry them by machine, but don't use soap, chlorine bleach, starch, or fabric softeners, which can damage or discolor fibers over time, or attract insects. Dry-clean any items that are specified as "dry clean only."

Do not store clothes in plastic bags or airtight containers that restrict the flow of air around the garments. Store everything in a well-ventilated area that is free of moisture, extreme temperature variations, and sunlight. So, storage in the attic, basement, or garage is not ideal. Try to find a storage area in your living area. Store the items flat or on padded or rounded hangers.

When you take the garments out of storage, put them in the dryer (if their care requirements allow) on the air-fluff setting to eliminate wrinkles.

Don't use wire hangers. They can rust, stain or snag the fabric. Remove any pins before storing garments — they can rust, stain, and snag, too.

flat storage *(for sweaters, knits and stretchy fabrics, delicate and fragile fabrics):* Fold wool sweaters and store them flat. Try to avoid creasing the items by layering them with acid-free tissue paper. Place the heaviest and bulkiest items on the bottom.

Use an acid-free box for long-term flat storage and a cedar chest for woolen items. Store heavily embellished garments, such as beaded gowns, flat. Stuff them with acid-free tissue paper to prevent crushing.

flat storage *(for heirloom-quality items):* To protect the fibers, store wedding dresses, holiday garments, and heirloom baby clothes flat. Clean the items first, then wrap them in buffered acid-free paper (for cotton and linen) or non-buffered acid-free paper (for silk and wool).

Stuff the sleeves, bodices, and upper part of skirts with tissue paper to avoid creasing the garment. Place the garment in an acid-free box, lined with a white sheet or muslin. Be sure there is enough room in the box that the garment isn't crushed.

hanging storage *(for jackets, suits, sheer blouses, dresses, tailored garments, window treatments, and outerwear):* Clean the items and remove any plastic dry-cleaning bags. Hang the garments or other items on padded, shaped hangers (in or out of clothes bags) in a well-ventilated closet. Allow space for air to circulate between garments. Button, zip, or otherwise fasten the garment so it holds its shape while stored.

fabric-cleaning products

There are many fabric-cleaning and stain-removal products on the market—but all you need are a few basics. These basic cleaning products are appropriate for clothes, carpets, and upholstery. Never mix stain-removal products—when combined, bleach and ammonia produce toxic fumes. Always store cleaning products safely out of the reach of young children.

laundry detergent: Detergent is available in liquid or powder form. Liquid detergent disperses better than powder and also works for on-the-spot stain removal (although detergents that contain fabric softener are not as effective at stain removal). Only use the amount recommended by the manufacturer.

enzyme cleaners and detergents: These products are great for removing food stains. They also remove surface fibers that cause pilling. Check the labels of your cleaning products, however, because some already contain enzymes.

liquid dishwashing detergent: Diluted with water, dishwashing liquid is remarkably versatile. Store it in a spray bottle and keep it on hand for quick stain removal on clothing, upholstery, and carpets.

bleach: Available in both chlorine and nonchlorine varieties, bleach helps to whiten whites and remove stains. But it's too harsh for everyday use and fades and wears out fabrics when overused. If you soak a stain in diluted bleach, it should come out in fifteen minutes. If it doesn't, nothing will get that stain out!

- Nonchlorine bleach is gentler than chlorine bleach and can be used on most fabrics.

  - Chlorine bleach is very strong and should be used sparingly, but does a great job whitening whites and removing stains on white items. Do not use it on acrylic, silk, spandex, linen, or wool fabrics.

    - Hydrogen peroxide is a mild bleach. When it's diluted with water you can use it on silk and wool.

absorbents: Powders such as white chalk, talcum powder, and corn starch absorb oil-based stains. Sprinkle one on the stain, let it set, and then brush off the powder.

prewash treatments: These laundry aids are available in gels, squeeze bottles, pump and aerosol sprays, and stick form. They enable you to pretreat a stain as soon as you notice it.

white distilled vinegar: Add vinegar to laundry rinse water to remove excess detergent and make clothes softer and fresher. It also reduces static electricity and odors. White vinegar removes fruit, wine, coffee, and tea stains. Don't use it on cotton, silk, acetate, or linen fabrics.

dry-cleaning solvents: For spot-cleaning dry-clean-only items, look for these solvents. The fumes are strong, so only use these products outdoors or in a well-ventilated area.

how to treat a stain

The sooner you attack the stain, the less time it has to react with the fabric fibers. Sunlight, hot water, heat, and time make it harder to remove stains. Always refer to the care label in the garment before trying any cleaning product or method.

1 Blot excess liquid with a clean towel or rag.

2 Gently scrape solids (mud, chewy candy, etc.) off the surface of fabric with a dull knife.

3 Sprinkle an absorbent powder on greasy spills (see page 278). Rinse nongreasy spills with cool water or club soda.

4 Before pretreating stains, test the cleaning product on a hidden area to be sure it won't affect the color. Choose from among the cleaning agents on page 278 to treat the stain.

5 Apply the cleaning agent. Do not rub a stained area. Rubbing can spread the stain and damage the fibers. Dab to blot, with a gentle touch. Rinse the item.

6 Let the item air-dry and then check to see that all traces of the stain are gone. If not, apply the cleaning agent again. Rinse and let air-dry. (Never put a stained item in the dryer or on a radiator—the heat might set the stain.)

7 When all traces of the stain are gone, machine-wash or dry-clean as usual.

Avoid washing stains with bar soap—this type of soap can sometimes set stains.

caring for carpets & upholstery

Routine cleaning is essential for maintaining upholstery fabrics and carpets—just as it is for clothing. Keep dirt and dust from accumulating by vacuuming your carpet once a week and your upholstery once a month. Rotate furniture cushions often and vacuum them, using your vacuum cleaner's upholstery nozzle and crevice tool.

Spot-Cleaning Carpets and Upholstery

If you get a spill on your upholstery or carpet, blot, don't rub, it immediately and remove any solid particles. Treat the stain as soon as you can, following the steps below. The longer you wait, the more likely it is that the stain will set permanently.

1 Select a cleaning solution. You may use a dry-cleaning solvent or pretreatment spot remover, diluted dish detergent, or mix a solution of half vinegar and half water. Test the cleaning solution in an inconspicuous area first to double-check that it doesn't damage the fabric or alter its color.

2 If the stained fabric or rug can be moved, lay it, face down, over a clean, absorbent white towel or rag, which will absorb the stain. Otherwise—for upholstered furniture or wall-to-wall carpet—work from the right side.

3 Dampen a towel with the cleaning solution you've chosen. Gently dab the stain from the wrong side, if possible, or from the right side. With small, light strokes, feather the outer edges of the stain to avoid creating a visible outline around the stained area.

4 Move the underlying towel, if present, so that a clean area is under the stain. This will help draw more of the stain out of the fabric. Repeat until the stain is gone.

5 Launder or dry-clean the item, if possible, to remove traces of the solvent.

Vacuum carpets along the wall carefully. Dust and dirt collect there and create dingy shadows.

stain removal chart

Always attend to stains as quickly as possible. Some stains require a combination of treatments. Treat for an oil or grease stain first, and then any other causes of the stain. This stain-removal chart is for washable fabrics only.

unknown stains: If you don't know the source of the stain, fill a small squirt bottle with cool water and a teaspoon of liquid hand dishwashing soap. Squirt the stain liberally and let it sit. Rinse with cool water. If this doesn't work, soak it in a mixture of one part white vinegar and two parts cool water.

fruit and beverage stains *(beer, wine, cologne, soft drinks, coffee, tea, berries):* Soak for 15 minutes in one quart of lukewarm water, one half teaspoon liquid dishwashing detergent and one tablespoon white vinegar. Rinse.

greasy stains *(butter, margarine, cooking oil, lotions, mayonnaise, salad dressing):* Sprinkle with cornstarch, cornmeal, or powder and let it set to absorb the grease. Brush it off after 15 to 30 minutes. Apply pretreatment stain remover. Spray types work better on greasy stains. Let it sit for a few minutes and then launder as soon as possible.

protein stains *(blood, eggs, vomit, milk products):* Scrape off the cause of the stain. Soak in cold water with one-half teaspoon liquid hand dishwashing detergent for fifteen minutes, rinse. If stain persists, soak in enzyme product and then launder. If it's necessary and safe for the fabric, wash with chlorine bleach.

stains from dyes *(cherry, blueberries, fabric dye bleeding, felt-tip markers, grass, artificial food colors):* These stains are challenging. Pretreat and then soak the stained item in water and nonchlorine bleach. If you can still see the stain, and the fabric is suitable, wash the entire item with chlorine bleach.

Stain Removal Chart

Stain	Treatment
Ballpoint Ink	Rub gently with a pen eraser. Dry cleaning solvent, rubbing alcohol, glycerin, or hairspray may also remove ink. If not, wet the stain and sponge it with mild detergent and a few drops of vinegar. Let it sit for 30 minutes. Rinse and wash as usual, hang to dry.
Blood	If the stain is fresh, soak it in cold water. Dab on diluted ammonia. Soak a dry blood stain in cold salt water for several hours, then rinse. If the stain persists, apply an enzyme prewash product and then a non-chlorine bleach.
Chocolate	Treat the spot with diluted hand dishwashing detergent or an enzyme detergent and water. Let it sit for 30 minutes, then rinse.

Stain Removal Chart

Stain	Treatment
Grass	Apply a paste of dishwasher detergent and water or pre-treatment product. Let it sit for 30 minutes. Rinse with cool water. Remove any remaining stain with diluted ammonia or nonchlorine bleach. Rinse and wash with an enzyme detergent in regular cycle with cool water. Don't machine dry until the stain is completely removed.
Lipstick	Scrape off the excess with a dull knife or the edge of a spoon. Apply a dry-cleaning solvent, let it dry, then brush it off. Wash with gentle detergent and cool water. If stain persists, dab with diluted ammonia. Rinse with cool water. If necessary and fabric allows, wash with diluted chlorine bleach.
Mildew	Apply a pretreatment product and wash with hottest water appropriate for the fabric. Spot treat with hydrogen peroxide. If mildew has formed on upholstery, sponge surface with liquid hand dishwashing detergent and minimal water. Dry in the sun if possible.
Mud	Let the mud dry, and shake or scrape off excess. Apply pretreatment product or diluted dishwashing detergent and soak. Wash with enzyme detergent.
Perspiration	Apply pretreatment product. Launder with enzyme detergent in hottest water recommended for the fabric. If stain persists, wash with oxygen bleach or vinegar.
Rust	The best remedy is a rust removal product. Or, sprinkle salt over the area and then spray it with lemon juice. Put it in the sun to dry, but make sure the lemon juice doesn't bleach the fabric by testing it on the wrong side first.
Urine	Rinse in cold water and wash in the regular cycle. To remove urine stains from mattresses, sponge the stain with a rag soaked with water and detergent or water and vinegar. Allow to air-dry.
Water Spots	Dampen the entire item with water and air dry. Or, hold the stain over the steam from a boiling kettle. Launder as usual.
Wax	Put the item in the freezer for 20 minutes to harden the wax. Scrape off the wax with a dull knife. Stretch the stained area over a bowl and pour boiling water over it to melt the remaining wax.
Wine, Red	Cover the stain with salt. Then stretch the stained area over a bowl and pour boiling water over it. If the stain persists, spray it with diluted white vinegar, or apply hydrogen peroxide.
Wine, White	A white wine stain can turn brown. Flush the area with cold water and liquid dishwashing detergent, or treat it with enzyme detergent and wash it in the regular cycle.

index

index

A

acetate, 118

appliqués, 261

B

backstitch, 67, 69

balloon shades, 167

basting, 70

basting tape, 70

basting thread, 21, 54

bathroom fashions, 153–155

bath towels, 153, 155

beads/beading, 29, 262–263

bed measurements, 148

bedroom fashions, 147–152

bed skirt, 147, 151–152

bedspreads, 147, 149–150

beeswax, 195

betweens, 17

bias binding, 13, 76, 265

bias tape, 28

bias trim, 77

blind stitch, 14

bobbins, 11, 44–45

body measurements, 34

boxed pillows, 138, 145–146

braid, 29

buttonholes, 106–107, 222–225

buttonhole stitch, 14, 68

buttons, 103, 108–110, 194, 219–225

C

café curtains, 169

camouflaging, 260–268

carpet cleaning, 280

casing, inserting elastic in, 82–83

chalk wedge, 20, 53, 196

closures

   pillow, 141, 144–146

   repairing, 219–225, 228–242

collars, 248

comforters, 147, 149. *see also* bedspreads

commercial patterns, 32

construction line, 38

construction stitches, 57–58

corners, stitching and mitering, 75

cornices, 167

cotton fabrics, 114

coverlet, 147

crewel needles, 17

cross stitch, 14

cuffs, 259

curtain rods, 171–173

curtains, 165–169, 183–189. *See also*
 window treatments

cutting line, 38

cutting tools, 19

D

darning, 200–205

darning needles, 195

darts, 74, 214

decorative hardware, 173

decorative stitching, 264

decorative trim, 29, 78–80, 217, 265

design ease, 35, 92

detail placement line, 38

detergents, 278

dots, 38

draperies, 165, 166

drawstrings, 230

dry cleaning, 275

drying, 274–275

dust ruffles, 147, 151–152

duvet covers, 147, 150

E

easing, 35, 92

edge finishes, 218

edge stitch, 57, 72

edge-to-edge lining, 180

elastic, 30

   inserting in casing, 82–83

   replacing, 226–227

   sewing to fabric, 81

embroidery, 264

embroidery needles, 17

eyelet, 29

F

fabric. *See also specific types*

   choosing, 42, 133–134

   cutting, 52, 136

   marking, 53–54

   piecing, 137

   for pillows, 139, 142

   plaid, striped, and print, 128–131

   preparing, 48

   sewing elastic to, 81

   tablecloth, 156–158

   for window treatments, 170, 178–179

fabric bows, 87

fabric-cleaning products, 278

fabric glue, 70

fabric grain, 49

fabric-marking pens, 20, 53, 196

fabric tucks, 254

fagoting, 14, 29

fasteners, 103–105, 194, 229

fit adjustments, 244–247, 252–259

flared garments, 256

fold line, 39

fold-over braid, 28

fringe, 29

frogs, 104, 105

fusibles, 24, 198–199

G

garment storage, 277

gathers, 89

gimp, 29

grainline, 38

H

hand-quilting thread, 21

hand-sewing, 17, 66–69

hand-washing, 275

hardware, for window treatments, 171–173

heading tapes, 187–189

hem line, 39

hems, 93–95, 258

    decorative edges, 255

    fixing, 249–253

    tablecloth, 160

home décor

    bathroom fashions, 153–155

    bedroom fashions, 147–152

    fabric, 133–134

    lining, 27

    pillows, 138–146

    table fashions, 156–164

    techniques, 136–137

    trims, 135

    window treatments, 165–189

hook-and-loop tapes, 104, 105, 229

hooks and eyes, 104, 105, 229

hourglass curtains, 166

I

instruction sheet, 37

interfacing, 24, 25, 194

interlining, 27

invisible thread, 21

ironing accidents, 276

iron-on patches, 207

irons, 22

J

jabots, 165, 166

jewel stones, 262–263

K

knife-edge pillows, 138, 143–144

knit fabrics, 113, 203, 273

L

lace, 29, 124–125, 265, 270

lace seam, 28

lapped zippers, 100–101, 237–238

leather, 271

length adjustments, 40, 254, 256–259

linen, 115

lining, 26–27, 180–182, 243

liquid fray preventer, 196

M

machine-drying, 274

machine embroidery thread, 21

machine-washing, 274

man-made fibers, 42

marking tools, 20

measuring tape, 195

measuring tools, 18, 195

mending and repairs

    assessing, 191

    buttons, 219–225

    checklist for, 192

    closures, 219–225, 228–242

    common, 193

    darning, 200–205

    decorative trim, 217

    edge finishes, 218

    with fusibles, 198–199

    general guidelines, 197

    hems, 249–253

    ironing accidents, 276

    knit fabrics, 273

    lace, 270

    leather and suede, 271

    lining, 243

    necklines, 248

    patches, 206–211

    pile fabrics, 272

    pockets, 215–216

    replacing elastic, 226–227

    seams, 213–214

    snaps, 228

    thread snags/pulls, 212

    tools, 195–196

    zippers, 231–242

metallic thread, 21

middy braid, 29

milliner's needles, 17

mounting boards, 174–175

multistitch zigzag, 14

N

napkins, 164

natural fibers, 42

necklines, 248

needle board, 22

needles

    darning, 195

    hand-sewing, 17, 195

    machine, 10

    threading, 66

needle threader, 195

notches, 38

notions, 194

O

overcast stitch, 14, 67

overlock machine (serger), 15

P

patches, 206–211

patch pockets, 215, 266

pattern adjustment lines, 39

pattern envelope, 36

pattern pieces, 38–39

patterns

    commercial, 32

    design and wearing ease, 35

    instruction sheet, 37

    length adjustments, 40

    pinning, 51

    preparing and laying out, 50

    sizing, 33–34

pick stitch, 68

pile fabrics, 272

pillows, 138–146

pillow shams, 147

pillow styles, 138

pinning, 51

pins, 17, 195

piping, 29, 86

placemats, 162–163

plaids, 128–131

plain weave, 112

pleated draperies, 166

pleating pins, 17

pleats, 91, 268

pockets, 215–216, 266–267

point presser, 22

preshrinking fabric, 48

presser feet, 12

pressing, 23

pressing tools, 22

print fabrics, 128–131

Q

quilting guide bar, 13

quilting pins, 17

R

rayon, 118

rhinestones, 263

ribbon, 29, 265

rib weave, 112

rickrack, 29

rod-pocket curtains, 167

roller shades, 169

Roman shades, 168

ruffled tablecloths, 161

ruffler, 13

ruffles/ruffling, 29, 90

running stitch, 67

S

safety pins, 17

satin stitch, 14

satin weave, 112

scallop stitch, 14

scissors, 19, 196

seam binding, 28

seam gauge, 18, 195

seam guide, 13

seam lines, 39

seam ripper, 19

seam roll, 22

seams, 59–65

    adjusting, 245–246

    finishes, 64–65

    repairing, 213–214

    trimming, 60

    types of, 61–63

seam tape, 194

sequins, 262–263

serger, 15

serger stitches, 16

serger thread, 21

sewing checklist, 55

sewing machines, 8–9, 71

    bobbins, 11

    built-in stitches, 72–73

    needles, 10

    presser feet, 12

    specialty accessories, 13

    stitch patterns, 14

    threading, 46

shades, 165–169

sharps, 17

shears, 19

sheer fabrics, 124–125

shortening, 254, 256

shower curtains, 153, 154

silk, 116

sizing, pattern, 33–34

sleeve board, 22

slippery fabrics, 122–123

slip stitch, 67

slits, 214

sloating stitch, 68

snaps, 104, 105, 228

snips, 54

soutache, 29

stabilizers, 24

stain removal, 278–282

staystitching, 57

stitches. *See also specific stitches*

    construction, 57–58

    hand, 67–69

    machine, 72–73

    removing, 197

    serger, 16

stitching lines, 39

stitch patterns, 14

stitch tension, 47

storage, 277

straight stitch, 14, 72

stretch fabrics, 120–121

stripes, 128–131

suede, 271

swags, 165, 166

synthetic fibers, 119

T

tablecloths, 156–161

table fashions, 156–164

table runners, 162–163

tab-top curtains, 169, 185–186

tacks, 54

tailor's ham, 22

tape measure, 18

tassels, 88

textured fabrics, 126–127

thimble, 195

thread, 21, 194

threading machine, 46

threading needles, 66

thread knots, 69

thread snags/pulls, 212

thread snips, 19

toggles, 104, 105

tools

    cutting, 19

    hand-sewing, 17

    marking, 20

measuring, 18, 195

mending, 195–196

pressing, 22

topstitching, 58, 73

topstitching thread, 21

t-pins, 17

tracing wheel/paper, 20, 54

transparent ruler, 18

triacetate, 118

trim, 28–29

    attaching, 78–80

    bias, 77

    decorative, 29, 78–80, 217, 265

    home décor, 135

    repairing, 217, 218

twill tape, 28

twill weave, 112

U

understitching, 57, 72

upholstery cleaning, 280

upholstery thread, 21

V

valances, 165, 169

velvet, 272

vents, 214

W

washing, 274–275

wearing ease, 35

welting, 84–85

window treatments, 165–189

    casual, 168–169

    fabrics, 170, 178–179

    formal, 166–167

    hardware, 171–173

    heading tapes, 187–189

    linings, 180–182

    measuring windows for, 176–177

    mounting boards, 174–175

    rod-pocket curtains, 183–184

    tab-top curtains, 185–186

wool, 117

work space preparation, 43

woven fabrics, 112

Y

yardstick, 18

Z

zigzag stitch, 14, 72

zippers, 96–102, 231–242

index